Karen focuses on, dissects, and gives excellent advice on how to address one of the most important weak points of conventional management: the lack of clarity. The need to operate with clarity permeates every aspect of what leaders and organizations do on a daily basis and is vital to be a high performer.

—Jeffrey Liker, bestselling author of *The Toyota Way*

In an effective organization, everybody should know at any given time what is the most important work they can do to contribute to its success, and how well they're doing at it. However, in many organizations we find a miasma of overwork, poor strategy and communication, ill-defined or inadequate processes, and frustrated employees. In this outstanding book, Karen Martin tackles the biggest dysfunction addressing organizations today—a lack of clarity—and shows how to implement change at every level, supported by her extensive experience and her magisterial command of Lean thinking. This book is essential reading for leaders and managers everywhere.

—Jez Humble, coauthor of *The DevOps Handbook,*
Lean Enterprise, and *Continuous Delivery*

Karen Martin does a masterful job of proving to readers why clarity is the key to outstanding performance, and showing what smart organizations can do to attain and sustain it. She maps a clear path to defining what winning is and how to get there. The chaos-cutting solutions and powerful clarity-enabling practices she shares are keenly relatable and immediately implementable. I was absolutely absorbed by each word, each page, each illuminating example and instructive concept.

—Billy R. Taylor, Director of North America
Commercial and Off Highway Manufacturing at
the Goodyear Tire and Rubber Company

Karen Martin writes, "Clarity exhibits many qualities, the most important of which are coherence, precision, and elegance." All are present in her latest book, *Clarity First*. Karen's take on this timely and timeless topic is accessible, experience-based, relevant, and actionable. It should be required reading for leaders at all levels of an organization.

—Julie Winkle Giulioni, coauthor of
Help Them Grow or Watch Them Go

Clarity First is a mantra for success—both now and in a future that increasingly rewards clarity and punishes certainty.

—Bob Johansen, PhD, Distinguished Fellow at the Institute
for the Future and author of *The New Leadership
Literacies* and *Leaders Make the Future*

Leading in the age of accelerated innovation, complexity, and speed relies on clarity. Clarity of thought, communication, and purpose enables leaders to achieve their desired outcomes, help others exceed their expectations, and create higher performance organizations at scale.

In this book, Karen highlights how clarity enables individuals and organizations to experiment, take necessary risks, and improve decision making to discover the breakthrough innovations of ongoing and future success.

Clarity First will equip you with concrete capabilities and skills to deal with the uncertainty and ambiguity inherent in innovation—and win.

—Barry O'Reilly, founder and CEO of ExecCamp
and coauthor of *Lean Enterprise*

Clarity First provides a much-needed conduit between an organization's purpose and performance, linking people development and the alignment of their goals across all levels, and helping create an environment where all employees understand their daily work and why they do it. This excellent book paves the path for long-term success and sustainability within any industry.

—Tracey Richardson, founder of Teaching Lean Inc. and coauthor of *The Toyota Engagement Equation*

At the heart of all good decisions and actions lies one of two factors: luck or clarity. We can hope that our employees, colleagues, or managers get lucky, or we can provide them with the information they need to be successful. Clarity is never easy to achieve. Indeed, every company I've worked with has had a crisis of clarity. In *Clarity First*, Karen Martin lays a course to provide a foundation of clarity for your company to build success in from the beginning.

—Jim Benson, author of *Personal Kanban*

Clarity is an essential but far too often overlooked foundation in the quest for success—both for organizations and individuals. Guided by this comprehensive and inspiring book, you will not fail.

—Joakim Ahlström, author of *How to Succeed with Continuous Improvement*

While most of *Clarity First* focuses on organizational clarity, the chapter that describes how to apply the concepts to the individual—from both personal and professional perspectives—is particularly powerful. As Karen puts it, "Organizational clarity begins with you." There are books that deal with self-help, and there are books that describe how to improve organizations, but it is, unfortunately, rare to find a book that truly forces the reader to confront the impact he or she directly has on the organization. Reflecting on this can lead to dramatic personal, and then organizational, clarity and improvement.

—Kevin Meyer, cofounder of Gemba Academy
and author of *The Simple Leader*

In this terrific book, Karen Martin not only makes the compelling argument that clarity is needed—indeed, key—for success but also offers many practical tips to learn to gain greater clarity in one's thinking and communicating. In this, clarity is a skill that can be practiced every day to better frame issues for oneself and to engage others and lead one's business to superior performance. A must-read for any serious manager.

—Michael Ballé, coauthor of *The Lean Strategy* and The Gold Mine trilogy

Nobody ever said, "I don't need more clarity in my company!" The reality is clarity can be elusive. But Karen Martin makes this essential outcome accessible, actionable, and possible. My favorite part is it's possible in a totally human way. Brilliant!

—Shawn Murphy, CEO of Switch & Shift and
author of *The Optimistic Workplace*

I coincidently finished reading *Clarity First* the day before going to Toyota Kyushu in South Japan. Although not by design, the timing was perfect and made all the examples described in the book even more vivid and validated during the plant visitation. Examples of the opposite are more abundant and not particular to any country or industry, but consequences are never positive. May this book be a guide for leaders who courageously seek achieving clarity first.

—Sammy Obara, CEO of Honsha.org

So often my work as a CEO is stymied because of confusion, chaos, and miscommunication. Too often these symptoms are not caused by external factors but because of a lack of clarity inside my own organization. In this book, Karen Martin provides a concise road map for how to improve clarity. I'm putting it into practice, and it is working! I know other leaders will benefit from more clarity, too.

—Daniel Wolcott, president and CEO of
Adventist Health Lodi Memorial

In *Clarity First*, Karen Martin takes a direct and often tough approach to pierce the clouds of ambiguity in our working world. By citing specific examples in recent business headlines, Karen illuminates the problem of what a lack of clarity can do to financially devastate and damage a company and its reputation. But more than a thorough examination of why a lack of clarity can cause so many serious problems, Karen provides a lucid path to clarity for any organization or individual to follow. *Clarity First* is a great guide to successfully navigating the challenging waters of today's uncertain business world.

—Jerry M. Wright, former Chairman of the Board of
the Association for Manufacturing Excellence

Clarity First is one of those rare books that captures timeless wisdom and makes it accessible to us all. If there is a single all-important element that is lacking in our organizations, as well as in our personal lives, it is clarity. This book effectively explores why clarity is essential to success, what we can do achieve it, and what steps we need to take to extend it throughout any organization. Bravo, Karen!

—Mike Orzen, coauthor of *Lean IT*

It is quite clear that Karen Martin understands what DePree meant when he said, "the first job of a leader is to define reality." To paraphrase Lewis Carroll, "If you don't know where you are going, any path will do."

Karen Martin gets it! She understands, because of many decades of working with top companies, that everyone must be on the same page and be clear on the mission.

—Roger Greaves, former Chairman and founding CEO of Health Net, Inc.

Every organization needs a Karen Martin! With deft precision, Karen draws a straight line between clarity, or a lack thereof, to organizational performance. Organizational clarity is a competitive advantage. A must-read packed with invaluable insights and easy-to-deploy solutions!

—Virginia Cattaneo, SVP Client Services at a Fortune 500 investment management organization

Karen Martin's *Clarity First* successfully drives home a point we all need to hear! The clearer we get—in our processes, our org charts, our metrics, and our minds—the better our organizations will run. Let me be clear: we can all benefit from Karen's in-depth look at what keeps us from getting clear and what we need to do to turn that around. Clarity is a gift, and Karen gives it to us with a wonderful intellectual and emotional generosity.

—Ari Weinzweig, cofounding partner of Zingerman's Community of Businesses and author of the Zingerman's Guide to Good Leading series

Karen Martin identifies a string of problems affecting organizations today: They do not see reality. They accept superficial understanding. They jump to conclusions. They do not investigate further. They tolerate inefficiency and mediocrity. Ultimately, they do not seek clarity. These organizations are at risk for survival. But Karen provides easily understood and necessary remedies, as well as sources and references for further reading, which will help any leader build a truly outstanding organization. *Clarity First* is an eye-opening and highly worthwhile practical guide for daily work.

—Chote Sophonpanich, Chairman of Green Spot Co. Ltd.

CLARITY
FIRST

CLARITY
FIRST

HOW SMART LEADERS AND ORGANIZATIONS
ACHIEVE OUTSTANDING PERFORMANCE

KAREN MARTIN

New York Chicago San Francisco Athens London Madrid
Mexico City Milan New Delhi Singapore Sydney Toronto

1 2 3 4 5 6 7 8 9   LCR   23 22 21 20 19 18

ISBN   978-1-259-83735-7
MHID   1-259-83735-1

e-ISBN   978-1-259-83736-4
e-MHID   1-259-83736-X

McGraw-Hill Education books are available at special quantity discounts to use as premiums and sales promotions or for use in corporate training programs. To contact a representative, please visit the Contact Us pages at www.mhprofessional.com.

To my brother, Craig, who is my rock.
Achieving clarity, and accepting what it reveals,
isn't always easy, but it's always
easier with you by my side.

Contents

Preface

Clarity: It's a simple concept and yet strikingly elusive. Lack of clarity collectively costs companies, educational institutions, government agencies, and nongovernmental organizations billions of dollars per year, inserts unnecessary risk into every decision or action, drains organizations of the energy needed for productive effort, and causes customers to question whether the organization is capable of delivering value.

I've been studying clarity for close to three decades. I spent my early career as a clinical scientist, which provided a ripe canvas from which to develop keen investigation and pattern detection skills. Several years later I transitioned from clinical diagnoses to building and managing rapid-growth business operations, using my diagnostic skills to create high-performance work environments. Eventually I found my way into consulting and built a team. The dominant diagnoses we[1] make in our consulting work directly relate to the presence or absence of clarity: high degrees of clarity create high-performing organizations; low clarity drags organizations into an abyss of poor performance with frustrated leaders, disengaged employees, dissatisfied customers, and disappointed shareholders.

---

[1] I and my team are the "we" I refer to in this book.

This pattern was so common that I dedicated a chapter to clarity in my earlier book, *The Outstanding Organization*.[2] From the moment it was released I began receiving notes from readers about clarity, and to this day that chapter receives far more attention, generates more questions, and evokes more emotion than any of the others. One of the more memorable notes came from a midcareer engineering manager who worked for one of our clients. He was a stiff-upper-lip kind of man and even-keeled during problem-solving efforts that sparked disagreements among the leadership team. He didn't tend to show much emotion, yet in his e-mail he wrote, "I'll admit—I actually cried when I read your chapter on clarity and realized how much the lack of clarity is dragging me and our organization down. Thank you for offering tangible solutions to reduce our pain." Shortly after that a book reviewer heralded clarity as the "*it*" leadership skill.

In the years since *The Outstanding Organization* was published, I have seen firsthand that a lack of clarity is responsible for far more organizational chaos than I had originally observed—more so than any of the other three conditions I addressed in that book. Based on reader and reviewer responses, as well as our continued work with organizations, I knew I had to dedicate an entire book to clarity.

Despite its contribution to chaos, ambiguity is often tacitly rewarded. We have witnessed firsthand as leaders issue unclear proclamations and requests that team members are reluctant to clarify, out of fear that they will receive "that look," or they will miss a deadline and be punished for it. We've seen people get fired or sidelined for revealing problems. We've been called in to help an organization develop problem-solving capabilities only to find that its cultural values reward people for leaving important questions unanswered.

---

[2] The book addresses the four fundamental behaviors and conditions—clarity, focus, discipline, and engagement—that create outstanding performance yet are strikingly absent from many organizations. The book addresses their importance and how to achieve them. For more information, see *The Outstanding Organization* (McGraw-Hill, 2012).

Lest you think the examples in this book represent a skewed sample of negative outliers who sought help because they needed it, let me be clear: we have worked with hundreds of organizations in nearly every industry and functional work area. These organizations make products that save lives, keep the power on, or help businesses do whatever they do faster, better, and less expensively. They are healthcare organizations, financial institutions, energy utilities, and technology firms. This problem doesn't exist solely in private-sector businesses. We see this fog in social service agencies, religious institutions, academia, law enforcement, and government. *Especially* government. They deliver professional services and provide transportation. They move dirt, keep planes in the air, and give us drinkable milk. These organizations are like yours. And perhaps like yours, a pervasive "fog" of ambiguity plays out in the form of market share loss, missed targets, productivity dips, creeping expenses, poor customer service, interpersonal and interdepartmental tension, and employee disengagement and turnover. Nearly every organization we have worked with was initially blind to the lack of clarity with which it was operating, and unaware of the pivotal role that ambiguity played in its inability to achieve the goals it set for itself to meet marketplace demands and provide breakthrough products.

The good news is that modern management methods offer powerful clarity-enabling practices that can turn the tide. In particular, Lean management principles, practices, and tools serve organizations by surfacing hidden issues and enabling clarity. We draw heavily from Lean management in our consulting work, and some of the methods that appear in the following chapters come straight from the Lean playbook. But this is not a book about Lean. It is a book about clarity—why you need it, why you don't have it, what you can do to get it.

Clarity-driven management enables your organization to reach a level of performance well beyond what you've experienced, while creating a work environment that attracts and retains top talent. Let's begin.

CLARITY
FIRST

1

More Than a Moment

It took me forty years on earth
To reach this sure conclusion:
There is no Heaven but clarity,
No Hell except confusion.

—JAN STRUTHER FROM THE POEM "CLEAR"[1]

We have all experienced those moments in life when hard realities present themselves with complete clarity. It's the moment
you realize that the dream job you worked hard to get has taken
you away from doing what you love, or that a relationship you've
invested years of your life in is shifting in a direction that's different from what you want. Too often, crisis—a near-miss accident
or a frightening diagnosis—is the catalyst that brings these revela-
tions. In those moments we are suddenly able to see the reality we
had avoided, hidden, or explained away. Those moments are hard,
in part because they present difficult choices: change what you are
doing, or continue as you have been with the knowledge that what

---

[1] Jan Struther, *A Pocketful of Pebbles* (Harcourt, Brace, and Company, 1946).

you have is all there will ever be. No surprise, then, that so many people avoid or ignore those moments of clarity.

No surprise, either, that organizations do the same. Ambiguity is the corporate default state, a condition so pervasive that "tolerance for ambiguity" has become a cliché of corporate job postings, a must-have character trait for candidates. Ambiguity is a condition we sink into because it is automatic and it provides short-term benefits that manifest in a number of ways. The manager who posts a vague job description is able to put off defining the specific responsibilities for the role. The project launched with ambiguous purpose leaves the project manager free to interpret results to his advantage. Ambiguity about customer requirements or preferences means you don't have to work to satisfy them. As John Lennon wrote in the song "Strawberry Fields Forever," "living is easy with eyes closed."[2]

But is it? The short-term benefits of ambiguous organizational behaviors come at enormous long-term cost. Ambiguity leads to substandard performance, as leaders and team members at all levels invest time and effort on priorities that don't bring significant benefit. Ambiguity causes people to reach inaccurate conclusions, make faulty decisions, or spin their wheels in nonproductive ways. The absence of clarity also creates an opportunity for biases and assumptions to influence how people interpret information. Ambiguity tempts organizations to be reactive: instead of addressing the most important issues, they address those attracting attention at this moment. Ambiguity prevents organizations from operating with focus, discipline, and engagement.

Lack of clarity insinuates itself into the organization in hundreds of ways, both obvious and insidious. Lack of clarity runs the meeting with no agenda. It worms its way into the customer complaint that goes unresolved. It allows product quality issues to persist to

---

[2] The Beatles, "Strawberry Fields Forever," *Magical Mystery Tour*.

the point of costly and reputation-sapping recalls, or market-share erosion. It weakens the decision you aren't sure you have the authority to make, and flashes the exit sign at the talented team members you can't promote because you still don't have budget approval four months into the fiscal year. It lurks in the background when you don't know which of the dozens of metrics really matter, and thus can't explain what success looks like or how you would know when you reach it. The individual and collective lack of clarity keeps leaders and organizations of all types and sizes from performing to their fullest potential.

It often requires a business crisis and a resulting moment of revelation for leaders to recognize how much ambiguity exists and how much it costs them. From that revelation, however, leaders need *more than a moment* of hard work to achieve the clarity needed for outstanding performance.

To demonstrate the difference between organizations operating with ambiguity and those operating with clarity, consider Figure 1.1. Let your gaze take in the whole picture at once. How many dots do you see? Two? Four? Eight? Different numbers depending on where you focus? Organizational ambiguity is like the lattice lines—it obscures or outright hides what matters, making relevant issues harder to see individually and nearly impossible to discern all together.

Investments in clarity are the organizational equivalent of removing the extraneous lattice lines in Figure 1.1 to reveal only dots, as in Figure 1.2. When organizations make clarity a cultural requirement, it's easier to discern relevance from irrelevance. It's clear which market factors, customer behaviors, technological advances, and current events truly affect the organization, and it is far easier to make good decisions about what to do about them.

The superior results are worth it. I have personally seen those results in the clarity-pursuing organizations we work with. For a more objective perspective, consider the evidence from research

FIGURE 1.1 Organizational ambiguity is similar to Akiyoshi Kitaoka's optical illusion

Figures 1.1 and 1.2 are part of a collection of optical illusions created by Akiyoshi Kitaoka, professor in the Department of Psychology, Ritsumeikan University, Kyoto, Japan. Image used with permission by Dr. Kitaoka.

conducted by Nicholas Bloom, an economist at Stanford University. Bloom, together with Rafaella Sandun of Harvard Business School and John Van Reenan of The MIT-Sloan School of Management, among others, spent more than a decade assessing whether specific management practices have a quantifiable impact on corporate performance, or whether differences in business success are connected with other factors.[3]

For their research, Bloom et al. looked at three clarity-enabling practices that I also address in this book: targets, incentives, and measurement. Targets refers to whether an organization has defined long-term goals that it achieves by setting shorter-term performance targets. Incentives refer to rewards, such as raises and promotions, given to employees based on objectively sound actions. Measurement refers to the ongoing collection of performance data to assess how the organization is doing, and to actively look for, and act on, areas needing improvement.

Bloom et al.'s dataset includes more than 8,000 companies in 20 countries. Through research studies and surveys, the researchers place the organizations they study on a management continuum from zero to five, with zero encompassing no adoption of sound management practices and five representing excellent practices. Overall, the findings reveal that clarity-inducing management matters—a one-point difference on the continuum translates into 23 percent higher operational productivity, 14 percent greater market capitalization, and 1.4 percent higher annual sales growth.

To understand more about what this looks like in practice, consider a randomized trial Bloom conducted in India in partnership with economists from the World Bank and involving a group of garment manufacturers. The researchers collected data on the management practices of all the manufacturers, but only

---

[3] Bloom et al. summarize their work in the following article: Nicholas Bloom, Rafaella Sandun, and John Van Reenen, "Does Management Really Work?" *Harvard Business Review*, November 2012.

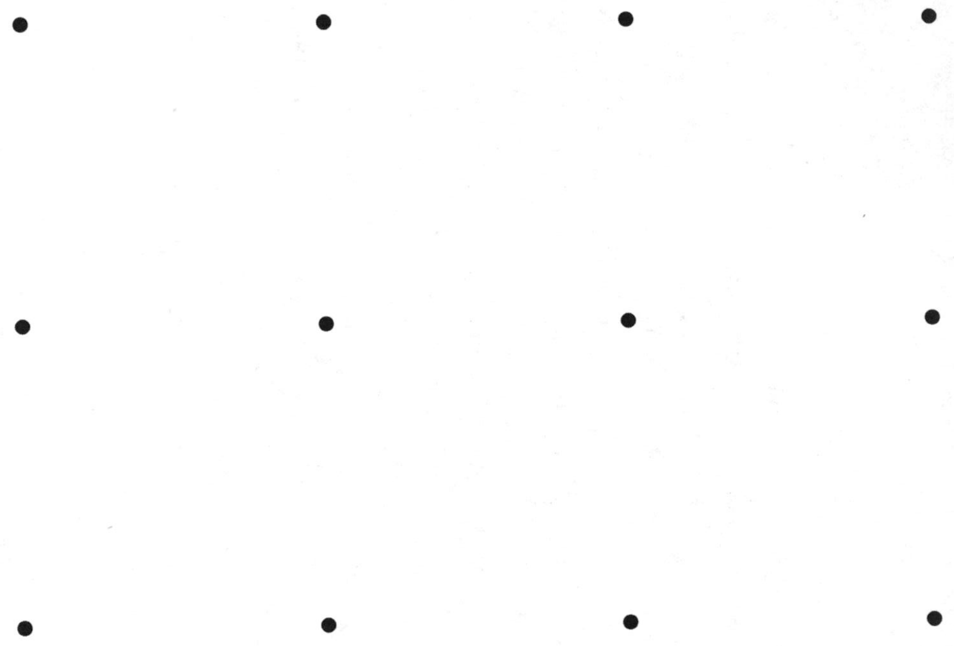

FIGURE 1.2 Clearing the lines of ambiguity
Image used with permission by Dr. Akiyoshi Kitaoka, Ritsumeikan University, Kyoto, Japan.

half—randomly selected from the 28 manufacturers who agreed to participate—received coaching in 38 Lean management practices. The coaching focused on clarity-inducing practices, including quality management, inventory management, staff recognition, and order management.[4] The coaches were consultants from a large and well-known management consulting firm; they worked with each firm half-time for five months, followed by a number of months of less intensive visits with the manufacturer to answer questions or give advice.

After the consultants finished, the researchers reassessed each organization's performance and found the manufacturing plants that received consulting on average cut product defects by 50 percent; reduced inventory by 20 percent; and raised output by 10 percent compared with the companies that received no consulting. Most critically, however, the senior executives of these businesses said that the companies were *easier to lead* after the intervention. That ease allowed the executives to expand faster, resulting in 30 percent higher profits.[5]

Viewed another way, the consultants helped the manufacturers adopt methods and approaches to increase clarity in the business. To be clear, the outstanding performance they achieved did not happen through luck or coincidence. It occurred through the confluence of demand for their service, product quality, competitive pricing, and by adopting a clarity-driven way of operating. By "operating," I'm referring to how leaders lead, how managers manage, and how frontline team members do the work. Clarity—or the

---

[4] The Lean practices used in this study included standard work, preventive maintenance, daily Lean management, visual management, right-sizing inventory, order segmentation, continuous formalized problem solving, and performance-based reward systems and staff recognition. For a complete list of the 38 Lean management practices they used, see the Appendix on pages 45–48 of the cited study.

[5] For specifics on the study Bloom and colleagues conducted in India, see: Nicholas Bloom, Benn Eifert, Aprajit Mahajan, David McKenzie, and John Roberts, "Does Management Matter? Evidence from India," *Quarterly Review of Economics* 128, no. 1 (February 2014).

lack thereof—lies at the core of how a business, government agency, or nonprofit operates. Clarity raises the organization up; ambiguity drags it down. Why?

Because people are responsible for delivering outstanding performance, and people need clarity if they are to make better decisions, deliver better service, innovate at higher levels, solve problems more effectively, develop more competent teams, and manage the work with greater skill—all in the service of providing greater value to customers, the true source of differentiation in the marketplace. People can often do their jobs without clarity; but rarely can they do their jobs well, and never can they perform at a level that is outstanding. I take it further: people have a fundamental right to expect clarity from the organizations they work for.

Clarity creates an environment in which people are able to perform at their best, and thereby enable higher levels of organizational performance. As shown in Figure 1.3, clarity is akin to the water and fertilizer that enable a tree to grow strong. When clarity is infused into the root system of the tree, the tree is able to develop a more robust trunk, strong branches, and vibrant foliage, with enough flexibility that they can flex with the winds of change. Clear operations make team members more efficient and engaged. Clarity also makes people feel more confident, capable, and connected to organizational purpose, priorities, processes, performance, and problem solving, as well as to their leaders and coworkers. Such connection, engagement, and confidence leads to increased employee agility, loyalty, and the drive to innovate.

This is not simply my opinion. When I asked more than 4,000 subscribers and social media connections to share their thoughts on clarity, their responses echoed what I have seen in our consulting work. I asked two questions: When you receive clear information (vs. unclear), how does that make you feel? And how does it affect your ability to perform? The results were consistent: clarity enables better performance by removing a *layer of doubt*.

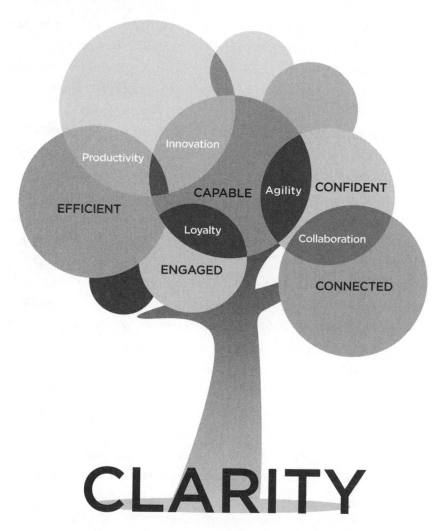

FIGURE 1.3 Clarity grows outstanding performance

Nearly every respondent said that clarity makes them feel confident that they understand the organization's goals, priorities, and the work itself, as well as expectations for their work. One respondent said, "Clarity helps me feel more confident that my decisions are in line with what the business wants." Another said, "Clarity reduces the risk of guessing or being wrong." Yet another said,

"Clear information feels like a path to 'right the first time.' Unclear feels like I'm being set up for failure."

Clarity doesn't just make people *feel* more capable. It actually makes them more capable and empowered when they know what is expected of them when performing a task.[6] In their book *The Progress Principle*, authors Teresa Amabile and Steven Kramer noted that the need to feel capable grows throughout life as people achieve more and more and compare those achievements with their "personal bests" and those of others. When people feel capable, they are more productive and creative. When they don't feel capable, their self-worth erodes, they become disengaged, and their work suffers.[7]

While Amabile and Kramer didn't explore the direct link between clarity and feeling capable, the survey respondents made a causal connection: "I'm able to perform better when I understand what's needed," one respondent wrote. Another: "With clarity, I don't need to ask trivial questions and waste so much time." And another: "Clarity helps me perform more accurately."

Of all of the responses, there were two that best summarized the power of clarity: "With unclear information, I feel lost, frustrated, prone to assumptions, confused, worried, distracted, and I lack confidence" and "Clarity makes me feel confident, powerful, and energized."

Which of those situations do you believe will help you deliver the greatest value to customers and help grow the business? Clarity enables greater productivity, stronger collaboration of all involved parties, and better ideas—all of which lead to better organizational performance.

---

[6] Marilyn Gist, "Self-Efficacy: Implications for Organizational Behavior and Human Resource Management," *The Academy of Management Review* 12, no. 3 (July 1987), 472–85.

[7] Teresa Amabile and Steven Kramer, *The Progress Principle* (Boston: Harvard Business Review Press, 2011), 68, 90.

WHAT IS CLARITY?

The simplest definition of clarity is *the quality of being easily and accurately understood*. Clarity in a business context goes deeper than that, however, since it exists in multiple forms: as an organizational value, a state of being, and an outcome.

When clarity exists as a value, individuals and the organizations they work for operate in a way that places a premium on clarity and rewards the people who seek it. In that environment leaders and team members pursue clarity in their daily activities, and cultivate an expectation of clarity throughout the organization.[8] An example of clarity as a value can be seen in Alan Mulally, the former CEO of Ford, who applauded members of his team when they called attention to drops in performance or other areas of the business that needed attention instead of staying silent.[9]

Alternatively, organizations can operate in a way that dismisses clarity and penalizes those people who seek it. At Wells Fargo, for example, employees were fired when they tried to report wrongdoing when they saw their peers opening false accounts in order to meet new account targets. Opening unauthorized accounts was reportedly condoned by bank leadership, and employees who refused to comply or actively worked to call the practice to light were penalized.[10]

Wells Fargo is an extreme example of how clarity might be discouraged or dismissed. More commonly, organizations are benignly ambiguous, operating with a lack of clarity because it seems to be easier and safer in the short term. Remember, ambiguity is the default stage—it is what happens automatically.

---

[8] The same is true when creating the conditions for operating with greater focus, discipline, and engagement.

[9] Jonathan Gifford, "100 Great Leadership Ideas," *Marshall Cavendish Business*, December 2010, 64–65.

[10] Matt Egan, "I Called the Wells Fargo Ethics Line and Was Fired," *CNN Money*, September 21, 2016.

Clarity, in contrast, requires work for a person to achieve it as a state of being, and it requires focused effort for a person to give clarity to others in the form of clear communication. Clarity can also be something you receive from others when they communicate clearly with you. In this sense, clarity exists inside a person's mind, as well as in the space between that person and another with whom he or she wants to share information.

What does clarity as a state of being look like? Clarity exhibits many qualities, the most important of which are coherence, precision, and elegance. Clarity as coherence comes through information that is both purposeful and logical. Precise information is succinct. Elegant information is crisp and easy for the intended recipient of the information to grasp.

Despite the multiple forms and multiple qualities that clarity possesses, there are also things clarity is not. Clarity is a close cousin to truth, for example, but they are not one and the same. A person or an organization can issue untruthful statements that are received as true because they have the coherence, precision, and elegance of clear communication. There is even a term for this—*agnotology*—coined by Stanford Professor Robert Proctor as the study of the willful act to spread ignorance or doubt.[11]

Clarity is also a close cousin to transparency, but they are not identical either. One can be clear with the information he chooses to share while withholding some of the details. Likewise, one can believe she's being transparent without being clear. Transparency is a noble goal in many situations, but it's not a "one size fits all" virtue. There are good reasons why the Healthcare Insurance Portability Protection Act (HIPPA) precludes healthcare providers from sharing private patient information outside the patient's direct care team, for example, but those reasons don't apply to doctors writing clear orders, or providing clear direction to their patient's treatment

---

[11] Robert Proctor, *The Making and Unmaking of Ignorance* (Stanford University Press, 2008).

team. Generally, though, transparency serves efforts to operate with greater clarity.

Finally, clarity is different from certainty. Certainty is not always possible, but achieving clarity nearly always is. For example, companies can't always predict when a competing product will rob them of market share, when a natural disaster will cut off access to a key supplier, or when political priorities will shift so that what they thought was tomorrow's concern becomes today's crisis. But organizations can improve their predictive powers and the speed with which they respond by gathering information, interpreting it, and communicating findings clearly. In this way, both clarity and uncertainty can coexist in the same environment. Similarly, certainty is a dangerous mindset in the early stages of problem solving, but it's essential to operate from a clear problem definition.

Organizations can also find themselves in a clear situation about which they communicate in an unclear way. Such was the case during the Fukushima Daiichi Nuclear Power Plant disaster that occurred in 2011. Fukushima staff members were certain that the earthquake and tsunami had damaged the plant to the point that it approached—and then entered—a full-fledged meltdown. Communications from the plant obscured that point, however, and thus made the situation seem less urgent. That lack of clarity grew out of an in-house policy prohibiting staff from using the words core "meltdown." The utility instead used the less serious phrase core "damage" for two months, which many believe delayed remedial actions that could have reduced the release of radioactive waste.[12]

Beyond what clarity is lies the positive results clarity can bring. Clarity enables every department to understand the organizational priorities and focus its resources on fulfilling them. Clarity ensures that people at least have the information, the processes, and the authority they need to do their jobs to the best of their ability.

---

[12] "Tepco Head Apologizes for 3/11 Ban Issued on 'Meltdown.'" *Japan Times*, June 21, 2016.

Clarity enables higher productivity, better decision making, more effective and timely problem solving, more relevant action, and better relationships—all of which lead to higher levels of performance for both the individual and the organization. Clarity thrills customers, increases profits, and lowers costs. It also makes the people within an organization happier and more engaged with their work.

Clarity, in short, is the key to outstanding performance. So why doesn't everyone seek and operate with it? Stated another way, if it's so good for us, why is it so rare?

WHY ISN'T CLARITY MORE COMMON?

I've been examining the question of why clarity isn't more common for decades, and the most distilled answer I have come to is that clarity is rare because it requires a lot more short-term work than does ambiguity. There's no way around it. Defining everything, from why your organization exists and what its priorities are, to how people must operate based on their clearly defined role, requires time and effort so that everyone understands the fundamentals and is working together to point in the same direction. Considering that it can take two people half a day to get clear on a question as trivial as what to eat for dinner, it's no wonder that many feel that the complexity of the organizational environment makes clarity seem impossible.

Which highlights another reason why clarity is so rare: because it's easy to rationalize why you don't have it. Uncertainty and complexity are facts of life and business. You will never know everything, and you are going to have to make the best decision you can anyway. Knowing that, people get trapped in a "we don't know and we can't possibly know" mindset. They confuse clarity with certainty or simplicity, and since they can't have the latter two they eschew the former as well. Such victim-like thinking can lead organizations to reject new ideas. Alternatively, they might jump on the bandwagon of a hot new product without defining what the organization brings to that market and what it hopes to get out of it. In either case, the organization is not positioned as well as it could be for outstanding performance.

I've also heard organizations justify ambiguity as necessary for creative work. The education scholar Laurence Peter reportedly quipped, "If a cluttered desk is a sign of a cluttered mind, of what, then, is an empty desk a sign?"[13] The implication is that you need to allow for some disorder if you hope to achieve something great. Tim Harford, author of the *New York Times* bestseller *Messy*, posits as well that creativity, innovation, and other types of performance are aided by some degree of messiness. People who operate in methodical ways or according to established norms, in contrast, may become constrained by them and fail to reach the highest levels of performance.[14]

But here, again, the tendency is to falsely equate mess with ambiguity, just as people equate certainty with clarity. Mess and ambiguity are not equivalents. They are peers. You can have a messy situation with many moving parts and utmost flexibility about how to explore it, *and* you can have complete ambiguity about why you are in that situation and what you hope to change about it. Alternatively, you can have that same messy situation and the same flexibility alongside clarity about why you are there and what—in general terms—you hope to accomplish. Ambiguity makes any kind of work harder to do, but it almost guarantees a disaster when it comes to messy work. Clarity, in contrast, makes messy work easier and more productive.

---

[13] This quote is often misattributed to Albert Einstein. Peter is the author of *The Peter Principle*. The quote on the cluttered desk can be found in *Peter's Quotations: Ideas for Our Times* (William Morrow, 1977), 339.

[14] Tim Harford, *Messy* (Riverhead Books, 2016).

Take problem solving and innovation. Both are messy. Both types of work put teams in a proverbial house of mirrors in which they have to try doors to see which ones open and what lies within. If teams do not enter the house with clear inputs in the form of current-state facts or customer requirements, they'll have no way of knowing if a pathway or a discovery is useful.[15] Clear inputs are enablers of effective creativity, and clear outputs are required for creative work to be properly appreciated and used.

Thoughts on VUCA

Introduced by the U.S. Army War College in the 1990s to describe the conditions it faced in Afghanistan and Iraq, the acronym VUCA—which stands for volatility, uncertainty, complexity, and ambiguity—is now a term tossed about in corporate boardrooms, in executive strategy sessions, and among management consultants. It is increasingly mentioned as a business condition that requires a different leadership approach.

Here's the problem: I hear far too many people use the term in a hand-wringing, shoulder-shrugging way, as though they're being held hostage by conditions over which they have no control. Some use it as an excuse for not setting their sights higher, not stretching farther, not working harder to retain or regain market share, and not striving for excellence. It's become an excuse for settling for less. Such defeatist thinking can negatively affect product development decisions, annual business plans, and strategy. I'm fairly

---

[15] For readers of my earlier book *The Outstanding Organization*, "messy" is different from the kind of organizational chaos I address in that book. Getting to the other side of messy work usually involves a deliberate, methodical, and controlled process, as with problem solving. Chaos, in contrast, is undisciplined and out of control.

certain that's not how the Army War College intended it, but that's how some in business are using it.

I see clarity as an antidote to the negatives of VUCA thinking, because with clarity, corporate executives can exhibit more control than they realize over the four VUCA "realities." Volatility is the toughest one to control and to see coming, but when leaders are clear about internal and external conditions it is easier to recognize volatility on its way and respond accordingly. Uncertainty is likewise a reality of business, but, again, far too many leaders assume that uncertainty is universal rather than taking the time to get clear on as many elements as they can. Complexity, for its part, creates an opportunity to simplify, as most complex situations and concepts can be broken down, clarified, and addressed.

Ambiguity is the one "reality" that doesn't belong in the acronym at all, since ambiguity is a man-made condition that exists within the other three. Nothing that's ambiguous needs to remain so. Its antidote is clarity. Let's rename it "VUC." We live in a VUC world.

In addition to the fact that ambiguity is easier in the short term and often justified as either normal or better, there are other reasons grounded in human behavior and psychology that explain why organizations and the people who work for them do not seek clarity in everything they do. These reasons, highlighted below, explain why managers do not understand the executive team's top priorities; why design teams make assumptions about customer preferences that don't pan out; and why companies are caught off guard when data paints a different performance picture than what they had assumed.

Ignorance

The first step in changing any habit is recognizing that you have it. This is harder than it seems with clarity. Since clarity lies in that middle state between communicated and received, it can be vulnerable to points of disconnect between what people say and what is heard. I might think an idea is perfectly clear, but fail to get it across to you. You, in turn, may think you understand something but in fact be ignorant—in the sense that you lack knowledge—about the nature and scope of the issue.

Consider a situation we recently encountered. A vice president at a financial institution was tasked by his CEO to create a continuous improvement (CI) culture in the organization, and contacted our firm to discuss a potential engagement. At the beginning of the conversation, he thought that his CEO's request was clear. But as I asked questions to understand the desired end state, he realized he lacked clarity on many of the fundamentals, such as: How was the CEO using the term "CI"? What did she mean by a "CI culture"? What does that look like to her? Was she prepared to champion an organization-wide shift from command-and-control leadership to delegating authority for tactical improvement to the frontline team members who are the experts in doing the work? Or did she want some other flavor of "CI"?

Such conversations are not rare in our line of work, and they expose the fact that clarity for one may breed ambiguity in another without either knowing that ambiguity is there. Situations like this fall into the category of *naive ignorance*, brought about when a person does not know what he or she does not know. The CEO likely thought she was clear, and so did the VP—at first. Only with additional questions and information did he realize that he needed to spend more time understanding what the CEO's true end goal was and reassess the options for achieving it.

Not all manifestations of ignorance are as innocent as this one. A second form of ignorance is what I refer to as *conditioned ignorance*, whereby people are likely aware that they don't have the full picture, but have been conditioned to look the other direction and not seek clarity. This can happen easily in business environments that make clear they do not value employees who ask questions or surface problems. Team members working for these organizations become conditioned to ignore ambiguity or look away from situations that invite scrutiny.

The third and last form of ignorance is *willful ignorance*, whereby a person makes a conscious and independent choice not to seek clarity about an issue. I say willful ignorance is a choice, but in some cases it is only a choice in the most literal sense, made at a deep psychological level. When family members collude in denying abuse or addiction, for example, they are engaging in willful ignorance.[16] The same happens when leaders refuse to acknowledge significant competitive threats, and instead dismiss them as irrelevant. For example, leadership of the now-defunct Blockbuster refused to accept that new competitor Netflix had a compelling offering that took advantage of customer frustration over Blockbuster's late return policy, as well as its reliance on the success of recent releases to generate demand for rentals. By the time Blockbuster leadership could no longer deny reality, Netflix had gained insurmountable momentum.[17]

The fact that many organizations and people have become habituated to ambiguity exacerbates the lack of awareness many have about what is clear and what isn't.

Lack of Curiosity

Another obstacle to clarity is a lack of curiosity about what you do not know. Lack of curiosity is not our natural state. As infants we emerge from the womb as curious and clarity-seeking beings.

---

[16] Daniel Goleman, "Insights Into Self-Deception," *New York Times*, May 12, 1985.

[17] Marc Graser, "Epic Fail: How Blockbuster Could Have Owned Netflix," *Variety.com*, November 12, 2013.

"Why?" is the most frequent question children ask, and reflects our innate desire to know. The second most common question—"Why not?"—allows us to test new ideas and challenge thinking. It pushes us to try things people say we can't accomplish or to differentiate between two options.

But many children, teens, and young adults have their innate curiosity drummed out of them by otherwise well-meaning parents, teachers, and early bosses who are overloaded or insecure. We get dismissed with a, "Because I said so," or "It just is," or "Stop asking questions!" Every time that happens a child is taught that it is bad to want to understand. As producer Brian Grazer puts it in his bestselling book *A Curious Mind*, "Curiosity has been strangled. It's considered a wild card. But that's exactly wrong."[18]

Popular culture likewise depicts curiosity as a negative, as in the saying "curiosity killed the cat," or in the fact that childhood's most famous emblem of curiosity—Curious George—always got into trouble and needed to be rescued by the Man with the Yellow Hat. Curiosity too often is presented as dangerous, childish, and something a person is supposed to grow out of.

Yet curiosity is necessary for innovation, for effective problem solving, and for any meaningful learning and improvement—as well as for strong leadership. Only by asking, Why? Why not? What if? and How could we? do organizations successfully tackle new problems and seek out new ideas. In fact, none of the large problems we face as humankind—climate change, intractable wars, antibiotic resistance, eroding water quality—can be solved without creative solutions that begin with curiosity.

Fortunately, organizations are filled with people with dormant curiosity waiting to be sparked. Many of those people have been habituated to the idea that curiosity is dangerous—it can uncover facts you'd just as soon not know, or worse: get you fired. Maybe

---

[18] Brian Grazer, *A Curious Mind* (New York: Simon & Schuster, 2015), 95.

they have seen that people who ask why and why not get punished or don't make it far.

Organizations can ignite that dormant curiosity. They need to be thoughtful about it, though. With a bit of coaxing, curiosity can reemerge *if* leaders create a safe environment in which asking why is both encouraged and rewarded.

Hubris

In the example I gave of the financial institution that wanted to develop a CI culture, the VP didn't realize that he lacked full clarity about his CEO's vision. When he realized he needed clarity, he went back to the CEO to get it. Not everyone has that response. Some people respond to clarifying questions by digging their heels in further, asserting what they think they know. In these cases, their hubris is an obstacle to clarity. They think they know, but they don't, and they aren't going to ask.

Hubris can also manifest in subtler ways. In the value stream transformation work we do with clients, for example, part of the diagnostic and design work involves a method known as value stream mapping. In these sessions, senior leaders who oversee the functions in a value stream work to understand how value moves through the organization toward the customer. At some point in nearly every session—and often at many points—a leader says, "Really?" in response to information provided by a peer in a different function. Leaders think they know how the organization delivers value to the customer, but these sessions universally reveal to participants that they don't have the full picture.

Organizations can address this obstacle first by adopting a growth mindset about the business. In her book *Mindset*, psychologist Carol Dweck describes her years of research on the psychological factors affecting learning and education. She finds that people can be categorized as having one of two mindsets. A person with a fixed mindset believes that intelligence is innate, and people are either "good at something" or not. A person with a growth mindset believes that intelligence can develop, and we can learn skills that allow us to get better at certain tasks than we were at the beginning.[19]

When she applies her findings to the personalities that often rise in the business world, she finds that many executives who ascend to the top ranks of their companies have a fixed mindset—they rose to the top of their field partly on account of their self-confidence and their decisive nature. They believe they are good at what they do, and they believe they *know* what matters. It's hard, if you are one of those people, to recognize that the very qualities that got you where you are may be keeping you from getting any further. It's equally difficult if you work with one of those people and they refuse to look deeper at an issue.

Fortunately, mindsets are malleable. People can adopt a growth mindset with reflection, coaching, and some work on the self. They can choose to let go of their belief that they know everything and start asking more curiosity-driven questions of more people.

I know leaders who have managed to do just that. Working on the self is necessary even for the most humble leaders. Leaders at Toyota, which has long promoted humility as a corporate value, learned that lesson during the recall of Toyota vehicles that began in 2009. Toyota had been receiving reports from drivers of "unintended acceleration" but dismissed them as technically impossible—Toyotas are built with redundant systems designed to prevent movement of the vehicle when the brake is pressed. Knowing that, Toyota leaders assumed that the incidences were entirely cases of user error. It took a fatal accident and an investigation before Toyota leaders looked again at the issue and used problem solving to uncover the true root causes: floor mats improperly sized or installed that caught the accelerator in some cases; and sticky accelerator pedals that did not come

---

[19] Carol Dweck, *Mindset* (Ballentine Books, 2007).

up when released in others.[20] That knowledge led Toyota to initiate programs, such as free first-year maintenance for owners of new Toyotas, to foster more direct contact with the customer.

Cognitive Biases

Psychologists Daniel Kahneman and Amos Tversky were the first academics to systematically study human decision making to determine whether the classical economics view of rationality was correct. What they found is that many decisions are subject to bias. Biases serve as filters for the brain—they sift through the thousands of pieces of information that come at us at any moment in the day and let through only the ones they deem important. "Important" for your brain refers mainly to the facts you need to stay safe.

Since Kahneman and Tversky conducted their first experiments in the 1970s, scientists have identified dozens of biases.[21] Biases allow you to process information and make quick assessments. Is this a good business deal? Can I count on this partner to deliver when they said they would? Biases are not inherently bad. But they can operate unconsciously, taking over when you don't have the time or the information to consider a decision carefully. Indeed, biases kick in most often when we haven't done the work to achieve clarity and make decisions steered by clear goals and available facts.

Biased decisions sometimes work out OK. When that happens, it reinforces the idea that all a leader has to do is "follow her instincts," a dangerous position not only because biases are unreliable by

---

[20] For a full account of the actions Toyota took during the 2008 financial crisis and the concurrent issues with unintended acceleration, see Jeff Liker and Timothy Ogden, *Toyota Under Fire: Lessons for Turning Crisis into Opportunity* (McGraw-Hill, 2011).

[21] Wikipedia currently lists 175 biases (https://en.wikipedia.org/wiki/List_of_cognitive_biases), which were categorized into four types by Buster Benson (https://betterhumans.coach .me/cognitive-bias-cheat-sheet-55a472476b18#.ptoavi4fs). Benson's categories have been beautifully arranged by John Manoogian III on his cognitive bias codex: https://en.wikipedia .org/wiki/List_of_cognitive_biases#/media/File:Cognitive_Bias_Codex_-_180%2B_biases,_ designed_by_John_Manoogian_III_(jm3).jpg.

definition, but because my biases may be different from yours, and yours from those of another leader in your organization. We are not all steering in the same direction if bias is driving us.

In particular, organizations need to beware of biases linked to past successes or failures. Organizations that once led their fields often have hardwired cultural practices that came to be during a past era and were positively reinforced by strong performance. In a changed context, however, those same practices may guide organizational decision making even though they have outlived their relevance. The same is true of decisions that did not work out—leaders may be biased against projects or partnerships that share some qualities with a failed effort, despite different circumstances.

Time Constraints

Organizations give people at all levels far more to do on a given day than they can reasonably achieve. People often feel like they don't have the time to stop, assess, and consider whether the actions they take by rote are the right ones. Furthermore, if we have a quota to fill or a deadline to meet, we work to fill the quota or meet the deadline—in truth, our performance evaluation usually depends on it.

Few of us are in control of our time to the extent that we can dictate how we spend every minute of it. But those who are, or who can influence how time is spent by others, should invest in giving people a percentage of their time for assessments and problem solving. One of the most wasteful organizational practices is rework. Over and over we see time spent redoing work that could have been done properly the first go-around, and the rework time is far greater than the time that could have been spent assuring clarity up front. When you take that perspective, you find that operating with greater clarity is more efficient for both the giver and receiver of information. Clarity requires the time and space to think through requests, needs, and ideas, but the resulting communication and actions will be more precise and purposeful.

Fear

All of the psychological and behavioral obstacles to clarity share a common cause: fear. Fear comes in many forms and has many roots. Clarity-related fear is nearly always centered on the fear of knowing, because what a person learns through the process of seeking clarity may be more painful in the short term than remaining in ignorance. Fear keeps people from speaking up when they believe that a problem exists. Fear keeps people from taking action because it could mean more work. People fear that they will be ridiculed or punished for calling attention to something. People may also experience situational apathy, whereby the risk of calling attention to an ambiguous situation outweighs the potential benefit. All of these fears may be well founded. Perhaps you have seen people in your organization get fired, demoted, or marginalized for asking difficult questions. Perhaps a past effort to get clear on a problem's cause called attention to one of your decisions or was blocked by someone who didn't want the truth revealed.

Yet in most cases the fear people feel about seeking clarity in the workplace is based on incomplete thinking. The problem you are avoiding exists whether you seek clarity on it or not. The longer you wait, the worse the consequences of that problem can become, requiring greater effort to fix. As Socrates said, "There is only one good, knowledge, and only one evil, ignorance."[22] The good news is that in most cases, the damage wrought by not knowing is far worse than the pain of knowing. Clarity is liberating, even if its results are hard to hear.

For a modern example, consider again how Ford's Alan Mulally applauded his team members for calling attention to drops in performance or other problems. In many ways, Mulally's leadership style echoes that of Toyota leaders. Part of the Toyota philosophy is that "no problem is a problem." At Toyota, this shortened version of

---

[22] Socrates, quoted in Diogenes Laertius, *Lives of Eminent Philosophers*, vol. 1 (3rd c. A.D.).

leader Taiichi Ohno's original quote means that problems—defined as a gap between where you are and where you'd like or need to be—are inevitable when you strive to reach higher levels of excellence. If there are no problems, you either aren't reaching far enough, or you haven't looked carefully at what's in front of you.

How Clear Is Your Organization?

Ford and Toyota—and a host of other clarity-centric organizations—offer compelling models for those in any industry who want to break through organizational ambiguity. They show how leaders and the organizations they run can embrace clarity, and in doing so break free from many of the factors that lead to ambiguous thinking.

To begin seeking greater clarity, I invite you to take a self-assessment to learn the extent to which your organization lacks clarity in its basic foundations.[23] Organizations fall into one of three categories when it comes to clarity, based on how actively or well the people within them work individually and collectively to overcome the factors outlined above: *clarity pursuers*, *clarity avoiders*, and the *clarity blind*.[24]

Organizations that are clarity pursuers view clarity as an organizational value. They institutionalize norms and behaviors that encourage people to seek clarity in both the information they deliver and the information they receive. The institutional investment firm Bridgewater Associates, and its outspoken leader Ray Dalio, has a reputation as a clarity-pursuing organization.[25] People are expected to be transparent, honest, and clear about the performance of their work and that of others—to the point of discomfort. Bridgewater

---

[23] To take a self-assessment, visit www.clarityfirstbook.com.

[24] These three categories apply to individuals as well. More about this in Chapter 7.

[25] Alexandra Stevenson and Matthew Goldstein, "Bridgewater's Culture Is Like a 'Nudist Camp' at First: 'Very Awkward,'" *New York Times*, March 7, 2017.

is an example of clarity-on-steroids; this extreme approach isn't what we suggest for our clients, but the idea of encouraging clarity is right on.

In contrast, clarity avoiders could be clear but choose not to be in one of three ways. Type 1 clarity avoiders use *intentional deceit* to achieve a defined purpose. An organization like Takata, the airbag supplier that pled guilty to knowingly distributing faulty products, is a classic Type 1 clarity avoider in that the organization actively set out to deceive people. During indictment proceedings, for example, court records revealed that the CEO directed a junior engineer to remove test data that revealed air bag ruptures from a report that was being sent to an automaker. The data manipulation practice was so common that Takata had a term for it: "XX-ing the data."[26]

Type 2 clarity avoiders operate, in contrast, with *strategic ambiguity* and avoid clarity on the grounds that clarity could force one side to take a position that damages a relationship, initiates a conflict, or limits future options. In the business world, strategic ambiguity may be used in contract negotiations as a technique to keep a potential supplier from knowing it "has it in the bag," which can result in a less favorable price. Strategic ambiguity has its use, but too often we see it applied to situations that don't warrant it. In one example, a client refused to share an organization chart with its staff, arguing that the information could be used by competitors to poach employees. In another, a company refused to post a diagram of its product roadmap. In both cases leaders argued that the information was competitive intelligence that they needed to keep secret, so they kept it ambiguous for everyone.

Type 3 clarity avoiders elevate *willful ignorance* into an organizational mandate. The example I gave above of Blockbuster earlier

---

[26] Hiroko Tabuchi and Neal Boudette, "3 Takata Executives Face Criminal Charges Over Exploding Airbags," *New York Times*, January 13, 2017.

in this chapter demonstrates the head-in-the-sand approach that can take over in organizations that avoid confronting the reality of slipping market share or falling performance. Willfully ignorant organizations are not usually nefarious. More often they are once-successful institutions whose way of operating no longer serves in a changed competitive landscape. Their way of working isn't working, but they don't know any other way and so avoid confronting reality.

Organizations that are clarity blind fall into two categories: those who don't recognize clarity's importance and those who do but can't perceive when they don't have it. Samsung, for example, exhibited clarity blindness when it thought that the cause for exploding batteries in its Galaxy Note 7 smartphone was a supply chain problem when it turned out to be a design flaw.[27]

No organization pursues clarity all the time, but few are as clear as they could be or should be to enable outstanding performance. Understanding your current state will put you in a strong position to take steps to inject clarity.

A Call to Action

How do we produce more than a few moments of clarity?

Begin by knowing the state of clarity in your organization, and understanding where you fit and the influence you have to encourage clarity in every realm you touch. The recommendations in this book are for leaders at all levels of an organization. Whether you lead a functional area, a project team, an improvement team, or lead the organization as a whole, you can improve your personal embrace of clarity and encourage it in your operations, as well as in those people within your realm of influence.

---

[27] Hayley Tsukayama, "Samsung Cites Two Separate Battery Issues for Its Note 7 Recall Woes," *Washington Post*, January 22, 2017.

The following chapters provide specific actions you can take to produce the greatest benefits in clarity. Since neither clarity nor organizational performance is strictly linear, no chapter stands fully on its own. It's the interrelationship of management practices—and the degree of clarity in each—that provides for overall clarity. That said, clarity pursuit can start anywhere you feel you can make the greatest impact.

Chapter 2 focuses on your organizational Purpose: why the organization exists, and how that *why* is communicated to all team members and embedded in what you do. Chapter 3 connects Purpose to the organizational Priorities you set by using a clarifying methodology for defining priorities, gaining consensus around them, and tracking progress toward achieving them. Chapter 4 addresses Process clarity, including the organization's value streams and the processes that support them. Chapter 5 highlights the methods and approaches you need to monitor and continuously improve organizational Performance. Chapter 6 offers instruction and coaching around Problem Solving as an organization-wide capability that everyone—from executive leadership to the frontline worker—needs to achieve outstanding performance. Chapter 7 addresses you as an individual and the work you need to do to achieve personal clarity. Chapter 8 summarizes the key points from the book and offers ways for you to begin your commitment to building a culture of clarity.

Clarity, like forming any new habit, requires practice if you want to overcome the default mode of ambiguity, and practice takes time. Just as you wouldn't become a concert pianist in the first month of taking piano lessons, you won't reach the goal of consistently pursuing and operating with clarity overnight. Changing an entire organization into one that pursues clarity takes even longer and requires classic behavior modification. The larger the organization and the more entrenched it is in ambiguity, the more time it will take to transform it. You need to fight every instinct that screams for faster results than are psychologically and socially possible. Patient persistence is key.

Some of the time you spend will be dedicated to creating a safe environment for clarity to emerge and thrive. Organizations have to dispel the fear people have of asking questions or displaying their curiosity and deploy the means to surface problems and deal with them swiftly and matter-of-factly.

In some organizations, fear can be fairly entrenched. To show people you are serious about pursuing clarity, create safe spaces for candid conversations and experiment with overtly rewarding curiosity and clarity. Successful experiments will help accelerate the removal of fear. Chip away at it until you've created an environment in which it's not only safe to be clear, it's also an expectation. But be warned: consistency is key. When someone faces criticism, ridicule, or any sort of punitive action for seeking or operating with clarity, you will find yourself back at square one. This requires that you take a hard look at your leadership team and assess fit for creating a clarity-pursuing work environment.

The final requirement for success is will. *You have to want it.* Building clarity into your daily practices and into your organization's culture will take some effort, and will is the glue that helps new behaviors stick. The more ambiguity your organization has operated with in the past, the more effort it will take to transform how it operates today. The strength of will—your unwavering commitment—will provide the tenacity you'll need to lead this type of change.

I recently said that to the CEO at a client that had been adopting clarity-inducing Lean management practices, but doing so in a half-hearted way. "You have to be all-in if you want results," I told him. Initially he was irritated by my comment, but later he shared with me that my frank words triggered a change in perspective. He said he thought I hadn't shown enough respect for the progress they had made, but then, "I realized you were right," he said. "I hadn't fully committed. I guess I was trying to see if I could get significant results without full commitment, and I see now that's not how it works."

Correct. Halfway is *not* how clarity works. Step-by-step, however, is.

I believe in the power of people to change themselves and lead change across an organization. I've seen it firsthand. With awareness, practice in a safe environment, time, and will, you can begin to realize the productivity-increasing, morale-boosting, and performance-enhancing benefits of clarity. Let's get to it.

2

Purpose

People don't buy what you do. They buy why you do it.

—Simon Sinek

Realizing the myriad benefits that come with organizational clarity requires that you be 100 percent clear on the most important, foundational question there is: What is your organization's purpose?

It seems like a simple question, yet many organizations wrestle with it. Purpose isn't *what* you do, though it's important to know that. Purpose is *why* you do what you do. Why are you in business? Why do you deliver your particular goods or services? Why does your organization exist?

I invite you to consider the question for a full minute before reading further.

How did you do? If you found yourself unsure of the answer, debating between two or three options, or at a complete loss, you're not alone. I can count on two hands the number of leaders who have been able to answer this question with conviction and without hesitation.

A skeptic might say those low numbers reflect a lack of necessity, but that has not been my experience. In fact, business performance experts as far back as W. Edwards Deming have addressed the importance of purpose as a way to establish cohesion in the organization. How else do you establish priorities and create focus? As Deming scholar William Scherkenbach wrote, "The wishes and hopes of top management for the future might be very noble, and in fact be on a course that could effectively meet customer needs and expectations except for one thing: the rest of the company is off somewhere else doing their best."[1]

Having a clear purpose ensures that no one is off doing their best at something that does not matter to the organization. With purpose, everyone understands the foundational reason why the company is in business or the organization exists. That said, such clarity is rare, not because it is nonessential but because companies don't take the time to achieve it. Mature organizations may be so many years from inception that they have lost sight of their original motivation. Large organizations may have gotten so diverse and far-flung that the disparate departments don't feel a unifying connection. Rapid-growth start-ups may be so caught up in day-to-day operations that they don't consider it.

Whether early or mature in an organization's life cycle, purpose is your *why*. It's the reason behind all that you do. It reflects what your organization believes in. Of course, organizations can survive for years—even decades—without clarity of purpose, but at some point you will find yourselves faced with a challenge you are not prepared to tackle and for which you lack a clear sense of direction. At those times, you need to understand your why.

Consider how a clear purpose might have helped United Airlines prevent the criticism it received when a passenger bumped from

---

[1] William Scherkenbach, *The Deming Route to Quality and Productivity* (CEEP Press Books, 1986), 13–14.

an overbooked flight refused to leave the aircraft. The staff working that flight called the airport's security guards to the scene, and they forcibly removed the passenger, an act captured on multiple cell phones and splashed across social media. The resulting uproar launched a much-needed conversation about airline booking practices and passenger rights, and it also prompted people to voice pent-up frustration with United Airlines.

Modern air travel is a hassle in the best of circumstances, but flying United—according to the bulk of customer comments—stood out on account of the indifferent service and overall lack of attention to the customer. There is no driving purpose guiding employees in a way that would make the act of forcibly removing a passenger unthinkable. As bestselling author and speaker Patrick Lencioni put it, "United is an organization without clarity. Clarity of purpose. Clarity of values. Clarity of strategy. And when an organization doesn't know why it exists, how it behaves, and what makes it unique, it falls back on policies and procedures, which is as demoralizing for customers looking for service as it is for the employees unable to use their judgment to make decisions."[2]

Consider as well the importance of purpose for a business analytics company that hired our firm to deploy performance improvement practices in its key operations. It had been experiencing rapid growth and was expecting to double its revenue that year. One of the executives had experience with Lean management and knew that, deployed properly, Lean could help the organization scale quickly and set the stage for continued financial strength when it entered a period of more modest growth.

The organization provides insights into safety practices for customers in high-risk industries. To uncover those insights, the company installs hardware to capture real-time data at the customer

---

[2] Patrick Lencioni, "United Airlines Was Broken Long Before That Doctor Was Dragged Off a Flight. Here's What It Can Do Next," *Inc.*, May 4, 2017.

site, and then analyzes the data using sophisticated software and algorithms. The resulting analyses produce real-time insights into worker behavior, which help customers learn how best to reduce risk.

Early in our engagements I ask three questions to assess organizational clarity: What do you do? (What good or service do you provide?) What do you *really* do? (What customer problem does that good or service solve?) Why do you do it? (What is your purpose?) (see Figure 2.1). I asked the first question— "What do you do?"—of two dozen managers and received two consistent, though inaccurate, responses: "We make hardware that tracks safety practices," and "We install hardware that tracks safety practices."

The first response implied that the company is a manufacturer, which it's not (a contract manufacturer makes the hardware). The

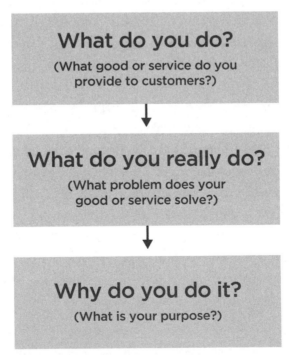

FIGURE 2.1 Three levels of knowing who you are as an organization

second response implied that it's an installation company, which it's not. It does install hardware, but for the purpose of capturing data on which to perform its analytics. Installation is merely a means to deliver value. Interestingly, when I asked the managers what type of company they were, the responses were unanimous: "We're a technology firm." That was a clear and accurate response, but no one caught the incongruence of "technology" with manufacturing or installations, and none of the responses captured the firm's true *what*: analytics and insights.

The lack of clarity this organization had about the fundamentals of its business—especially below the executive level—is not unusual. On the contrary, this exercise with client groups often reveals disparity in the way team members understand what the organization does, the customer problems it solves, and—most important—why it chooses to solve those particular problems over others.

If you're in an industry that produces a tangible good, the answer to the question *what* you do usually begins with, "We assemble, build, grow, make, mine, produce, etc.," and ends with a description of the tangible physical good you manufacture, assemble, extract, or build: We make circuit breakers. We build roads. We extract coal. We produce soy milk. We raise cattle. We grow carrots.

If you're in the service sector, the answer to this question likely begins with, "We deliver, design, manage, provide, repair, sell, teach, transport, write, etc.," and ends with a description of the service the organization provides: We deliver healthcare. We provide overnight accommodations. We manage investments. We repair refrigeration systems. We design marketing campaigns. We store data. We enforce the law.

Notwithstanding the inconsistency in the answers provided by the junior team members at our technology client, most senior leaders either have or can quickly get clarity about *what* they do. This is particularly true for companies that I refer to as being "in love with their products." Love of product is common in technology and manufacturing firms with a long history of market domination, but it can happen to any company that gets too focused on the specifics of the product without a higher level understanding of what that product does for its customer.

Knowing *what* your organization does is important, but knowing one's purpose requires answers to the next question: "What problem(s) does your product solve?" The answers from the tech firm managers were consistent on this one: "We help our customers reduce insurance expenses." Indeed, one of the rotating images on the flat screen monitor in the firm's front lobby highlighted the cost savings achieved when its customers have fewer accidents, and therefore pay lower insurance premiums, and experience reduced equipment repair costs and fewer employees receiving disability. This is a good example of clarifying the problem a good or service helps a customer solve. Clarity about the problem is a deeper form of what. It is not far enough, though.

To understand *why*, our client needed to go deeper still. I asked the managers to reflect on their description of the problem: "We help our customer reduce insurance expenses." There's clear value in that. Understanding the customer's problem is critical if the company wishes to develop products to solve it. But is clarity around the problem enough to motivate people and to continuously improve the business? How does clarity about the problem make you feel about what the firm does? Are you moved by it? Would you be willing to work until 10 p.m. four nights in a row to help your customer reduce insurance expenses? Does helping customers save money—an important benefit—inspire you?

With that question of motivation top of mind, I asked the third question: "Why are you in business?"

Silence.

A few people answered by repeating the problem that their product solved (saving money). One person added that their product also helped customers meet regulatory requirements. While that's true and it's good that they were moving toward a deeper form of "what," it still didn't explain *why* the company exists. In fact, they didn't arrive at an answer to the question during that session. Instead, it was a few days later when one of the managers showed up for a meeting wearing a T-shirt with large, bold letters that said: WE SAVE LIVES.

The T-shirt was part of a product launch that had taken place a few months earlier. Though the tagline hadn't been incorporated into the company's broader operations, it provided the answer to *why. Saving lives* was its true purpose.

Consider the qualities of that statement for a moment: We save lives. No one could argue the importance of it. No one who cares about others and about work that contributes to others could fail to be moved by it. Saving lives matters. It is emotional. It has meaning. It is also definitive. It can guide decisions. It can help leaders decide whether an initiative, a business opportunity, or a proposed partnership serves the organization's purpose or distracts from it. As leadership and business performance guru Simon Sinek has said, "If you don't know *why*, you can't know *how*.[3] I'll add that if you don't know why, you may not even get *what* right.

Why Is It So Hard to Know Why?

The example of our tech client helps make concrete how a competitive company providing a high-value service can still lack clarity about the fundamentals of what it does and why it does it. I shared its story not because its challenges are unique but because they are ubiquitous. Why is it so hard to know why? I've noticed some patterns.

---

[3] Simon Sinek, *Start with Why* (Portfolio, 2009), 70.

The first pattern I've seen is that organizations confuse purpose with its cousins: mission, vision, values, and guiding principles. Each of these elements is different, but I regularly see them used interchangeably with each other, and with purpose. They are not the same. My definitions, in simple terms:

- Mission is a statement of *what*. We provide . . . , We make . . . , etc. You complete the sentence with the name of a good or service: a noun.
- Vision is a description of where you are heading as a company. A destination is also a noun.
- Values—also nouns—provide clarity about the behaviors and work attitudes that are acceptable.
- Guiding principles are a more specific version of values. They provide specific "rules" (in verb/noun format) about how the organization will conduct its business.
- Purpose is a *verb* that reflects why you have a mission, vision, values, or guiding principles.

As these definitions make clear, mission, vision, values, guiding principles, and purpose are distinct from each other. I see a lot of confusion, however, even from organizational leaders, and there needn't be. Each provides positive guidance, but in a distinct way.

The oil and gas giant Chevron has done an outstanding job of defining its mission, vision, and values in distinct terms. Chevron's mission—its *what*—is to "develop the energy that improves lives and powers the world forward." Its vision is "to be the global energy company most admired for its people, partnership, and performance." And its values are to "conduct our business in a socially and environmentally responsible manner, respecting the law and universal human rights to benefit the communities where we work."[4]

---

[4] https://www.chevron.com/about/the-chevron-way

Each of these statements is distinct, but together they are coherent. It makes clear where Chevron chooses to position itself in an industry under pressure for its environmental impact and association with corruption. Chevron's purpose of improving people's lives is embedded in its mission. To make purpose more powerful, Chevron could provide specifics about how in practice it improves the lives of its customers, but overall the company does a good job.

Marc Benioff, the founder, chairman, and CEO of Salesforce.com, has been lauded for the way he imbues social purpose into his for-profit organization. Benioff has advocated for a 1-1-1 model whereby the company commits 1 percent of its equity, 1 percent of employee time, and 1 percent of product to nonprofit work. In his words, "We had a vision from the beginning that not only would we have a new technology model, which was the cloud, not only would we have a new business model, which was subscription, but we'd have a new philanthropic model, which is 1-1-1."

The 1-1-1 commitment ensures that Salesforce is about more than business. Benioff believes that connecting the company to communities through philanthropy makes his employees feel engaged and inspired, and helps him expand his horizons as a leader. Salesforce, with all its clarity about why it does what it does, calls that *why* a mission: "To leverage Salesforce's technology, people, and resources to help improve communities around the world." That's a purpose—a *why*, not a *what*—and illustrates that even organizations with purpose may define their why within the mission/vision/values mix.

To be clear, the semantics matter less than the results. I do not believe that a company needs to define all five statements: mission, vision, values, guiding principles, and purpose. They're all useful if they're clearly defined, true to the intent (which many aren't), and understood by all (which many aren't). Purpose is the most important. Purpose is emotional, and since humans are emotional beings it carries far more weight. I'm not suggesting that it's OK to cry at the drop of a hat or share every private feeling you have in the workplace. I do mean that everyone wants his or her contribution to mean something and bring benefit. Purpose generates emotional resonance, which is one of the best ways to attract and retain top talent. People want to be part of something larger than themselves, and a well-defined purpose fulfills this human need.

Ironically, emotion is a second reason why organizations have trouble with purpose. Emotions—often unwelcome in business—represent uncomfortable territory for a lot of companies. For many leaders it's not natural to describe their business in those terms. They prefer to speak in terms of product features and benefits.

The third reason why it is hard to clarify purpose is that it requires leaders to get to the core of what makes the organization tick—what *truly* drives decisions, customer relationships, prioritization, and management practices. Mining of this nature can be difficult for a number of reasons. Sometimes it uncovers decisions made without much rationale. It can expose political decisions made to benefit a group of leaders or a department and not the company as a whole. It can reveal a lack of clarity about goals or ways of operating the organization thought were totally clear. It can uncover inconsistencies between the company's stated values and its actions. It can, in short, feel like exposing a naked emperor, and no one wants to do that.

The last reason why purpose is so hard in the context of a for-profit company is because many think they have one—to make money. Nobel Prize–winning economist Milton Friedman once said that the social responsibility of a business is to increase its profits. He was responding to the debate, still raging in business circles, about how far businesses should go to operate in a way that provides social benefits. His position is popular among many who believe that profitable companies, the taxes they pay, and the employment opportunities they create achieve purpose simply because they exist. Friedmanites see profit as purpose enough, but it isn't.

Profit Is Not Your Purpose

If you answered "Why does your organization exist?" with the response, "To make money," you're not clear about your purpose.

Making money is an *outcome* of providing a desired or needed good or service in a way that meets the quality and price expectations of your customers. Making money is not the sole reason to do it, however. Nonprofit organizations focused on a social or environmental service, as well as government organizations with direct citizen-facing functions, usually find it easier to keep their beneficiaries at the center of what they do. For them it can be difficult or even unseemly to talk about money beyond acknowledging the importance of stable and sustainable financing. Yet even publicly traded, for-profit organizations shouldn't put profit as their sole raison d'être. In practice, business founders are more often driven by a passion to fulfill an unmet desire or need or solve a vexing problem.

Those few businesses that do truly exist only to make money often crumble when they face their first significant business challenge. For instance, a colleague once told me that when he asked the CEO of a prospective client what the organization's mission was, the CEO said: "To make money. And our vision is to make *lots* of money." The company filed for Chapter 11 bankruptcy protection two years later and was acquired for pennies on the dollar. The new owner did not retain the CEO. A former Toyota executive, in contrast, summed up

Toyota's profitability motive in this way: "The emphasis on profitability is because we need the profits to grow and meet our social needs and not from shareholder pressures."[5]

Organizations that focus on money consider only the needs of a narrow set of stakeholders. The only people who care deeply about how much money an organization makes are its investors and shareholders. Customers and employees—the two groups that contribute directly to a company's success—are indifferent to how much a company makes, so long as there is enough to ensure reasonable product availability and job security.

Customers want their suppliers to help *them* make money by reducing their expenses, improving their productivity, easing their effort, improving the quality of their products, or adding features that will enable them to capture greater market share. Reflect for a moment: What value does your organization provide? That's what customers care about. Peter Drucker nailed this idea when he said the purpose of a business is to create a customer.[6] I'm with Drucker. Companies that take this responsibility seriously win.

Employees, in turn, typically care about how much money their employer makes only in so far as it reduces the risk of layoffs, ensures higher bonuses,[7] and provides budgets that allow teams to accomplish high-quality output.

---

[5] Shankar Basu, *Corporate Purpose: Why It Matters More Than Strategy* (Routledge, 1999), 101. Note: For readers who enjoy studying Toyota, the book covers Toyota's roots and business philosophy more deeply than most and does a very good job in showing how Toyota's purpose came to be and has been consistently adhered to. The book is currently out of print, but you can find some of its content online.

[6] Peter F. Drucker, *The Practice of Management* (Harper Business, originally published in 1954, reissued 2006), 37.

[7] This is one of many reasons why bonuses and incentive packages should be based on overall company performance versus the performance of individuals or functional work teams. Bonuses do matter, but many bonus structures create a "me-first" culture that hurts rather than helps an organization achieve its goals.

There is a final reason why making money isn't an appropriate why: Most people aren't inspired by it. They may want and need it, but that's different. People are motivated by feeling that they are part of something larger than themselves. Millennials in particular look for work with deeper meaning and purpose, but this trend is evident in all age groups.[8] Purpose is a cross-generational, fundamental human need. Organizations that take time to ensure that team members have a strong connection to purpose create enthusiastic brand ambassadors who are deeply committed to helping the organization succeed.

WHY KNOW WHY?

It should be clear by now what purpose is and why it may not have been top of mind before now. Next we tackle in more detail why you need to care about it—how does clarity of purpose benefit you? Purpose matters from three perspectives: your organization's, your employees', and your customers'.

Purpose and Your Organization

Organizations operating with a clear purpose gain a competitive advantage.[9] It is simply easier to make decisions and pursue value-creating opportunities when the purpose they are serving is clear and consistent. Without such clarity, organizations confronted with new trends or competitors can lose focus and launch competing efforts that pull the company in conflicting directions.

---

[8] In my view, Millennials have it right, and I'm grateful for how they're questioning workplace traditions and voting with their feet. See *State of the American Workplace*, Gallup, Inc., 2017, 5.

[9] Nate Dvorak and Bryant Ott, "A Company's Purpose Has to Be a Lot More Than Words," *Gallup Business Journal*, July 28, 2015.

Having clarity of purpose acts as an anchor that keeps your ship from being dashed against the rocks or floating out to sea toward an unknown destination. Purpose is also an elixir that tames organizational attention deficit disorder and self-inflicted chaos. Being clear about purpose helps prevent you from flip-flopping on branding issues, or overlooking a customer need, or pursuing a random acquisition or other investment. With clear purpose, priorities are easier to set, creativity can be funneled in the best directions, and problems are easier to surface. Knowing why you do what you do contributes to clarity about how to handle an emerging problem or business opportunity.

Consider how purpose may influence decisions at a company like Seventh Generation, a maker of household consumer packaged goods like hand soap and toilet paper. The company derives its purpose from a Native American tradition of considering the impact of its actions on the next seven generations. With that purpose, Seventh Generation manufactures its products to use few resources and no toxins, all toward the end of making useful products that are gentle to the user and to the earth. Having such clear purpose acts as a filter for deciding which suppliers to work with or prioritizing new products to develop. This purpose has paid off for Seventh Generation in financial returns. The company saw double-digit compound annual sales growth from 2006 until 2016, when it was purchased by Unilever.[10]

In contrast, consider how a lack of purpose prevented an energy utility I worked with in the mid-2000s from responding to change on the horizon. Leaders had not defined a clear purpose for the organization, and thus had not defined why it supplied energy. There was little discussion of the importance of lights or heat for the customers it served, and far more emphasis on the *what* of

---

[10] Jack Nef, "Unilever Agrees to Buy Seventh Generation," *Adage*, September 16, 2016.

energy resources and costs. As a result, the organization was reactive when it came to short-term fluctuations in energy supply and costs. Within that as context, the leaders believed wind energy was not relevant to the business, and that the challenge of storing and transmitting renewables would prevent wind development over their three-year planning horizon. They were wrong. From 2000 to 2010 installed wind energy capacity grew by 8,000 percent, according to the U.S. Department of Energy, and became highly relevant in this company's service area.[11] Without a clear purpose, the utility had no lens for thinking about how it wanted to prepare itself and its customers for a rapidly changing energy landscape. The utility lost two years of development and innovation—and potential revenue—trying to figure itself out. Fortunately it has caught up and is a market leader. But it nearly missed an important business wave and expended a lot of rushed effort in its catch-up period.

It's no coincidence when for-profit organizations that clarify and embed purpose into the DNA of the organization also see strong financial returns: A 2014 study conducted jointly by Harvard Business Review Analytic Services and Ernst & Young's Beacon Institute found that companies with a strong sense of purpose outperformed both those with no stated purpose and those in the early stages of mining for meaning.[12] When an organization's behavior aligns with a compelling purpose and brand promise, customers give that company twice as much share of their wallet over companies that don't operate from an anchor of purpose.[13] The competitive edge increases over time because true embedded purpose is difficult to replicate, whereas "me too" products are not.

---

[11] U.S. Department of Energy, *2010 Wind Technologies Market Report*, https://www1.eere.energy.gov/wind/pdfs/51783.pdf.

[12] "The Business Case for Purpose," Harvard Business Review Analytic Services Report, 2015, https://hbr.org/resources/pdfs/comm/ey/19392HBRReportEY.pdf.

[13] Dvorak and Ott, p. 2.

Purpose and Employees

From an employee's perspective, purpose matters too—a lot. It is human nature to want to be part of something bigger than oneself. This is doubly true of work given how much time we spend in the workplace. Gallup's ongoing research into the role employee engagement plays in business performance validates this. Their surveys consistently find that when organizations are silent or ambiguous about their purpose, or when organizations communicate a purpose with which employees do not connect, employees disengage.[14]

Ensuring you get the best ideas and performance and longest tenure out of your employees therefore requires investments in making the organization the kind of place people want to be associated with. Job perks are definitely part of this equation. Tuition reimbursements, free lunches, onsite child care—employees find these benefits attractive, but they don't guarantee employee loyalty. Even investments in employee engagement yield little if they are not connected to a larger set of cultural norms and behaviors.

In a study of 250 companies, for example, business author Jacob Morgan found that many companies try to spur engagement through serial investments in one-off events like bonuses or team-building events. He finds companies that address engagement in this way still receive consistently low marks from their employees. In contrast, companies that make cohesive and long-term investments in the employee *experience*—which he defines as including the cultural, technological, and physical environment in which people work—look better in the eyes of employees. Not surprisingly, those organizations earn stronger financial returns.[15]

Findings on the impact of employee investment like those from Gallup and Morgan offer evidence for the idea that employees want a deeper connection to the company, the work it does, how it does

---

[14] *State of the American Workplace*, Gallup, Inc., 2017, 5.

[15] Jacob Morgan, *The Employee Experience Advantage* (Wiley, 2017).

it, and why. The greater an employee's connection to purpose, the more engaged and loyal that employee will be.

I do not mean to suggest that salary and benefits don't matter. They do. All employees care about getting paid what they see as their worth, receiving benefits that fit their needs, and having perks that align with their interests. Organizations that want to attract and keep the best talent cannot rely solely on salary and benefits to engage their stars, however. They need an "emotional hook." Practical concerns will quickly drive a valued employee to a competitor offering higher pay or better benefits *unless* the employee has nonpractical reasons to stay that balance his or her practical ones. Practical reasons don't have feelings. When there's no emotion at stake, it's an easy choice to simply go where the money is.

You want employees to care because caring is the most important psychological "must" for engaging people. But caring requires you to have a clear purpose. Such clarity allows you to attract and retain people specifically drawn to your organizational why.[16]

Consider how you might react if you were a prospective employee. Take a moment and pretend you're considering a role with my business analytics client described early in this chapter. Pay attention to how you feel—not what you *think*—knowing that the company makes and installs hardware.

Now put that aside.

Pay attention to how you *feel* knowing that the company's greatest value lies in the software it designs to analyze client data.

Now put that aside and pay attention to how you *feel* knowing that the company helps its customers save money.

Now put that aside and pay attention to how you feel about saving lives.

---

[16] As addressed in Chapter 5 of *The Outstanding Organization*, if your employees aren't engaged, it's you, not them. People want to engage. You have to establish the conditions for them to engage.

Are you tempted to go onto Monster or LinkedIn right now and look for a company where you can help save lives? Are you eager to roll up your sleeves and get to work? I don't know about you, but they had me at "we save lives."

That brings us to an important point about employees and purpose—you have to communicate with them about it. Over and over and over again. Don't underestimate how much work this requires. The Harvard-Beacon Institute study I referenced earlier found that nearly all of the 474 global executives surveyed saw the connection between purpose and organizational performance, but fewer than half felt their company had clearly articulated it. Only a few of the companies had embedded their purpose deeply enough in the organization to reap its full potential.[17] The story about the technology firm earlier in the chapter highlights this common reality: most of the executives were clear about the firm's purpose, but the work teams weren't.

Purpose and Customers

Does having a strong sense of organizational purpose matter to *customers*? I believe that, in some cases, it does—though keep in mind that purpose operates differently for customers than it does inside the organization. The benefits of purpose for customers are mostly indirect. They come to a customer through products that are easy to use and solve a clear problem. They come to customers through service processes that are simple and direct and result in a clear resolution to a problem. Customers may not be able to see the connection between a company's purpose and their experience with it, but they will definitely feel it if their interactions with you breed frustration, confusion, and wasted time spent solving a problem that shouldn't have existed in the first place. In fact, your organization's

---

[17] "The Business Case for Purpose," Harvard Business Review Analytic Services.

customer service metrics are an excellent purpose diagnostic. If you find that customers are not giving you consistently high marks for customer service, look to your purpose. Achieving clarity of purpose puts you in a better position to improve the customer experience.

In addition to the widespread indirect effects of purpose on customers, there are also some direct effects, though they do not apply in the same way in every circumstance. When purpose works directly on customers, there is often an ideological or service-oriented issue wrapped up in the identity of the organization. For instance, Starbucks is a leading buyer of Fair Trade coffee beans, continually redesigns its cups to reduce paper waste, adjusts processes to reduce water consumption, and provides generous benefits to its workers.

Dozens of companies have likewise highlighted social purpose as part of their raison d'être. Nike has become a leading proponent of transparent supply chains and fair labor practices after one of its suppliers was exposed for using child laborers in its factories.[18] SolarCity works to make solar power more widespread and affordable. TOMS makes shoes with a "buy one donate one" business model, in which every pair of shoes purchased results in the donation of a second pair to a needy community.

These are just a few examples of companies wearing their purpose quite openly. These companies still have to make products that customers want, of course. But customers arguably stay with them and continue to buy from them because they believe in the company, feel proud of what the company does, and want to support it. When organizational purpose aligns with customer values, customers are more likely to try a product and, if it addresses their needs, more likely to continue buying it.

---

[18] Ashley Lutz, "How Nike Shed Its Sweatshop Image to Dominate the Shoe Industry," *Business Insider*, June 6.

Consider how this relationship between customers and organizational purpose has played out in the aftermath of recent automotive recalls. Research that compared pre- and post-recall customer loyalty for Ford, GM, Hyundai, and Toyota found that the post-recall reduction in customer loyalty ranged from 3.3 percent to 11.2 percent, with Toyota faring the best and GM the worst.[19] Why? The study did not attempt to answer this question, but I have a hypothesis.

Toyota has been clear for decades about its commitment to the quality of its cars, and the need to attract and retain excellent people to make them. This commitment is reflected in its communications about purpose: "It's our belief that our cars should do more than help you go places on the road, they should also help you go places in life."[20]

Though the quality gap between Toyota cars and those of other manufacturers has narrowed in the last 20 years, no manufacturer has placed quite the same public emphasis on quality and how it keeps drivers on the road as Toyota. I believe that clarity of purpose, and the consistency with which Toyota pursues it, contributes to sustained customer loyalty even in the face of a recall. Purpose does not mean that Toyota did not make mistakes that led to the recalls—it did, and has apologized for not reacting quickly enough to identify the root causes of problems. But its emphasis on the purpose of helping people get where they are going perhaps gave its customers more confidence that it would solve its recall problems.

---

[19] Robert Passikoff, "Brand Loyalty Recalls: Ford, General Motors, Hyundai, & Toyota," *Forbes*, April 30, 2014.

[20] "Let's Go Places," http://www.toyota.com/usa/our-story/.

Purpose at Toyota

Toyota's people- and society-driven purpose was introduced in 1935 when Kiichiro Toyoda, son of founder Sakichi Toyoda, published the Toyoda Precepts developed by his father. Those evolved into the corporate polices and guiding principles that have been updated every few years to reflect the company's current thinking.

In studying Toyota's evolution as a company from a fledgling automotive manufacturer in 1937 through its rise to global dominance and its current neck-and-neck position with Volkswagen,[21] you can see minor shifts in the emphasis it places on how it wishes to conduct business. But the one unwavering principle has been its emphasis on people, both in its strong focus on developing employees and its obsessiveness over customer value.

The Toyoda Precepts (1935)

1. Be contributive to the development and welfare of the country by working together, despite position, in faithfully fulfilling your duties.
2. Be at the vanguard of the times through endless creativity, inquisitiveness and purpose of improvement.
3. Be practical and avoid frivolity.
4. Be kind and generous; strive to create a warm, homelike atmosphere.
5. Be reverent, and show gratitude for things great and small in thought and deed.[22]

---

[21] Bertel Schmitt, "It's Official: Volkswagen Is World's Largest Automaker in 2016. Or Maybe Toyota," *Forbes*, January 30, 2017.

[22] Basu, *Corporate Purpose*, 77.

Toyota Corporate Policy (1989)

1. Consider the customer first, and create products always offering outstanding quality, value, and technology by sticking to the basics of sound manufacturing.
2. Strive for progress through openness and creativity, based on mutual trust among all members of the company.
3. Join hands for mutual success, drawing on the vitality of the worldwide Toyota family.
4. Contribute to economic growth and greater quality of life through responsible corporate citizenship in every corner of the globe.
5. Constantly pursue self-development, and always keep in step with market and societal changes.[23]

Guiding Principles (1992)

1. Be a company of the world.
2. Serve the greater good of people everywhere by devoting careful attention to safety and to the environment.
3. Assert leadership in technology and in customer satisfaction.
4. Become a contributing member of the community in every nation.
5. Foster a corporate culture that honors individuality while promoting teamwork.
6. Pursue continuing growth through efficient, global management.
7. Build lasting relationships with business partners around the world.[24]

---

[23] Basu, *Corporate Purpose*, 82.

[24] Basu, *Corporate Purpose*, 84.

When then-president Shoichiro Toyoda released the Guiding Principles above, his cover letter stated: "I want to call on everyone at Toyota to take part individually and collectively in reinforcing our corporate identity as a company where the greater good of society is the first consideration in all endeavors." Throughout its 80 years in business, one principle Toyota has never wavered on is that people come first. Now that's clarity!

The bottom line on clarity of purpose for your organization, the employees, and the customer is that every executive, senior leader, middle manager, supervisor, team lead, frontline worker, support staff, job applicant, board member, shareholder, in most cases customer, and supplier should know—clearly and unequivocally—why the organization exists. They should be able to articulate it in language that is consistent across the organization, and they should be able to use it to guide decisions and interactions.

Until you nail your purpose, there's no chance that your organization will operate with the level of clarity needed to reach your potential. Knowing your collective why is the first step to unleashing the power and potential that lies within your organization.

FINDING YOUR PURPOSE

Now that you understand the benefits of purpose, it's time to get to the business of finding yours. Clarifying your why may sound like a simple task—and it is. But simple isn't always easy. In some organizations it can take two to three months of focused effort to define purpose, and obtain organization-wide input, feedback, and socialization of it.

Begin the discussion with the executive team. You may also include investors and your board of directors. It helps to involve a facilitator with deep experience working with organizations to define their purpose. (Note that mining for purpose is different from creating a strategy and often requires a different type of facilitator.)

The work will involve going deep into the three questions presented at the beginning of this chapter: the what, what *really*, and why of the organization. I would also be remiss if I failed to remind you of the obvious—you need to be clear on *who* you're doing it for.

Know Thy Customer

Your why is inextricably linked to the identity of your core customer. How does your customer think and behave? What's his or her daily life like? How does the good or service you provide affect that daily life? You need this knowledge to codify your customers' needs and determine the best ways to deliver value to them.

One technique you can use to achieve clarity about your customers and their needs is to spend time at the customer location—also known as the *gemba* or "the real place" where the action happens—gathering deep insights into the customer experience. You need to observe customers—*lots of them!*—using the goods you make or the services you provide.

Many executives never do this, to their peril. They rely instead on surveys, which are notoriously poor vehicles for getting to know your customers. A case in point: I recently had to call the customer service department of my local cable company with a service issue. The agent could not solve my problem on the phone, and scheduled an appointment with a technician. Still, when we ended the call she asked me to complete the customer survey, adding that at her company "anything less than a five is considered a low mark" that would negatively affect her review. Why ask if you don't want clarity? Other surveys ask such vague questions that they don't provide meaningful insights. That's what I mean when I say that customer surveys communicate poor information. Too many of them are designed in a way that fails to garner honest feedback on what the customer needs. Either that or they are too simplistic in design—for example by focusing only on the "net promoter" score or some other reductive, context-free metric. Don't rely on them. Every single leader on your executive team needs to have deep customer understanding. Everyone, not just your sales and marketing executives. Ask the customers questions as they're using the product. Learn what they *really* think versus what your annual survey reveals.

Armed with this meaningful information, build a "customer persona" for your primary target group. Having a specific persona in mind when developing products or pursuing new markets leads to better decisions about product features, marketing campaigns, and quality, pricing, and service expectations.

Some of the organizations we've worked with nonetheless balk at this suggestion. They believe that creating a customer persona will force them to oversimplify the needs of the customer, resulting in product development and service decisions that ignore important segments of their customer pool.

While it's true that no two customers are exactly alike, they vary a lot less when you're clear about your core customer and the problem(s) your product solves for him or her. If you have not done the heavy lifting of clarifying who you're serving and why, it's more difficult to identify the subsegments with differing needs. The goal is not to box you into a limited and generic set of actions and decisions. The goal is to define the core group. From there you are in a position to identify variation—and you may find that your customers aren't as varied as you thought.

This is not a one-and-done exercise. The definition of your core customer will change over time as market conditions evolve. Grocery retailer Trader Joe's, for example, has extreme clarity about its purpose and mission, in large part because it knows its customer very well. In the past the company described its target customer as an "unemployed college professor who drives a very, very used Volvo."[25] The professor's needs and sensibilities were taken into account for buying, packaging, and marketing decisions. Having a specific persona in mind allowed leaders to create one of the most consistent brands out there.

Yet over time, the persona has evolved. A manager at my local Trader Joe's recently described its current target customer as "well educated and seeking high quality value." That's not as specific a description as the Volvo-driving, out-of-work professor, but it's still very clear that the company is not serving the teen market, nor is it going after customers in all socioeconomic strata.

Even if you serve multiple distinct customer groups, you can develop personae to capture each of them. For example, former Urban Outfitters CEO Richard Haynes has described Urban's core customer as an upscale 18- to 26-year-old renter who carries a little bit of angst. He described subsidiary Anthropologie's customer as a more polished, older homeowner who is likely married with children. Subsidiary Free People's core customer loves spring festivals—Coachella and Wanderlust most of all.[26]

Similarly, a food producer we've worked with describes one of its three core customer groups as, "30 to 49-year-old middle-income parents with children between the ages of five and nine years old, who value quality over price and, because their time is limited, place high value on convenience." That's a mouthful, but clarity about this key customer group makes for far more consistent messaging, brand identity, and product development decisions.

Clarity-seeking organizations define either one core customer or a small number of core customer types and use that understanding

---

[25] Chip and Dan Health, "The Curse of Knowledge," *Harvard Business Review*, December 2006.

[26] Analyst Day webcast, www.edge.media-server.com, September 2012.

to drive decision making and maintain alignment around product development, marketing strategies, service needs, and so on. When you combine the power of a clear purpose with a clear target customer, it becomes far easier to achieve outstanding performance.

From What to Why

Once you've confirmed that you know who you serve, you can dig more deeply into the work of finding your why. Whether you wish to do this work on your own or lay the groundwork with an objective facilitator, you can use the questions below to get started, beginning with the easiest question, What?, moving to the more complex question, What *really*?, and then to the most difficult question, Why? These questions appear linear, but gaining clarity is often an iterative process. You may find that answers to later questions reveal the need to modify responses given earlier.

Level 1: What do you do?
- What products (goods and/or services) do you provide?
- To which market segments?
- Who's your competition?
- What's unique about your products compared to those of the competition?

Level 2: What *really* do you do?
- What problems do your goods or services solve? Be specific here. Don't stop at the first level problem, but dig more deeply to uncover the most fundamental customer problems your product solves.

Level 3: Why do you do it?
- Why does your organization provide your service or good?
- Why that good or service and not another?
- What need or desire does that good or service fulfill?

■ What outcome(s) does your good or service enable? In other words, what does your good or service enable your customers to know, feel, or accomplish that they wouldn't otherwise be able to?

Pay close attention as you move through the questions to the emotional reaction you have to the responses. Level 1 *what* answers are usually straightforward and clear. If you react to them at all, it will likely be at an intellectual level. You make, provide, design, or repair, etc.

Level 2 questions should produce a bit more of an emotional response. After all, no matter what type of business you're in, you don't make, provide, design, or repair for nothing, but rather to solve customer problems. If you're not solving a problem—or if you're creating a problem—you have no business being in business.

Does thinking about the problems you solve make you feel more engaged? It should. Even if a problem is vexing, most people ultimately love finding a solution to it. The clearer you can get on the problem or range of problems your organization solves, the more energy you and your teams will feel.

Level 3 is the real emotional hook, the level at which you should be digging to uncover the resonant reason why your organization exists. If you are a tax accountant, do you process tax returns? No, your *real* what is to help people meet a complex legal obligation they may not have the time or knowledge to meet on their own. And your why? Maybe you give people control over their money, or the ability to invest in the future, or peace of mind that they won't get into trouble.

Allow me to demonstrate how powerful this set of questions can be for an organization through a client example. Several years back I was working with a greeting card manufacturer to redesign how it delivered value to customers. When I opened the session by asking the leaders in the room what they do, they looked at me like I had lost my marbles. "We make greeting cards," one participant said. "Good," I replied, "I see I'm at the right company."

Then I asked, "What value do you deliver to your customers?" They explained that they had the very best designers and that they used high-quality raw materials (ink, paper, glitter, bows, and so on), which allowed their cards to earn high scores in focus groups that compared their products against their competitors'. These are all examples of how this company fulfills its *what*, but we were still not at the *why*.

"Why do people buy your cards?" I asked. The marketing executive said, "Because our cards are very high quality for the price." I agreed that the look and quality of the card matter, but the real customer value lies in the problem a card solves, so I asked the question that way: "What problem do your cards solve?" Silence. After a few minutes of thinking, someone mentioned feelings, which launched the group into a talking about how greeting cards allow people to express an emotion—love, gratitude, remorse, or support—or to fulfill a real or perceived obligation. Greeting cards often serve as a proxy for people who feel awkward expressing their emotions face-to-face in their own words. Discussions continued along those lines for a while, ultimately landing on the following purpose: We connect people and strengthen relationships.

Now imagine you're an employee of that greeting card company. Which inspires you more? Going to work every day to produce a high-quality card made of the best materials, or going to work every day to connect people and strengthen relationships? Do you see how what you do takes on a very different feel when you consider the problems that you're solving and why you solve them?

Kellogg has a great purpose statement: "Nourishing families so they can flourish and thrive."[27] The financial services company ING

---

[27] "Staying Focused. Going Further." http://www.kelloggcompany.com/en_US/our-vision-purpose.html.

also has a good purpose statement: "Empowering people to stay a step ahead in life and business." It's a bit vague about what "a step ahead" means, but at least it's customer focused.

You can develop a clear purpose statement, too, but be patient. The outputs from your discussions should be viewed as purpose-in-progress. They are initial drafts that you share with leaders and managers at all levels of the organization. Listen *very carefully* to their comments and reconvene to discuss and incorporate their views into the final purpose description.

YOU KNOW YOUR ORGANIZATION'S PURPOSE: NOW WHAT?

Once you know your organization's purpose, you need to communicate it frequently and with great clarity. Integrate it into your job postings so that prospective employees understand what you are about and can decide proactively if they want to be part of it. Integrate it into the onboarding of new employees so they understand the standard upon which all actions and decisions will be based. Place it front and center on your organization's website and your intranet home page. Add it to your security badges. Physically post it on visual information boards. Include it prominently in your annual report to key stakeholders and in marketing campaigns. Come back to it in every discussion about a key business decision.

You want everyone at all levels of the organization to know your purpose. More important, you want them to make decisions based on it. You want to get to the point where purpose is fully integrated into decision making.

Since purpose operates in different ways at different levels of the organization, you might need to adjust how you apply it, depending on where you sit. Here are some questions that trigger discussion to help you think through that process of applying purpose at different levels:

1. Organization: Why does the organization exist?
2. Groups: Why does your team exist?
3. Individuals: Why are you here? What is your personal purpose?
4. Requests: Why do you want/need me to take the requested action?
5. Gatherings: Why are we meeting?
6. Priorities: Why are these the priorities?
7. Process: Why do we do it this way?
8. Problems: Why do we need to solve this problem? Why do we need to solve this problem *now*? Why does this problem exist?
9. Improvement: Why is this improvement necessary?[28]
10. Reports and data: Why is this needed?

Now that you know your purpose, it is time to use it to get clear on your priorities.

---

[28] Using a well-crafted charter is one of the best ways to infuse clarity into work that's often ambiguous. A charter not only answers the *why*, but it also clarifies scope (what's the area of focus, and what does the team *not* have the authority to do?), how success will be defined (via measurable objectives), who's involved, and what the expectations are. Visit www.ksmartin.com/clarity-first to download a sample charter.

3

Priorities

If you chase two rabbits, you will lose them both.

—Native American saying

Target CIO Mike McNamara is known for his impeccable focus. When McNamara arrived at Target in 2015, he conducted an assessment of the IT operations. He established three strategic priorities for himself and his team—not five or ten, three. One of these priorities was to reduce from 800 to 80 the number of special projects actively underway or in queue. McNamara said, "Even a company as big as Target doesn't have 800 priorities."[1]

If 800 seems like an impossible number, I can tell you from experience that Target's mammoth IT inventory is not so shocking. When a midsize health system client took the time to look, it found 417 projects that were actively underway, waiting in queue, or started and abandoned. The count included a number of "stealth" or "rogue" projects that were more or less unknown to leadership,

---

[1] Kavita Kumar, "Target's IT Chief Set a New Direction, Starting with Smaller Budget," *Star Tribune*, July 30, 2016.

but had been consuming time and resources. Companies in every industry confront the runaway project list. A manufacturing client found 132. A financial services company stopped counting at 200.[2] At that volume, it's inevitable that people are pulled in multiple directions at once, and lack the perspective needed to do the work that will bring the most strategic benefit first. If you want clarity, you have to narrow it down. Smart leaders prioritize.

You need to develop the ability to say no or not yet to dozens of problems to be solved and ideas to explore—even very good ones—in order to concentrate resources on what matters most *now*. Without clarity on priorities, the organization wastes time and resources solving the wrong problems, or starting, stopping, and restarting projects as the newest, shiniest idea absorbs budget and talent. Such lack of clarity results in efforts that consume money and attention but never achieve any returns. It creates an environment in which strategic efforts, deadlines, and budget limits are viewed as arbitrary and irrelevant.

This chapter focuses on the importance of setting clear priorities. The following sections walk through the process we use with clients at the highest level to identify all the work they would like the organization to accomplish in a given fiscal year, define that work according to the problems it solves and the strategic benefit it brings the organization, and create a priority list to guide what gets done first, what can wait, and what should not be done at all. You will learn methods for assessing where you are now in terms of priority setting, and how to narrow in on the "relevant few" priorities that matter for organizational success.

---

[2] In my earlier book *The Outstanding Organization*, I mentioned that clients often produce lists with 30 to 70 active projects or initiatives (p. 80, Chapter 3, "Focus"). As we continued to work with clients, we discovered that most organizations had far more going on than what leaders initially reported. We also found that clients were only considering "projects" as work that takes many months to complete. In reality, resources are limited and anything over and above "the course of doing normal work" must be considered when setting priorities.

The priority-setting process we use assumes your organization has a defined strategy with *consensus*[3] from all members of the senior leadership team. The process and methods described here for setting and executing priorities use that strategy as a foundation to guide decisions about which actions and efforts will allow the organization to reach its strategic goals. Likewise, the organization should have defined key performance indicators (KPIs) for measuring organizational performance against the strategy. I talk about KPIs in detail in Chapter 5.

And what if you lack a clear strategy? The information in this chapter will provide useful context, but before you can apply it you will need to do the hard work of defining strategy so that the priorities you set all point toward the same goal. Setting clear strategy is a book in and of itself, and beyond the scope of this one. A. G. Lafley and Roger Martin's book *Playing to Win* is a useful resource to begin.[4]

The priority setting process is furthermore designed for application *first* at the highest level of the organization, so that all the actions underway in functional areas or business units line up to a single "True North" strategic direction. The metaphor of True North in Lean vernacular refers to the organizational compass that points everyone in the same direction toward a desired state, defined by a clear strategy and achieved through continuous performance improvement.[5] Leaders in organizations that have not set clear organization-level priorities can still use the process in their area of influence, but with the understanding that the clarity-inducing results will be local, not widespread.

With those clarifications, let's prioritize!

---

[3] We define consensus as commitment to a decision or action versus necessarily agreeing with it. Leaders may disagree about priorities but need to fully commit to a plan.

[4] A. G. Lafley and Roger Martin, *Playing to Win* (Harvard Business Review Press) 2013.

[5] For more information on the meaning of True North in Lean, see Tim McMahon, "What Do We Mean by True North," A Lean Journey (blog), January 22, 2014, http://www.alean journey.com/2014/01/what-do-we-mean-by-true-north.html.

WHY PRIORITIZE?

Prioritize—it seems like common sense that an organization would need to. And many leaders believe that they *do* prioritize. After all, there are only so many work hours in a day, and only so many talented leaders and team members. Leaders need to make sure that everyone's time is spent on the most important issues. Yet in practice, "most important" can get very muddy. What's most important to one leader may not be most important to other leaders or stakeholders whom the work will serve. This is one reason why organizations find themselves with 800 priorities as Target did. Or 132, 200, or 417.

Not only do most of the organizations we work with lack alignment and consensus around priorities, they have too many priorities to begin with. Some are important and relevant projects, while some came into being through a combination of reactivity, wishful thinking, and sloppy problem-solving practices, leading to priorities that were neither vetted against the organization's goals nor framed in terms of a specific problem to be solved. Many of these priorities are never killed or completed, leaving a lingering residue of work.

The activities an organization performs over the course of a year fall into two primary buckets. The first bucket includes the work it takes to run the organization on a daily basis. Work performed in the normal course of delivering value to customers (and planning to offer new types of value) belongs in this bucket. Work performed by support areas such as finance, information technology, marketing, legal, human resources, and so on is also included in this bucket.[6] Ongoing innovation work performed by research and development or new product development teams also goes in this bucket. The defining characteristic here is that the work happens on a regular, consistent basis.

---

[6] As you'll learn about more in Chapter 4, we are strong advocates of viewing both value-delivery work and work that supports value delivery in *value streams* for the purposes of designing, improving, and managing work at a macro level.

The second bucket is the "special effort" bucket, and includes problems that need to be solved or that the organization is in the process of solving, and special projects of all sorts—including software implementation and rollout, merger integrations—basically everything that is *not* part of the day-to-day work of serving customers, but requires time, resources, and "mental bandwidth" over and above that which leaders and team members contribute as part of their daily jobs. The work in this second bucket is the type I focus on in this chapter.

Because leaders often confuse "regular work" with "special effort," we loosely define work that belongs on a priority list as that which: (1) takes place outside of and *in addition to* the regular day-to-day tasks that are performed consistently to deliver value to customers and run the business; (2) takes more than two weeks to complete from start to finish; and (3) involves more than four people. This definition helps differentiate a "special effort" priority from "daily improvement," for example. But this is not a hard-and-fast rule; each organization has to use judgment.

The fact that organizations need to invest time to explore how much "special effort" the organization has under way at any given time should make clear that, at the outset, few leaders are aware of the volume of special effort in their realm of influence, and dramatically underestimate the time and effort it absorbs. Moreover, leaders rarely appreciate the way in which long priority lists pull the organization in too many, often conflicting directions, producing significant ambiguity around which efforts make the biggest contribution to the strategy. A growing list of uncompleted to-dos gnaws at people, and creates cognitive drain that colleagues Jim Benson and Tonianne DeBerry aptly refer to as "existential overhead."[7] Large and ambiguous priority lists also contribute to the organizational ADD I addressed in *The Outstanding Organization*. Without

---

[7] Jim Benson and Tonianne DeMaria Barry, *Personal Kanban* (CreateSpace, 2011), 23.

clear priorities, the most important issue is always the one making the most noise in the moment.

Long priority lists and too many simultaneous priorities create another undesirable organization condition: productivity drain due to excessive *task switching*, or shifting one's attention from one task to another. The research on task switching has generated compelling and consistent results. This research applies as much to senior leaders taking on multiple urgent issues at once as it does to middle managers leading a dozen employees, or skilled problem solvers tasked with an array of complex problems. Leaders at every level experience the cognitive strain of having too much to do with too few hours of the day. All of it feels important, yet none of it gets the best and clearest thinking because the leader is shifting his or her attention back and forth between them rather than taking the time to step back and consider each in turn.

It may seem counterintuitive, but the one-at-a-time approach is key for achieving results. Professor David Meyer, director of the University of Michigan's Brain, Cognition and Action Laboratory, was a member of one of the first research teams to prove that the brain can only focus on one cognitive activity at a time. Humans might be able to successfully eat and listen to a news commentator at the same time, but they can't listen to the commentator and simultaneously read the ticker tape information on the bottom of the TV screen and process both pieces of information equally well. The research conducted by Meyer and his team showed that when people think they are multitasking they are actually task switching. Brains need time to reset with each switch, resulting in the loss of up to 40 percent of total productive time per work session, depending on the complexity of the tasks involved.[8]

---

[8] Joshua Rubinstein, David Meyer, and Jeffrey Evans, "Executive Control of Cognitive Processes in Task Switching," *Journal of Experimental Psychology: Human Perception and Performance* 27, no. 4 (2001): 763–97.

Eight years after Meyer and his team conducted the first studies on task switching, a Stanford University team conducted similar studies, with a twist. They looked at people who frequently used different forms of media (TV, telephone, e-mail, text) and compared performance between those who used different forms simultaneously and those who preferred to complete one task at a time. The Stanford study showed that the multitaskers believed that the practice boosted their performance, but found that they performed worse than the solo taskers. They were less able to filter out irrelevant information and organize their thoughts, which resulted in slower performance.[9] Consider how that applies to the executive sitting in the leadership meeting while also responding to e-mail on her iPad. How effectively is she processing the latest information about customer satisfaction, employee safety, and sales in a new market? When she makes a decision, how clear is her thinking about it?

It also turns out that the burden of task switching affects both manual and cognitive tasks. A team at Carnegie Mellon looked at how the brain processes information while driving. The study measured activity in the parietal lobe—an area of the brain that processes spatial information. Researchers compared the brain activity of participants driving on a curvy road in silence (focused driving) to that of participants driving the same road while listening to spoken sentences they had to judge as true or false (distracted driving). The study found that the distracted drivers had 37 percent less parietal lobe activity when listening to the sentences.[10] This finding suggests that distraction decreases a person's ability to

---

[9] Eyal Ophir, Clifford Nass, and Anthony Wagner, "Cognitive Control in Media Multitaskers," *Proceedings of the National Academy of Sciences*. See also http://news.stanford.edu/2009/08/24/multitask-research-study-082409/.

[10] Marcel Just, Timothy Keller, and Jacquelyn Cynkar, "A Decrease in Brain Activation Associated with Driving When Listening to Someone Speak," Research Showcase at CMU, January 2008.

process visual information, causing slower reactions and even mistakes when new or unexpected visual inputs appear.

And a more recent study from Carnegie Mellon's Human-Computer Interaction Lab confirmed that when people are interrupted while completing a task, they make far more errors than people who complete the task without interruption.[11] This study's findings shed significant light onto the ever-vexing problem of reducing human error. The conclusion: people get more work done more accurately when they can do it with a minimum of interruptions.

To get a sense of the degree to which task switching affects performance and productivity, consider a conservative example: assume that only half of your workforce serve in roles for which task switching and interruptions are the norm; and that the average task switcher loses only 15 minutes of productive time with each switch and that interruptions or other task switching triggers occur only five times a day on average (instead of Meyer's findings of between five and eight times resulting in up to 40 percent loss of productivity).

For a company with 500 full-time employees, that's 250 people experiencing daily productivity losses of 75 minutes each, which add up to nearly one work day per week! Spread out over a year, that productivity loss is equivalent to paying 37 full-time employees to do nothing. Assuming fully loaded labor costs of $80,000 per employee, that's $2,960,000—nearly three million dollars—in labor expense that could be used to absorb growth, invest in innovation, provide greater customer value, and improve how the organization operates.

When you consider the impact of task switching on most large-scale projects, the numbers are even more stunning. Assume that an eight-person project team meets once a week for 48 weeks of the year. Assume as well that it takes the team 15 minutes to get their minds fully focused on the project during the meeting and then,

---

[11] Bob Sullivan and Hugh Thompson, "Brain, Interrupted," *New York Times*, May 3, 2013.

when they get back to their desks, another 15 minutes for each team member to get back into the regular flow of work. That level of task switching alone produces an annual productivity drain equivalent to 5.5 full-time employees for *just one project*. Imagine how many project teams there are in an organization with thousands of employees! Complex projects require longer "mental ramp up" and "recovery time" to get one's mind refocused on the mission at hand, resulting in even greater organizational drag.

These are just some of costs organizations incur when leaders and individual contributors are put in a position in which they constantly have to switch tasks. People will always have multiple responsibilities, or have unexpected distractions—it's a reality of life. The goal is to make sure that the activities the organization has under way are worth the costs of task switching and to reduce task switching by working on fewer priorities at once. Next, I'll show how you do it.

STRATEGY DEPLOYMENT

Strategy deployment is a methodology for clarifying priorities and gaining organization-wide consensus and commitment to them. Quality management professor Kaoru Ishikawa conceptualized the methodology in the 1950s;[12] Professor Yoji Akao, a planning specialist, then codified and popularized it. The practice is also referred to as *hoshin kanri, hoshin* planning, and in some circles, policy deployment.

Nearly all leaders I've spoken with say their organization "does" strategy deployment. What they often mean when they say that is their organization has some form of strategy (though that strategy is often unclear or poorly communicated) and the leaders take actions

---

[12] This is the same professor who created the popular root-cause analysis brainstorming tool, the cause-and-effect or fishbone diagram.

of some sort during the fiscal year in the service of that strategy. But that is *not* strategy deployment. Strategy deployment is a specific, formalized, collaborative, and disciplined approach for setting a clear direction based on the organization's strategy. Using strategy deployment, organizations define priorities, create a clear action plan, build widespread consensus around that plan, and manage the plan in a way to ensure focused efforts and results.

At its core, strategy deployment is a macro-level problem-solving methodology. Chapter 6 is dedicated to the subject of problem solving, but the brief point to understand for the purposes of strategy deployment is that problems are gaps between where an organization is and where it would like to be or needs to be. With that context, the priorities included on a strategy deployment plan are framed in problem terms—as gaps to be closed—not as predetermined solutions. This is a shift for many leaders. Most companies frame priorities as actions to be taken, things to be done, changes to be made, and so on. A problem orientation injects clarity into the process, because everyone can see for each priority what the starting point is and where the organization wants to go. There is no room for pet projects or fuzzy "solutions" unconnected to a corresponding problem.

Without this form of disciplined prioritization, many organizations spend their limited resources on activities that don't enable them to achieve their strategy as quickly and elegantly as they otherwise could, and they attempt far more—whether aligned with strategy or not—than the organization can reasonably handle. The result? Spinning wheels, fighting for resources, inadequate problem solving, and outcomes that lack punch. "Too much" is a recipe for ambiguity. When organizational ADD sets in, people are forced to react to the most immediate item, not the most important one.

In a situation like Target's, narrowing a priority list from 800 to 80 is great. So is—in the case of the health system I mentioned earlier—narrowing a project list from 417 to 18. But it's still not enough if people are unclear about the organization's strategy and why the organization chose certain priorities over others.

Though organizations often set strategy for 2, 5, or 10 years, the strategy *deployment* plan defines the priorities for a limited period of time—often the fiscal year. Some of the more complex needs will naturally stretch beyond one year. If a priority involves construction, for example, it may take multiple years to find land, get permits, break ground, complete construction, and ramp up to full operations. In cases like these, the strategy deployment plan carries that priority into the next annual cycle.

The ideal order of events is that the organization creates its strategy deployment plan *prior to* starting its budget planning cycle. After all, how do you develop a proper budget if you don't know the work that needs to be done? Despite the logic of this sequence, however, many organizations attempt to tackle these activities in reverse or concurrent order. Get your priorities clear and then begin your budgeting process.

If you happen to be reading this book when you're already well into your fiscal year, you should still start now and create a plan for the remainder of the year, and then reset to align with the next annual planning cycle. Doing that may mean that you begin the next planning cycle immediately after rolling out your partial-year plan. But that beats waiting. You want to start as soon as you can to reduce ambiguity and gain organizational alignment about what matters *now*.

With that in mind, I'll explain the strategy deployment process that will help you gain the organizational clarity and focus you seek.

CREATING A STRATEGY DEPLOYMENT PLAN

The following section outlines the steps to create and manage a strategy deployment plan. But first, a warning: like building any new muscle, creating an effective strategy deployment plan takes time, especially in the first year. This type of planning is typically very new for organizations and tests both leadership and culture in fundamental ways. Rushing results in a failed process, frustrated leaders, and disengaged workers.

For organizations in their first year of strategy plan development, we recommend three months of fairly aggressive focus and effort, and two months thereafter for the full process from concept to a final plan.[13] It should be widely communicated *at the beginning* of the strategy deployment cycle that the organization is working to set clear priorities and will be communicating along the way to gather insights from business unit managers, team leaders, and frontline workers, and sharing information about the status of the plan. The goal is to operate in an environment of open and frequent communication from the outset. If leaders do that, team members will be primed to hear about the suggested priorities and contribute their views. Team members need a way to share their experience as they relate to the suggested priorities, challenge them, and provide feedback for ways those priorities should be refined by leadership.

The following sections walk through the phases of strategy deployment: year one prework, plan development, plan management, and annual reflection.

Year One Prework: Conducting a "Special Effort" Inventory

The first year of strategy deployment begins with a challenge: what to do with the myriad "special effort" projects and initiatives that are already in play, but may not be the most important issues to move the organization's strategy forward. Unfocused activity and

---

[13] One important activity that makes a plan quicker to create in subsequent years is the adoption of "leader standard work," which includes regular "gemba visits"—going to where the work is done—a management practice described in each of the next two chapters.

solutions in search of problems create "organizational noise" that needs to be addressed in order for the strategy deployment plan to be successfully executed. Until organizations deal with this noise squarely and courageously, they won't have enough resources to put into the real priorities. Conducting a *special effort inventory* assessment and deciding what to keep working on and what to delay or eliminate is essential prework for organizations in their first year of strategy deployment.[14]

The prework period typically takes between three and six weeks, depending on the organization's size and maturity, and culminates with a list of special effort activities (projects, initiatives, improvement activities, ideas, problem-solving efforts that are planned, in progress, or stalled) that *take place outside of and in addition to the regular day-to-day activities needed to run the business.*

To create this list, leaders survey the areas they oversee and document all of the special effort activities they find. We recommend that leaders also include in their list all of the special effort activities they are aware of in other parts of the organization.

As leaders compile the list, place each special effort item in one of the following categories:

1. **Active.** Special effort that has begun and is in process, no matter how slow the progress.
2. **Stalled.** Special effort that was started but then stopped for some reason.
3. **In queue.** Special effort for which substantive work has not yet begun.
4. **Stealth (or rogue).** Active effort that the leader overseeing the work area did not know about until he or she began asking staff to list special effort projects. In some cases, the

---

[14] If your organization has tried strategy deployment and hasn't had tremendous success, I suggest trying again with this prework phase built in. It may be your organization did not adequately address the noise the first time.

leader had actively vetoed the effort and someone began it anyway.

5. **New ideas.** Problems to be solved and improvement ideas that team members suggest during the inventory process.

Leaders must personally lead this assessment and include all areas of the organization they oversee. Few activities that fall into the category of special effort reside in only one functional area, so it is important for each leader to do his or her own forensics. It is also important that leaders get personally engaged in learning about the sheer volume of work their teams are engaged in above and beyond the course of normal work. This prework should not be delegated to junior or administrative staff, or to an in-house improvement team. Leaders need to gather the special effort information from their direct reports; junior staff and administrative staff can populate a spreadsheet with the findings.

After the special effort inventory has been completed, the leader should eliminate duplicates therein and combine activities that are closely related. *Again, this is not a job for an administrative or executive assistant.* This requires someone who understands business and the organization well enough to discern between one project and another.

Developing the Strategy Deployment Plan

Now the organization is ready to develop the first draft of its strategy deployment plan. We facilitate plan development with our clients during a two- to three-day sequestered strategy deployment planning session for the senior leadership team. Depending on the size of the organization, the team includes vice presidents and C-level leaders (or equivalent); in others, the team also includes director-level leaders. Some clients choose to include investors and board members as well. The initial group should not exceed 16 people.

The three days should take place in the office and not in an off-site hotel or conference center. Clients are often surprised by this latter recommendation—they believe they will be able to focus more easily if they are away from the office. We generally discourage off-site meetings because learning to focus and create clarity *in an environment rife with potential distraction* is necessary for achieving outstanding business performance. We want clients to develop those clarity and focus muscles from the very first session. Also, questions may come up during this session that can be addressed in real time by people on-site, and the leadership team needs to be able to access them easily via telephone, webcam, or in person.

These planning sessions should be animated, interactive, and hands-on. Tactically, we cover a wall with 36-inch-wide paper, or use large whiteboards that we divide into four sections labeled "Now," "Not Yet," "Never," and "Maybe." Beside or above the paper or whiteboards, we post the organization's strategy and macro-level Key Performance Indicators (KPIs). Physically posting this information serves as a visual reminder throughout the plan development process of the "True North" direction the priorities are intended to serve. Each special effort inventory item is written on a sticky note and placed in the "Maybe" section. Yes, there may be 200 sticky notes! We use different color sticky notes for each of the five categories (active, stalled, etc.). We use this physical and visual approach to allow all participants to easily move them around in a way everyone can see. We call this "working at the wall," and it creates a level of engagement and collective involvement that is difficult to replicate when one person controls a computer and others watch passively as items are moved around a computer screen. Active participation results in stronger collaboration and deeper consensus on what matters.

Now it's time to select the priorities that will make it onto the organization's strategy deployment plan. I noted earlier in the chapter that strategy deployment is at its core a macro-level problem-solving cycle, and as a result each item on the strategy deployment priority list should be framed as a problem to be solved. Two benefits come from applying a problem-solving lens. The first is that leaders are able to eliminate far more projects on the first pass than they would have otherwise because they can see when an item is a "solution in search of a problem." The second benefit is that leaders experience salience about how much time and expense the organization has been putting into work that does not move it toward its goals. Pain is often an excellent teacher!

It's important to take a firm stand and resist the urge to "grandfather" in existing activity that does not serve the True North organizational strategy and annual business goals, unless it fits one of three exceptions: (1) it is more than 50 percent complete; (2) the organization has made a significant financial investment it cannot recoup; or (3) the organization is contractually bound to continue.[15]

With that context, the leadership team focuses attention on its strategy and the related annual KPIs that have been established, and considers its priorities in light of the problems that need to be solved organizationally to achieve the strategic goals. First, identify the items that *must* be done in the short term and place them in the "Now" section of the paper or board. This step typically goes quickly, as there's often consensus on the high-priority items. Some of the special effort items captured during the prework phase will qualify as important priorities based on their relevance to strategy and can be moved to the "Now" section. Leaders may also add items they now realize are needed to achieve the strategy, that weren't already on the inventory. Leaders should write these new items on sticky notes (we recommend using a different color than the sticky

---

[15] It's good to apply this "hard-line" approach even to commitments that involve smaller dollars. If a project didn't make the key priorities list, it's often more expensive in the long run to continue to tie up resources with it.

notes with the inventory items) and add them to the "Now" section. Keep in mind that the strategy deployment plan includes problems to be solved or work to be accomplished *during the fiscal year for which the plan is being developed* (or partial fiscal year if the first planning cycle occurs mid–fiscal year).

Once the team has decided which activities will best enable it to realize the strategy, turn to the opposite task: look for items that aren't aligned with the strategy, or are low priority. The sticky notes listing these items are placed on the "Never" and "Not Yet" sections of the wall or board, respectively. "Not Yet" includes activities the leaders think should still happen in the future, without defining exactly when. Since there is often agreement around which items to eliminate, this step usually also goes rather quickly.

The next step is the most difficult: deciding where to place the remaining items in the Maybe section of the paper or whiteboard that did not make the "Now" or "Never" lists. There is no science that can be applied here. This is a judgment call based on the maturity of the organization, the amount of available resources, how difficult the "Now" priorities will be to achieve, and a host of other considerations.

At the end of the planning session, all items must be placed in either "Now," "Never," or "Not Yet." "Maybe" is only a holding zone to be used during the planning session, not a long-term category. It is normal during the planning meeting to go back to the list several times to winnow down the "Now" priorities and recategorize to "Not Yet." In our experience, leaders want to eat too much at the "buffet" in front of them. The "Now" list fills up quickly, and leaders must confront the reality that many projects they once considered high priority will have to wait. Even active projects with good momentum may need to be delayed to free resources for work that is better aligned with the organization's strategy. Leaders attempt all sorts of lobbying and deal making at this point,

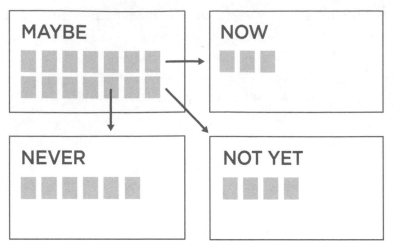

FIGURE 3.1 Dispositioning the "Maybe"
category of existing "special efforts"

but the fact remains that there are limited resources in the form of
time, people, equipment, and money available to accomplish work
and they have to choose. Figure 3.1 provides a visual for how the
sticky notes and paper or whiteboard facilitate this winnowing
process.

There may be moments during the session when the team needs
to pause. Maybe the team got through the process of deciding which
efforts to keep and which to abandon without serious disagreement.
In our experience, however, the plan development session can be
arduous for some leadership teams. Leaders have often uncovered
more work than they expected to find, much of it undertaken without clarity about the problem it was intended to solve and whether
it served the organization's strategy. The degree of organizational
dysfunction is laid out in ways that are impossible to ignore, which
can produce conflict. It doesn't serve the organization to gloss over
that reality. Strategy deployment is designed to reduce the number
of solutions-without-a-problem circling through the organization.
Years two and three typically reveal far fewer of these. Leaders will

have seen firsthand how much wasted work was under way, and with that awareness should have taken steps to keep from doing it again.

Before the team finalizes its proposed first draft priorities, we've found it helpful for the leadership team to consider the level of effort each of the "Now" priorities will require as a reality check before finalizing those high-level activities on which the organization will focus its effort. Figure 3.2 shows a *level of effort grid*, which we often include as part of the strategy deployment plan. The ratings are an estimate of the degree of involvement each functional area will have in solving each problem or completing each project on the strategy deployment plan. Priorities are ranked in terms of the effort that will be required to accomplish them, and color coded to make

Level of Effort Grid											
Priority	IT	Mktg	Ops	Fin	HR	CEO	QC	COM	AM	PD	JD
1	2	3	3		3	2	3	3		1	3
2	2			3	3	1					3
3		2			3		3				2
4	1	3		1			2	3	3	3	
5		2					2				3
6	1	1				1	2		3		
7						3					2
8		2		1			3				3
9	3	1							1	2	1
10	2			3							
11	1	1	1	3	1	1	1	1	1	1	1
12			3			3	1	1	1	1	1

3 Heavy - more than 240 hours total work effort
2 Medium - 16-240 hours total work effort
1 Light - 16 hours or less total work effort

FIGURE 3.2 Level of effort grid for "Now" priorities

very clear which teams will be most taxed by which priorities. The purpose of the grid is to help leaders make realistic decisions that do not overburden one functional area and prevent success.

Reaching Consensus

In the next step, the senior leadership team takes the priority list developed during the three-day session to their individual teams or areas of influence for discussion, feedback, and to develop consensus. To reiterate, consensus does not mean that everyone fully agrees and has the same opinions about the prioritized choices. Consensus means that within a context of differing opinions, all people fully commit to the plan in its ultimate form.

The term *catchball* is used in Lean management to describe this process because of the back-and-forth that should take place between leaders and their teams as they throw the priority "ball" back and forth. Think of catchball as an exercise in clarity culture building. Leaders ask their teams for their views, listen to them, and then bring these views back to the larger senior leadership team for consideration and discussion as they work to convert the priority list into a real executable plan. There's a two-way give-and-take to catchball that is critical for engaging the entire organization in priority setting. This is very different from "cascading goals" as it has been conventionally practiced—namely one-way from top to bottom in the organization. We often coach leaders to help them set the right tone of safe sharing and communication during catchball sessions, and to hear what their team members share about the priorities.

The catchball process is sequential. First, top leaders engage in catchball with their teams. Leaders may glean information from direct reports that forces them back to their peers to make changes. Once they come to consensus at the executive–to–senior management level, senior managers bring the revised priority list to their teams and engage in catchball at that level (see Figure 3.3).

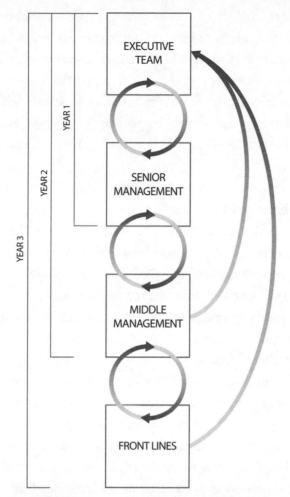

FIGURE 3.3 The catchball process for achieving
understanding and building consensus

In the first year of using strategy deployment, we recommend
that organizations only engage in catchball between executive
leaders and their senior managers. Organizations often need to
experience the back-and-forth of the process once or twice and
build collaborative muscles before they can effectively apply it down
another level, and then another until they are engaging in catchball
all the way through the organization. Over time, the organization

should use catchball from top to bottom. At each successive level of catchball, the involved team members get more granular about the specific projects that survive under the defined priorities.

There are a few dos and don'ts to keep in mind as organizations move through this process. *Do* ask for and expect debate, and *do* treat the debate process with respect and patience. People should question whether the priorities are the right ones and ask for the rationale.

Senior leaders of a manufacturing client of mine, for instance, wanted to expand into emerging markets. There was little debate on that, but when leaders named Brazil as the initial focus, several sales managers pushed back hard. In the views of one manager the executives weren't considering the full range of costs and political challenges the company would face in Brazil. An uncertain regulatory environment and difficulty finding talent to fill key roles canceled out the labor cost benefits, in his opinion. His views encouraged the executives to reframe the priority in exploration terms versus execution terms. Everyone agreed with this priority. As it turned out, the resulting analysis, shaped by the sales managers' concerns, showed that the cost benefits—while lower than they had originally estimated—still made Brazil an attractive market. In the end, both the executive team and the sales management team agreed that Brazil was a good market to move into, but both were better informed for the exchange and felt involved in and committed to the decision-making process.

Debates such as this can also reveal lack of alignment across a leadership team. If catchball uncovers such misalignment, take the time to work through it with respect for others and for the consensus process. Don't lose patience. I've seen leaders make all the right moves up to this point, and then—when debate flares—make an executive decision to prioritize an activity without consensus. This decision is typically futile; priorities that lack consensus limp along but never get sufficient attention from team members to get to the finish line. I've seen this happen with priorities such as a rebrand-ing initiative that senior leaders tagged for Now but the next level down saw as noncritical; or an ISO-9000 effort that got relegated to the Never list but was never fully dismantled and continued to suck resources without any benefit.

Be willing to go back to the table if catchball uncovers some new surprises. For example, a manufacturer we worked with had gone through the process up to this point, but when the leaders started catchball an executive heard from people one level down that the COO had a major project underway that he had been keeping a secret from everyone—and was still keeping secret even as he partic-ipated in the special effort inventory and plan development process. Such a discovery not only reveals when a leader has participated in bad faith, it also invalidates the spirit of strategy deployment. In this case, the COO's pet project was terminated and, a few months later, he left the company.

Don't present the leaders' Now list as if it's a finished prod-uct. It's a draft. Leaders are not mandating these priorities to their teams, but rather inviting people to weigh in, provide feedback, and even challenge executives' assumptions about what matters to cus-tomers and the organization.

Some leaders find it hard to do this with the right spirit of ongo-ing collaboration and revision. Some people one level down likewise find it difficult to speak up when they think their leaders have got-ten something wrong. Both parties have a responsibility to speak their views and listen to others for clarity. Catchball can expose when an organization's culture is not primed for that kind of open communication.

Consider the experience of a health system client of ours: The senior leaders had been an authoritative group and used to calling the shots. Only one of them was in the habit of seeking informa-tion and feedback from junior leaders. As a result, when the leaders sat down with the team members in positions one level down from them, they didn't expect anyone to express disagreement with their chosen priorities. When one manager shared how a named priority could produce problems, the senior leader responsible for that area responded negatively. He didn't overtly say that her idea was invalid, but his tone was snippy and defensive and caused her to shut down.

When I met with the leaders to debrief after the session, I asked them about that exchange. The leader involved hadn't thought anything of it at the time—that was the way he always operated. Only by my calling attention to it did he realize that his comment was likely interpreted by the team member as a clear signal that her input wasn't desired. The exchange gave the entire leadership team insight into why no one tended to push back on their ideas. They had created a team of "yes people."

I share this story to highlight a vital component to successful strategy deployment that's often missed: leaders have to enter the process with a strong desire for collaboration and learning and be open to the transformation that can occur *inside them* as a result of working in this way. They need to have a questioning mind. We used to introduce strategy deployment to any organization that asked for it. No longer. If we sense an organization's leadership team doesn't have the proper mindset for successful strategy deployment, we begin by building that mindset or we don't begin at all.

Once leaders have engaged in catchball and completed the appropriate number of plan iterations, senior leaders reconvene for final confirmation of priorities and an approved plan. The final plan should be captured in a document that lists each priority as a line item—again, ideally framed as a problem to be solved— that includes related metrics that the problem owner will track to determine whether the priority execution is achieving the desired targets. The plan will also document the name of the problem owner (the person accountable for results for each priority item), the approximate time frame during which the work will occur, and the real-time status for each line item. Each priority will later spawn a dedicated A3 report that priority owners will use to communicate about the problem-solving process. A3 reports are a type of story-board that presents in visual form the necessary facts about individual priorities. I go into more details on A3s in Chapter 6 on Problem Solving.

Moving down into the organization, the priorities should manifest as a manageable set of activities for the year, with defined staff, budget, timelines, and collaboration needs with other departments. When viewed as a whole, the priorities should present a clear path for the organization to follow to fulfill its True North strategy.

Communicating the Plan

Once the strategy deployment plan is finalized, *everyone* needs to know what the priorities are and how their work fits into them. Team members at all levels and in all functional areas need to know—and be able to articulate—why the priorities matter, how their department is working to fulfill them, and what to do if new needs arise or a rogue project emerges.

Senior leaders should play an active role in communicating the final priorities and explaining how they came to be. Don't delegate this task to junior staff, business unit managers, or improvement professionals. People need to see and hear *their leaders'* commitment to the process.

Communicating the finalized priorities should happen through in-person meetings. Global organizations or those with remote workforces can use video streaming technologies that allow leaders to "attend" meetings with distant work groups. But in person is always best.

Once communicated verbally, the priorities should be posted in high-traffic locations. Organizations can use physical priority boards or posters, or flash them on flat screen monitors throughout their locations. Priorities lose visibility and importance when they reside solely in computers or on boardroom walls.

Occasionally, executives resist displaying the company's priorities publicly. They are concerned the information might be used for competitive intelligence. These concerns should not be dismissed out of hand, but they are often overblown. The work gets done at a much more granular and specific level than will be captured in those visual reminders.

Managing the Strategy Deployment Plan

Once the strategy deployment plan is properly communicated, the strategy deployment effort shifts from planning to executing the plan. This is a big deal. Anyone who has ever tried to change a personal trait or learn a new skill understands how hard it is to maintain the habits needed to create lasting change. The early stages, while difficult, carry enough excitement to create momentum. Once leadership teams have the strategy plan in hand, however, the reality sinks in: they really *do* need to pull the plug on that pet project everyone was so excited about; the organization really *is* going to have to do that heavy lift, high-investment, no-fun work that will improve performance for everyone.

Strong strategy deployment plan management helps keep organizations on track through the "reality" period—the longer-term, less exciting period defined by prolonged and disciplined execution of the plan. Effective management helps the organization stick to the plan. The management process can also uncover obstacles so leaders can help remove them. And it reveals the mini-successes experienced along the way. These give teams cause to celebrate and highlight what works to keep the organization clear and on target.

Visual tools focus the discussion. A board that displays the priorities and provides a visual reflection of how much progress has been made in reaching KPIs is a necessary plan management tool. A3 reports are another. I discuss KPIs in more detail in Chapter 5 on Performance and A3s in Chapter 6 on Problem Solving.

Another important aspect of strategy deployment plan management is holding regular strategy deployment plan status sessions. These should take place every two weeks in the first year, and can go to once a month in the second if appropriate. At all levels, strategy deployment plan status sessions should follow the same general agenda to address the following questions at the relevant level of specificity:

- Is the strategy deployment plan on target based on the established timelines and metrics?
- If no, why is it off target, and what are we doing about it?
- What support can senior leaders provide?
- Have any new problems, opportunities, or changes to the business context emerged that require senior leaders to consider reprioritizing?

That last question provides flexibility so the organization can make adjustments when warranted. Organizations operate in a dynamic environment, and events will occur that may force leaders to suddenly and legitimately shift priorities.

Consider as an example the impact of a natural disaster like the earthquake and tsunami that hit Japan and cut off access to suppliers operating in the most affected region. If your organization depended on an affected supplier for a key input, it would have had to shift priorities to identify a new supplier and build a new supply chain process to integrate it into the business—either that or risk losing sales due to failure to deliver. A leadership team would be foolish to limit its efforts to a list of Now priorities in such a situation. The same is true when faced with an unexpected opportunity, such as a new large-scale contract, the fulfillment of which would require major capacity upgrades.

With that acknowledgment, I want to make clear that reprioritization should be rare. I am not saying that change is rare. I *am* saying that just because a change occurs doesn't mean an organization needs to muster a major response to it. In fact, external events rarely warrant wholesale shifts in the strategy deployment plan. Leaders sometimes act as if they do, though. We have seen organizations change course or add a new priority at the first unexpected circumstance, even when they don't need to. Such reactivity is the single largest execution threat that we see.

Do not succumb. Senior leaders are the first line of defense. Develop the discipline to study changes to the environment and consider whether or not they truly warrant a change to the strategy deployment plan. Put a new idea through the same paces that all the others had to go through before bloating up the priority list. And be careful of "I told you so" thinking. Some priority shifts are actually reversals that occur when a leader did not fully accept the Now list and uses a disruptive event to make a new case for a sponsored project that didn't make the cut.

Year-End Reflection

Short periods of reflection should be part of each strategy deployment status meeting. Leaders should ask and answer questions such as: What's going well? What adjustments are needed? How are we performing differently as an organization? What are we learning? In addition to those frequent reflections, leaders should initiate a more formal year-end reflection to study and communicate the collective insights of the year. This should happen at the beginning of an organization's cycle for creating the strategy deployment plan for the next fiscal year, and in preparation for the next wave of priority setting.

Questions to ask include: How did the organization do? Was it able to stick with the Now priorities it set at the beginning, or did it make adjustments? Were replacements or additions truly warranted, or were they a reflection of carryover habits and organizational ADD? Did the organization miss key opportunities? What is the overall feeling about the priority-setting process? Were there benefits in terms of clarity? Did that clarity lead to greater focus? Did the organization accomplish more and accomplish it in a more effective way than in the past? What does the organization need to adjust?

As you consider the process as a whole, also look at the priorities themselves. Some Now efforts will likely be complete, while others may still be under way—are there any salient differences in the organization's success rate compared to previous years? Taking the time to reflect and discuss the experience will facilitate the process in the subsequent year.

Year two is typically much easier, reflecting increased maturity. The priorities inventory should not only be smaller; leaders should also find it easier to narrow the Now list to the relevant few priorities it knows the organization can successfully complete. Catchball also gets better and more productive, and leaders are able to add catchball cycles with lower-level team members. Best of all, if the organization set priorities in midyear or off-cycle, the second year gets it back in sync with fiscal year budget setting so that it can prioritize before submitting proposed budgets. To reiterate, having a strategy deployment plan in hand *before* setting a budget makes realizing those priorities much easier.

CONCLUSION

Disciplined prioritization focused on a clear strategy sets the stage for results like the growth experienced by automaker Ford. *Forbes* magazine dubbed former CEO Alan Mulally Mr. Discipline for his never-take-your-eye-off-the-ball leadership.[16] Under his watch, Ford went from losing $5.8 billion in a quarter to having 19 consecutive

---

[16] Bill Koenig, "Alan Mulally: Ford's Mr. Discipline," *Forbes*, May 1, 2014.

profitable quarters. Mulally reportedly held weekly business plan reviews with his team as one technique for maintaining an eye on organizational priorities and addressing any issues that came up in the preceding week that might require a pivot. Mulally's Ford also distributed cards to all employees that described the current business plan—a clarity tool that provided everyone at all levels with the information to understand the organization's priorities.

Strategy deployment is one of the most transformative, culture-shifting management practices there is. When leaders commit to strategy deployment they almost universally see the benefits in the form of clear priorities and focused effort. From there, they are in a far more powerful position to examine how the organization delivers value to its customers through processes—the subject of the next chapter.

4

Process

*So much of what we call management consists
of making it difficult for people to work.*

—PETER DRUCKER

When I ask leaders to define what makes an organization great, they invariably talk about outstanding goods or services. There's good reason for that. The most valuable companies in the world deliver known and recognizable products to millions of customers. But how did those products come to be? How did the product get into the hands of the customer? What happens if a customer has a problem and needs help? Goods and services offer such a tangible link to an organization that we often forget all the activity that takes place behind the scenes enabling and supporting them. Without robust, seamless processes for product development, supply chain management, fulfillment, customer service, and hundreds of other activities, the product would never reach a customer. It is the processes underneath that enable greatness.

Consider how this applies to Apple, one of the world's most valuable businesses and creator of some of our most indispensable electronics. When people talk about Steve Jobs they often refer to the meticulous attention he paid to the details of Apple products, from the introduction of the mouse as an easy way for users to choose where they wanted to go, to the exact shade of blue used for the first iMac, to the slight curve in the base of the iPad to enable easy pickup. Jobs cared about those details. He also cared passionately about the processes that enabled those products to come to fruition, enough to study with quality management evangelist Dr. Joseph Juran. On processes, Jobs said:

> In my opinion, the largest contribution of quality thinking is to approach . . . processes scientifically. Where there's a theory behind why we do them, there's a description of what we do, and most importantly, there's an opportunity to always question what we do. This is a radically different approach to business processes than the traditional one: "Because it's always done this way." That single shift is everything, . . . because in that shift is an optimistic point of view about the people that work in a company. It says these people are very smart. They're not pawns. If given the opportunity to change and improve, they will. They will improve the processes if there's a mechanism for it. That optimistic humanism I find very appealing. We have countless examples that it works.[1]

Jobs's comments struck me in part because it is rare for any business leader—let alone one of Jobs's fame and charisma—to stand up

---

[1] American Society for Quality, interview with Steve Jobs during the production of *An Immigrant's Gift*, a documentary about quality management leader Joseph Juran. The segment quoted begins at 8:07. https://www.youtube.com/watch?v=XbkMcvnNq3g&=77s.

and make a case for processes and the people behind them. In the context of clarity, processes are a series of actions or steps taken to achieve a particular end. Everything a business does—in fact, everything in life—occurs as a result of processes. Yet few leaders overtly advocate for process to the extent needed for clarity.

On the contrary, it is far more common to see eyes glaze over when a meeting agenda turns to process. You can almost see *unfun* flash like a neon sign through people's minds. Many leaders believe they have better uses of their time. The next deal awaits. Innovation is our future. And so on. Many leaders think that getting involved in process design and management is too granular for them, too "in the weeds" of the business. In some ways they are right—as a leader, you shouldn't be so involved in process design that you dictate how the work is done. That's not the job of the leader. However, it *is* a leader's job to have a working understanding of the processes that touch his or her domain of influence, how those processes affect the customer, and how to direct process design, management, and improvement. In fact, I would argue that one of the most high-impact activities for a leader is to understand and improve the processes under his or her control.

There is a long-standing misconception that the term "manager" refers to someone who manages people. That is a fallacy. You can't manage people. You lead people. You can manage processes, products, and projects. If processes, products, and projects are well managed, the people and the resulting performance of the organization take care of themselves.

Your organization and those who work for it need clear, well-designed, well-executed, and well-managed processes in order to excel. Ignore that fact if you will, but understand this: your organization will only ever be as successful as its processes.

And you can be *so* successful! Danaher Corporation presents an outstanding example of what can happen if an organization embraces process centricity. Since 1980 the company's cumulative total return to investors has topped 70,000 percent,[2] and since 1996 Danaher stock has outperformed the Standard & Poor's 500 Index by more than 2,000 percent.[3] Many variables go into stock performance, but Danaher's leaders, former leaders, and employees often attribute Danaher's success to the Danaher Business System, a variation on the process-oriented Toyota Production System. The Danaher Business System provides clarity for everyone in the organization on how to operate, make decisions, prioritize work, and deliver value to customers. In a word, the system provides clear *processes* and a disciplined means for continuously improving them. Leaders at all levels of the organization talk about the clarity they have because of those processes. If Danaher can achieve this level of clarity and structure in a company with more than 60,000 global employees, your organization with 25,000, 10,000, 5,000, 500, or 50 employees can do it too.

Processes either keep customers coming back or drive them away. Processes can enable businesses to scale profitably, or they can cause profit to flatline from the expense of patch-fixing broken links in the work systems that enable value delivery. Processes allow talented people to perform at their best, or pull them down into the muck of inefficiency. Process design and management will either deliver quality or create organizational drag. Processes can enable positive and productive relationships or cause friction within and among work teams. Processes either motivate people by providing them with clarity about what they need to do, how to do it, and how to advocate for a better way, or they break the spirits of otherwise well-meaning team members. Processes either

---

[2] Justin Fox, "What Makes Danaher Corp. Such a Star?," *Bloomberg View*, May 19, 2015, https://www.bloomberg.com/view/articles/2015-05-19/what-makes-danaher-corp-such-a-stock-market-star-.

[3] Danaher Corporation, LinkedIn, https://www.linkedin.com/company-beta/157261/, accessed March 8, 2017.

allow people to perform at their best or they create untenable work environments filled with blame, frustration, and high levels of stress.

A business is the sum of its processes. Yet many organizations are the anti-Danaher. They limp along with ambiguous, undocumented, wasteful, and poorly managed processes. In fact, whenever we ask new clients for the percentage of processes that are documented, current, followed, measured, and continuously improved, the universal answer is close to 0 percent—they have very few processes that meet all five criteria. Instead of enabling work that is consistent, productive, and successful, they create self-inflicted chaos that forces workers at best to solve the same problems over and over, at worst to make avoidable mistakes that result in significant losses.

Consider the process gaffe that afflicted NASA's Mars Climate Orbiter. September 23, 1999, was supposed to be a banner day for NASA and space exploration. The whole world watched as a rocket launched the much-anticipated $125 million Mars Climate Orbiter into space. The mission, five years in the making, aimed to send the spacecraft to Mars to orbit the planet, gather data, and report it back to earth. But mission control lost contact with the orbiter en route to the Red Planet, and never regained it. What happened?

It turns out that NASA experienced a significant process fail. Multiple engineering teams worked on the Mars Climate Orbiter, but the project specs did not clarify a standard system of measurement. As a result, one engineering team used Imperial measurement while the other used the metric system. Inaccurate calculations caused the craft to approach Mars at an altitude that put it inside the planet's volatile atmosphere. The Orbiter was not designed to withstand such a rough ride and did not survive it. A flubbed unit conversion cost the space program a $125 million spacecraft and five years of hard work, culminating in an embarrassing failure from which NASA took years to recover.

The Mars Orbiter offers a dramatic, large-scale example of what happens at a micro level across dozens of processes in your organization. On any given day, half your people are metaphorically calculating with Imperial measures while the other half are on the metric system, and neither side knows it.

There is another way. Smart leaders recognize that achieving clarity requires clear processes. Leaders need to get involved in process at the level necessary to advocate for effective process design and management. To help you, this chapter provides a primer on analyzing the state of your processes, and what leaders need to know about them. I make clear how detailed your involvement should be and include some context for you to go deeper when the situation calls for it.[4]

WHY DON'T ORGANIZATIONS PAY ATTENTION TO PROCESSES?

Effective processes create such a dramatic boon, and broken processes such a significant bane, that I have long reflected on why process design and management as a discipline doesn't get more attention. Over time I have discovered myriad reasons, subreasons, and sub-subreasons why, which together come down to a hard reality: most leaders lack foundational skills in process design and management, and don't view them as institutionally important enough to learn. That may sound harsh, but it's true. There are three reasons why.

First, many processes are invisible. They happen behind the scenes or beneath the visible aspects of the business. Most of them function well enough that problems are like a pin leak in a larger

---

[4] A note on scope: this chapter focuses on what you need to know about processes for the purposes of clarity. A thorough treatment on process improvement warrants a book of its own, and is beyond the scope of this one.

pipe. The loss immediately affects those close to the leak, but is less visible at the end of the line. People acclimate to that kind of slow leak.

The second reason why leaders and the organizations they work for have not invested more in having clear, high-functioning processes is lack of experience. Building proficiency in any endeavor—whether golf, guitar, or gastroenterology—requires practice, experience, and knowing what good looks like. Yet gaining that experience can be challenging because the models are few and far between. Process design and management are not part of the core business curriculum offered at most universities and graduate programs. When young professionals graduate into the workforce, the organizations they work for likely aren't process-centric enough to fill in those education gaps. Fast forward 10, 20, 30 years and those young professionals have become leaders who have never thought much about processes and don't know what well-designed and well-managed processes look like, let alone how to create them.

Career-long lack of exposure metastasizes quickly to produce the third reason why organizations pay less attention to processes than they need to for clarity: they have a specialist mentality. Leaders' lack of direct experience has led them to believe that process design and management must be complex and difficult, and thus requires a specialist to do well.

The Six Sigma movement has encouraged specialist thinking with the "belt" concept. Similar to karate and other martial arts, belt ranks signal proficiency for the Six Sigma practitioner, with "master black belt" denoting the highest credential. On the supply side, people at all levels now mistakenly believe that they need a black belt, green belt, yellow belt, or purple polka-dot belt to understand how to design and manage processes. On the demand side, organizations that become more process aware hire various types of belts in the mistaken belief that the credential necessarily equates to skill. It doesn't. Green belts, in particular, get very light exposure to some of the most critical elements of designing, managing, and improving processes. I've met hundreds of belt holders who don't know how to map a value stream, design a pull scheduling system, or apply proper psychology to reduce resistance to new ideas—all standard skills that people leading improvement need to possess.

Six Sigma isn't the only improvement approach to suffer from specialist-itis. The advent of Kaizen Promotion Offices (KPOs) and similarly named improvement teams has created a double-edged sword for the Lean management movement as well. Having full-time, dedicated resources available to facilitate improvement is a helpful first step as an organization begins its journey toward treating improvement as part of the work itself and not an activity separate from the work. A problem occurs when improvement team members don't serve as teachers, but instead own improvement, either through their own doing or by the organization believing that specialists should do the work of improvement. It's a danger-ous Catch-22 that many organizations with KPOs haven't navigated successfully. The "first step" becomes a permanent step.

More damaging than the idea that belt holders and Lean cham-pions are experts, however, is the corollary that non–belt holders must not be. I can't express strongly enough how false that idea is. Knowledge, practice, and results—those factors matter, in that order. Any frontline team member, team lead, supervisor, or man-ager can—*and should*—become proficient in process design and management. It's not rocket science, and it doesn't require a belt. Most people have the capability to learn how to do it.

Leaders should avoid overreliance on specialists to do the busi-ness of managing a business—because that's what processes are: the business. Toyota Motor Corporation is arguably a better per-forming company than many, and it doesn't have a large body of people with "belt" designation. Neither does Danaher. Nor did we have specialists when I was at Health Net, a leading health insur-ance company and one of my early employers. Roger Greaves, a process-centric CEO, led the company when I was there. Under his watch Health Net aspired to perfection in process excellence, and that focus allowed the company to absorb rapid growth without losing control or faltering.

The evidence is in the numbers: In 1986 Health Net had 200 employees and revenues of $350 million; when Centene acquired it in 2016, it employed 5,500 people and its revenues were $17.6 billion. I credit much of that growth to the clear processes that defined how the organization operated. Roger agrees with my assessment, adding, "Without clear processes you have chaos. Everyone works to their own ends, not necessarily that of the organization."[5]

Since it was my first corporate role, I had no basis for comparing my experience at Health Net with other companies. After I amassed more work experience, I saw that unclear and unmanaged processes were the norm and the process centricity of Health Net the exception.

The degree of detail that any individual needs about the processes that make work happen throughout the organization differs depending on the level at which he or she operates. Leaders at all levels need high-level understanding of how value flows to customers. Directors (or equivalent leadership level) need that same level of clarity, and they also need to understand the critical processes in the departments or functions they oversee that form the value stream. Middle managers, supervisors, and team leaders need to understand an even finer level of detail: the individual process steps involved in their realm of influence, and so on.

How Value Flows

Value streams include all of the activities involved in delivering value to the customer in the form of a good or service. Every leader

---

[5] E-mail correspondence with Roger Greaves on March 30, 2017.

should understand and be able to explain how value flows—or in many cases, doesn't flow—through the organization. I spoke recently with an improvement executive who had stepped into a new role at a large company in the hospitality industry. This person has deep knowledge of improvement methods, and still he was stymied. "Karen," he said, "I can't figure out what our value streams are. We have food. We have accommodations. We have entertainment. We have customers who use all or only some of those services, but I can't figure out how it all flows together."

His experience reflects the reality that many organizations don't know what they do, or how they do it. Senior leaders bristle at this comment, for obvious reasons, but they see that it's true when I ask them to describe how they deliver value to their customer—the high-level serial and concurrent processes that constitute "work"— and they can't do it.

It's difficult to overstate how important it is for leaders to have absolute clarity about the organization's value streams and how each of them perform. When we facilitate value stream analysis and design sessions as part of a systemic value stream transformation effort, senior leaders are surprised to see how the organization delivers value to its customers compared with their perceptions. The greatest shock comes when leaders realize that the organization's current work systems don't support what they've promised customers, and that the work environment prevents team members from performing their jobs successfully.

Sessions like these shine a light into the organization's corners and highlight the cobwebs that have accumulated there. They are incredibly powerful. The clarity senior leaders get about the realities of the organization—warts and all—is foundational for making strategic decisions that affect value delivery. It's not solely about process, either. Many value stream analysis and design sessions uncover golden market opportunities that our clients execute to great success.

Figure 4.1 depicts a value stream map for a technology firm that performed complex analyses for its customers. Our client wanted to shorten the lead time, improve service quality, and reduce the work effort for its primary value stream.

You'll notice that there are three primary components to the map: information flow in and out of IT systems, the handoffs as work passes from function to function, and a timeline that shows the amount of work effort (process time) and the lead time (also referred to as throughput or turnaround time) for each process. The image also shows Percent Complete and Accurate (%C&A)—a quality metric that's described later in the chapter—for each process in the value stream. The summary data block at the bottom right shows the lead time for the entire value stream, the total process time, the ratio between the two of them (which reflects the degree of flow), and a product of the %C&A measures for each process block, which reflects the degree of rework in the value stream.

Of all of the improvement methodologies and operational design strategies I've learned and used in my career, proper value stream analysis, design, and management is without question the most powerful and transformative methodology I've seen. It all begins with gaining clarity about current state operations by visualizing how value flows to customers with a high-level value stream map. Only with this degree of clarity can leaders then design better work systems and prioritize improvements that will have the greatest impact.[6]

---

[6] For information about why, when, and how to create value stream and process-level maps (mentioned later in the chapter), see Karen Martin and Mike Osterling's *Value Stream Mapping* (McGraw-Hill, 2014), *Metrics-Based Process Mapping* (Productivity Press, 2012), and Karen's recorded webinars at www.ksmartin.com/webinars.

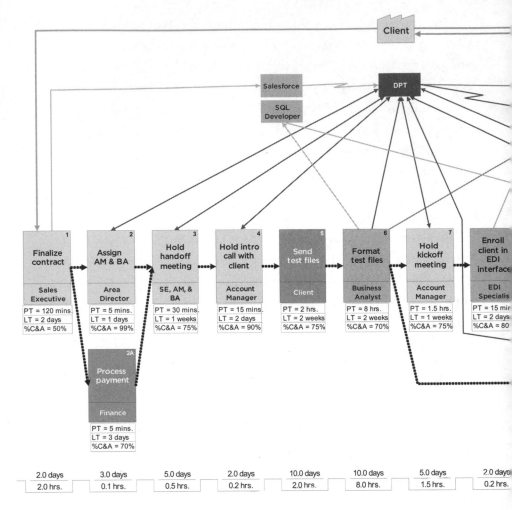

FIGURE 4.1 Current state value stream map for new customer implementation

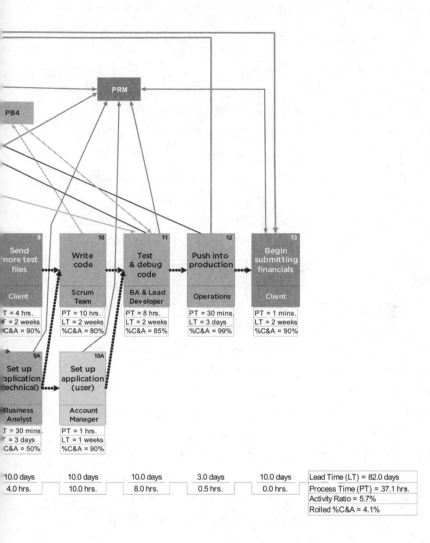

How Do I Contribute to Value Delivery?

Value stream maps offer an underutilized side benefit besides visualizing operations: they help employees at all levels understand how they contribute to delivering value by showing where they fit in the work systems. This context is critical for new hires in non-customer-facing roles, and especially critical in companies that are organized according to function.

We saw this during a problem-solving session at a defense contractor, where we used the firm's previously created value stream map to orient the team to the problem. During a break I overheard a middle manager from the finance department say that, until that day, he had never understood his connection to the firm's customers, nor to other internal departments. Used in this way, value stream maps serve as the organizational equivalent of the "you are here" notations on posted maps in airports, cities, and shopping malls.

Clarity about one's role in delivering customer value helps people become more engaged in solving problems. We saw this type of "awakening" occur when a City Hall clerk saw where she "sat" on her organization's value stream map. Before then, she had never understood how her work processing building permit applications affected the budgets and time projections of contractors and property owners. Her director had described her as "asleep at the wheel." Once she understood how her role delivered value, she took an active role in improving the way her department served its customers.

It should be said, however, that value stream maps don't create engagement. They provide context. The organization still has to engage people and give them opportunities to contribute in an environment of continuous improvement. If the environment isn't primed to receive a person's contribution, no degree of clarity will help.

From Value Streams to Processes

Value streams are comprised of processes and subprocesses that make or break your organizational performance. Figure 4.2 provides an example of this relationship from the healthcare industry, which may be familiar to anyone who has received a CT scan. The image lays out the entire value stream from order to delivery, and then focuses on two specific processes within that stream to show the relationship between the levels. There are other levels of granularity above, in between, and below the two levels depicted in this figure, but this offers a general picture of the macro work system and micro processes that form it.

The bar for the degree of clarity an organization needs about its processes is even higher than it is for value stream clarity, because the tactical execution of work resides in processes. Ambiguity about the specific steps needed to deliver outstanding value is the largest contributor to poor customer experience, runaway costs, and potentially dangerous mistakes. Clarity by itself does not make outstanding processes, but no process can reach outstanding levels without absolute clarity in its design, execution, and management. The following section focuses on the necessary systems organizations need put into place to achieve process clarity.

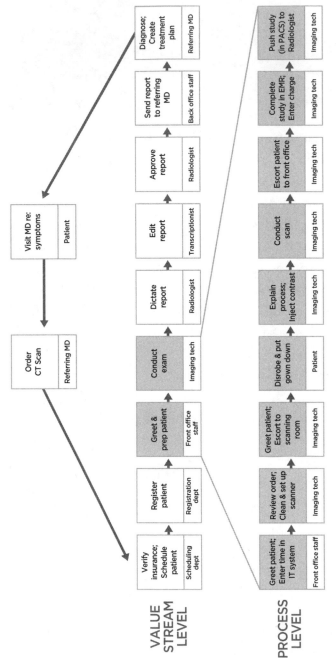

FIGURE 4.2 Performing CT scans: value stream and process-level views

WHAT MAKES A PROCESS OUTSTANDING?

Outstanding processes require attention to three key elements: design, execution, and management. Process design covers the details of the process itself: how tasks are completed, in what sequence what inputs and outputs are expected, and to what standards. Process execution focuses on the clarity people need do the work, including the skills they need to be successful doing the work. Process management, in turn, allows organizations to assess on an ongoing basis how well their processes serve the needs of the business, and to continuously improve processes to reflect the dynamic environment within which work exists.

The Well-Designed Process

Process clarity begins with well-designed processes that share the following characteristics:

- **They are safe.** They are ergonomically sound and can be performed without placing the customer or team member in danger. This includes eliminating the risk of psychological stress and repetitive stress injuries.
- **They are efficient and effective.** A team member can perform the work and produce consistent and high-quality results without heroics or excessive effort. In Lean management, efficient and effective processes are free of three productivity-robbing "enemies": muda, muri, and mura. *Muda* refers to all forms of waste, including overproduction, overprocessing, errors, rework, excessive inventory, waiting, excess motion, excess transportation, and underutilization of people. *Muri* refers to overburden on equipment and people. *Mura* refers to unevenness. Efficient and effective processes are also designed so that information passed to the next person in a process is unambiguous, as measured by

percent complete and accurate (%C&A). See the sidebar for more details on %C&A.

- **They are easy to understand.** The steps for performing tasks are clearly defined and unambiguous in meaning.
- **They are easy to perform successfully.** Assuming a team member with the right skills is assigned to the task and well trained for the work, the process is designed and documented in a way that he or she can be successful at it.

Each of the elements of safety, efficiency and effectiveness, ease of understanding, and successful execution is foundationally about designing a process so that the person performing it is put in the best position possible to do his or her best. One of the primary tenets in Lean management is respect for humanity, also referred to as respect for people. The first definition for respect in Oxford Dictionaries is "a feeling of deep admiration for someone or something elicited by their abilities, qualities, or achievements," and the second is "due regard for the feelings, wishes, or rights of others."[7] In Lean, respect goes deep and focuses on creating work environments that allow each person to become the best version of him or herself, and to perform work successfully. All too often people get blamed for performance, where in reality the performance gap is caused by poorly designed processes. So the next time you begin to think that John, Sally, or a specific team is a problem, look again. In nearly 100 percent of the cases, the problem lies with the work environment and underlying processes.

Incomplete and Ambiguous Process Information

An underemphasized aspect of process design concerns the information that accompanies work that is passed from

---

[7] https://en.oxforddictionaries.com/definition/respect, accessed September 23, 2017.

person to person in a process. Much of the time the information is incomplete and/or ambiguous and requires the receiving party to rework the information before the task can be performed. In-process rework of this nature includes correcting information, adding missing information that should have been provided, and clarifying information that could have been clear to begin with. I'm not suggesting that people should stop correcting, adding, or clarifying information; I'm suggesting that when a process is well designed and well executed, the need to rework incomplete, error-prone, or unclear information drops dramatically. This type of rework is a major source of added cost, slow output, and poor morale.

The need to rework information is so prevalent that many leaders mistakenly believe that it is an unavoidable by-product of complex work—a simple cost of doing business. Not so. Rework erodes productivity and adds unnecessary expense. It produces no value, and it's a lousy use of your team's brain power—especially knowledge workers. Rework is one of the greatest contributors to staff frustration, stress, and interpersonal and interdepartmental tension.

Fortunately there's a metric that allows leaders to surface the problem and measure improvement as they insert clarity into the organization's processes. *Percent Complete and Accurate* (%C&A) measures the percentage of the time that work is passed to a team member or work group that does not require the receiving party to correct, add, or clarify information.[8]

---

[8] %C&A was first developed by Beau Keyte and Drew Locher, who defined rework as correcting and adding information (*The Complete Lean Enterprise*, 2nd ed. [New York: Productivity Press, 2015], p. 30). Mike Osterling and I added clarification to the definition of rework after we began discovering how rampant the lack of clear information was. Our books *Value-Stream Mapping*, *The Kaizen Event Planner*, and *Metrics-Based Process Mapping* all provide detailed information about how to use this metric to surface problems..

When Mike Osterling and I began experimenting with %C&A in 2004, it turned the process design conversation on its ear. With coaching in using this metric, our clients were able to confront significant process design problems that had been hidden from view. %C&A allows people engaged in improvement to clearly see how pervasive and extensive rework is, and how much drag it puts on the organization. While it's not a precise, scientifically derived measurement, it's a powerful directional metric that reveals the "hidden beast," as Mike dubs it. The insights gained from looking at work through this lens—especially service, transactional, knowledge, and creative work—have done more to improve productivity and create capacity than any other measurement we've used to date.

%C&A is also a powerful tool for reducing stress and creating stronger collaboration across functional areas. Poor work relationships drag everyone down, and poorly designed processes rife with unclear information are significant contributors to poor work relationships. Take the time to analyze the quality of the information handed off from step to step in a process and you will see what I mean. Once you know the truth about the current state and dig a little into root causes, the countermeasures for handing off clear information readily appear.

The Well-Executed Process

A well-designed process creates the potential for success, but execution determines whether the design is fulfilled in such a way that it meets its potential. And execution is wholly dependent upon whether the organization has people with the necessary level of skill, experience, and authority doing the work.

Design ensures that the process is safe and easy, but "easy" in this context means that people who have the skill can do it without taking unnecessary time or expending unnecessary effort. "Easy" does not mean that an unqualified or untrained person lacking the necessary organizational resources will get results. Thus, getting the right people in the right role, training them properly, and providing them with access to necessary information is critical for process excellence. To do that, an organization needs clarity about the level of skill needed to fulfill a process. To get that clarity, organizations need to have up-to-date organization charts with clear lines of authority and clear job descriptions, and they need current skills matrices. These foundational tools are not processes themselves, but they are process enablers, necessary for any organization that aspires to be outstanding. They are as important for complex knowledge work as they are for technical and transactional work. The following sections touch on what those enablers should look like for absolute clarity.

Organization Charts

An accurate and up-to-date org chart provides necessary clarity about who oversees which work areas, critical knowledge for process execution. Unfortunately in many organizations org charts are undervalued and underutilized. Organizations often don't have them at all, or they have charts that are so out of date they are useless. In the world of clarity it doesn't get much simpler than an org chart, and having one that is up to date and accessible makes it much easier for people to determine who should be involved when a question arises about a process.

This is particularly true within so-called "matrixed" organizations or other kinds of "flat" organizational structures. In these environments, org charts are sometimes viewed as a relic of hierarchical business structures, but they are even more necessary because the internal relationships are unclear. Matrixed organizations often create a disorienting level of ambiguity, because it's difficult to learn who has the authority to make decisions about processes or the people who do the work. There are a few shining examples of successful matrix structures—McKinsey & Company and W.L. Gore among them. More often, however, organizations that say they have a matrixed structure don't. What they have is a mess, resulting in people feeling *less* able to perform successfully because they don't know where to go for basic resources and decision making

I'm not advocating for or against a particular organizational structure. I am saying that regardless of your structure, people should have fast, easy ways to learn who to turn to for information or decisions needed to get work done. Don't make them guess.

Job Descriptions

Another simple, accessible resource organizations need to enable process execution is job descriptions. A job description answers fundamental questions for people: What are my primary responsibilities? What should I spend my time doing? More importantly, a job description indirectly answers the question: What should I *not* spend my time doing? Despite how practical this seems, we've seen a significant drop in the level of specificity—and, therefore, clarity—captured by job descriptions. When we talk with people inside organizations, they give common explanations for the decline.

For one, job descriptions are increasingly written by human resources staff (HR), not by hiring managers looking to fill a role. That shift means that job descriptions may hit all the right notes when it comes to protecting the organization against legal challenges, but they often lack clarity and specificity about the skills required and responsibilities to be fulfilled. Another reason for the lack of specificity in job descriptions is that organizations increasingly look for people with diverse skills and believe that specific job descriptions may limit their applicant pool to those with narrower skill sets.

There are also less well-meaning reasons why job descriptions are vague. Some leaders fear structure and don't want to be held to it. Some want to be able to ask their teams to do whatever they please, whether or not it's their job or they are qualified. Others don't want specificity because that would require the hiring manager to commit to a set of actions and outcomes.

Last, some leaders falsely believe that new hires want vague job descriptions to avoid being painted into a corner. That's not at all what we find, but if that is what you believe, you may have misunderstood what Millennials are saying about their expectations of the organizations for which they work. A number of studies on the professional lives of millennial workers show they expect more flexibility around when they work and where they work than did previous generations. Telecommuting and flexible hours are of high interest for talented millennial professionals, as is gender equity with regard to family leave, and more opportunities for engagement in social causes.[9] But flexibility does not mean vague—if anything, flexibility requires organizations to have even greater clarity about what people need to be doing when they are at work.

Regardless of why job descriptions have gotten so fuzzy, it's not a good practice for general clarity or for ensuring that processes are executed successfully. People already in your organization and expected to fulfill a process role need to know what they were hired to do. People considering a job with you want to know how they're likely to spend the majority of their time. How else can they decide if the job is right for them? How else, once in the role, will they be able to prioritize requests and know what level of authority they have, if they don't understand their role?

---

[9] See the Case Foundation *Millennial Impact Report 2015: Cause, Influence and the Next Generation Workforce*; the Pew Research Center's Social Trends Research, *Millennials in Adulthood*; and PwC's Millennials Survey: *Millennials at Work: Reshaping the Workforce*.

Skills Matrix

Once people are in a role, there are other details they need—and the organization needs—to ensure that they are qualified to do the job they were hired for on the one hand, and that the talents they have are fully utilized on the other. Organizations set themselves up for process failure when they hire people or assign them to a task for which they lack experience and proficiency. People want to feel confident and competent in their jobs, but too often the organization creates an environment of ambiguity around skill development.

Case in point: an energy firm went through a massive improvement effort in one of its service lines. To properly roll out the improved process, the organization needed to train 90 employees in four functional areas, and assigned the job of communication and training to a woman—I'll call her Jeanne—who had no experience in designing or facilitating adult learning sessions.

The results did not show respect for people: team members who attended the training walked away unclear about how their work was changing; the learning materials Jeanne developed contained two major errors; and the affected people who needed new levels of access in the company's IT systems did not get them in time to perform according to the new standard work. In the context of so much ambiguity, a rumor started that two departments were being merged.

These situations are unfair to people like Jeanne, and they are unfair to those who need clear and specific information about process changes. If the organization had made use of a skills matrix, it could have identified someone with skills in training, facilitation, and communication to lead the rollout. If it wanted to develop those skills in Jeanne, it could have matched her with that more skilled professional as one aspect of a larger effort to develop her training skills.

Figure 4.3 offers an example of a skills matrix, sometimes referred to as a learning and development matrix or a training matrix.

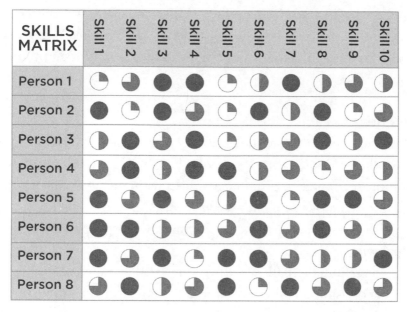

FIGURE **4.3** Skills matrix

Skills matrices can be created with a narrow focus on people within a specific work group, or they can be created for a broader group of people to visually depict the range of proficiency needed to perform various types of work. They can be used strategically to plan people development across the organization, and they can be used as a tactical scheduling and work assignment tool. For example, if a team member is out for the day, a skills matrix clearly shows who can do the work in that person's absence because there is an at-a-glance reference of team members with comparable skills. Leaders can also use it to match less experienced team members with those who have greater expertise in a particular area.

The example I give here in Figure 4.3 uses pie shapes to represent skill level. We sometimes use colors (red and green) and numbers (0% to 100%) to reflect skill proficiency. Whichever format you choose and however you define the "buckets" you place team members in, avoid overcomplicating it and crossing the line from clear to confusing.

Authorization and Decision Clarity

Closely related to the need for clarity about roles and responsibilities is the need for clarity about who has decision-making authority to improve a process, promote a valued team member, make policy exceptions, authorize money to be spent, and so on. The list is long. Sluggish process performance is common when people don't clearly know who gets to decide.

Clients initially balk when we suggest they take the guesswork out of decision making by creating standardized authorization matrices. These matrices identify common decisions made in the course of executing a process, set standards for who makes those decisions, and even determine what the decision should be in some cases. "But each decision is unique," some clients say. Others say, "You can't standardize situational leadership." Yet the organizations that develop decision matrices are almost always able to standardize the 20 percent of decisions that absorb 80 percent of leadership time and attention. Defining the relevant few decisions helped one client free 450 hours of leadership time per year.

Another useful way to simplify decision making is to become more intentional about who has what role in the decision-making process. Carolyn Taylor, author of *Walking the Talk*,[10] offers a useful decision taxonomy for the degrees of involvement and authority people have:

1. I decide
2. You provide input and I decide

---

[10] Carolyn Taylor, personal e-mail correspondence and PowerPoint slides adapted from *Walking the Talk*, 2nd ed. (Random House Business Books, 2015, originally published in 2005).

3. We discuss and decide together
4. I provide input and you decide
5. You decide

I've been using Taylor's approach, and it's working well. It's even helped surface a habit I had of asking for input without making clear that I was seeking different views (#2), not joint decision making (#3), which some assumed I was. I've seen that when people understand the level of involvement you are looking for, they are less likely to be confused or frustrated when your decision is different from what they thought you should do.

The reverse is true as well. When I want a true partner in making a decision (#3), I can better clarify that expectation to others. That definition has reduced frustration on my part when someone doesn't participate to the degree I expected. With this degree of clarity up front, I know if a person doesn't help it's because he or she didn't want to, not that I didn't ask for it. Leaders and improvement teams are finding Taylor's taxonomy helpful as well.

The Well-Managed Process

Change is a constant in organizations, and the conditions for which a process was originally designed do not hold indefinitely. Much the way the human body will put the pounds back on after weight loss unless the person maintains good diet and exercise habits, so too must processes be maintained through active management or they will undergo entropy and revert to their natural state of chaos.[11]

The only way to avoid entropy is to manage processes relentlessly, from the initial rollout to ongoing measurement and continuous improvement intended to improve performance or respond to changing conditions. Process management ensures that the process

---

[11] For additional learning, refer to the Discipline chapter in my earlier book *The Outstanding Organization* (McGraw-Hill, 2010).

is doing its job of producing the desired outputs in a way that is safe, clear, efficient and effective, and easy.

For the purpose of clarity, managing processes gives the organization critical insights. How else could an organization know how it is performing if it does not manage its processes? How can team members be clear on how to do the work if they don't have a way to confirm it? The answer: only through rigorous process management, which ensures people are not reacting to whatever is most immediate, but instead doing work that matters.

Well-managed processes are:

- **Documented.** Not only are the process steps captured, but so are the descriptions of how the work should be performed within each step. This documentation should be clear, visual, and user-friendly. "Standard work" also includes the specific criteria (work standards) that must be met in performing the work. Job aids such as checklists, memory aids, laminated process "cheat sheets" and so on are helpful forms of supplemental documentation.
- **Current.** The documentation reflects the way the work should be performed *today*, not how it was performed last month or last year.
- **Followed.** Workers have been thoroughly trained in the process, and adhere to it until the process is improved and new standard work is released.
- **Consistently monitored.** Process performance is measured against relevant key performance indicators (KPIs are discussed in greater detail in Chapter 5) to ensure that it performs as designed and meets the requirements of safety, efficiency, and effectiveness.
- **Regularly improved.** Processes that consistently meet KPI targets are analyzed to identify performance gaps with the goal of setting new, more aggressive targets, and identify

process changes necessary to meet them. Processes also need
to go through a cycle of problem solving and improvement
when conditions change or performance begins to
deteriorate.

To repeat, the goal of outstanding process design, execution,
and management is to create an environment in which people can
be successful at their jobs. When individuals perform at outstanding
levels, those results roll up to produce high levels of organizational
success.

Fujio Cho, honorary chairman of the Toyota Motor Corporation, reportedly said that one of Toyota's key differentiators is its
relentless focus on designing and managing processes. According to
Toyota insiders, Chairman Cho got himself into a bind when a comment he made was misinterpreted. He said that Toyota's laser focus
on process and work systems allowed Toyota to get brilliant results
from average people. But Cho did not mean that Toyota employees
are only average, as many assumed he did. He meant that the company spends significant time on process design and management so
that even a person with average skills can still perform brilliantly.

Average or below-average processes require heroics and brute
force delivered by top performers to achieve high levels of performance. Yet job pools contain a range of people with varying
skills—that is the reality within which all organizations work. Processes that are impeccably designed, clearly understood, relentlessly
followed, and regularly improved don't require heroics. People with
average skill sets can still perform them at high levels. Taking a
clarity-driven process view offers a practical way to operate a business, one that displays a remarkable amount of respect for people.

Finally, effective process management requires ownership.
Someone in the organization must be responsible for the process as
a whole and have the authority to improve the process across the
entire range of functions it touches, when conditions warrant it.

CONCLUSION

I opened this chapter by talking about Steve Jobs and the rare emphasis he placed on strong processes. The proof is in the pudding. A study by the management consulting firm Bain & Company found that Apple—as well as Google, Dell, and Netflix—is 40 percent more productive than the average company. When Bain partner Michael Mankins and his team dug deeper to understand why, they discovered the answer: processes. It is not that these companies have more talented employees; it is that the employees produce more because the processes enable greater productivity and output, resulting in profit margins that are between 30 percent and 50 percent higher than industry averages.[12] I can't think of a stronger case for working to achieve process excellence than 30 percent higher profit margins. Results like that are available to your organization if you take the steps to understand your processes and commit to improving them and managing them in a clarity-driven way.

Begin your journey toward greater process centricity in one division or area of the organization. Work on the processes in that area to learn about and improve your methods for designing, documenting, training, measuring, and improving them. Pay close attention to the results you reap from greater clarity. Do you see improvements in the quality of the work performed? In the stress levels of the workers involved? Then roll out your refined process design and management approach to other areas of the organization.

Next, we take a deeper look into organizational performance.

---

[12] Michael Mankins and Eric Garton, *Time, Talent, Energy: Overcome Organizational Drag and Unleash Your Team's Productive Power* (Harvard Business Review Press, 2017).

5

Performance

It is an immutable law in business that words are words,
explanations are explanations, promises are promises—
but only performance is reality.

—HAROLD GENEEN

Imagine attending an American football game in a stadium with no scoreboard. For spectators to have any clarity about the game's progress, someone would need to provide them with important numbers: the score, which down it is, how many yards remain for the next down, and so on. If an announcer broadcast the information over a loudspeaker, there would be a risk that some might not hear it clearly. If more than one person relayed the score and game status to spectators, there would be a risk of misinformation.

The absence of a scoreboard puts the teams at an even greater disadvantage. What if the quarterback thought it was the second down with 18 yards to go, instead of third down with 3 yards to go? He wouldn't know which play to run. A scoreboard fixes that. It's visual. It's easy to see. It contains important details without which no one can determine how the team is doing. A scoreboard allows all stakeholders—spectators, referees, coaches, and the players themselves—to operate from the same place. Everyone knows how the team is performing at any given moment, and those insights guide decisions and actions.

Like those football stakeholders, organizations need metrics in order to understand the state of play and to make decisions about where to focus. The first question we typically ask when we begin an engagement with a new client is, "How are you doing?" We don't mean this in a generic, "How are you feeling today?" or, "How was your weekend?" way. We mean, "How are you performing as an organization or work team?" "What does 'good' look like to every leader and every employee?" "Are you on track or off track?" We word our question broadly because the responses give us quick insights into whether leaders are tuned in to performance measurement, and the level of clarity leaders have about current performance.

Most leaders can't answer the question without thinking a bit, and many can't answer it at all. Those leaders who *can* answer the question without hesitating nearly always quote financial results: sales gains or losses, burn rate, market capitalization, and so on. They rarely quote performance in terms that reflect operations, the customer experience, or the employee experience (e.g., lead time, productivity, quality, on-time delivery, first call resolution, product returns, employee turnover, and so on). If the leader answers solely in financial terms, there's a good chance that the organization lacks balance in how it measures performance. Emphasizing financial metrics at the expense of others also shows a lack of understanding of how operational efficiency and effectiveness and the work environment lead to financial results.

Another common problem is that companies don't always think about performance in concrete terms of where they are now and where they aim to go—a measurable gap—and therefore don't track the metrics that allow them to describe performance in clear "from-to" (gap) terms: "improve quality from 93 percent to 97 percent," or "increase weekly sales from $1.6 million to $2 million." Measuring and communicating performance through a balanced from-to lens allows organizations to more easily answer the second question we ask, which is: "What problem or problems do you most need or want to solve?"

Putting it back in terms of that football game, many organizations aren't keeping score—at least not the type of score that fuels a journey to sustainable excellence. Organizations and the leaders who run them are information deprived. Information is the sum of useful data plus the actionable insights that come from analyzing that data. Information deprivation leads to inaccurate conclusions, incorrect assumptions, poor decisions—and no clarity. That lack of clarity prevents leaders from focusing talent in ways that produce top value for customers, investors, and other stakeholders. This chapter will help you change that. I'll show how to create clarity by taking steps to understand the current state performance—not what leaders think the performance is or what they wish it to be, but what it *is*. If your organization is not interested in making improvements and solving problems, don't waste your time getting clear about your performance. If improvement is your game, however, read on.

So Much Data, So Little Information

Any discussion about performance measurement needs to begin by addressing the thorny subject of data. In modern business, data generates equal amounts of enthusiasm and trepidation, due, in large part, to the ability to capture so much more data today than in the past. The lure of Big Data—a catchall term referring to the ability to capture, store, and analyze data from both inside and outside the organization to extract useful insights and predict the future needs and behaviors of people, machines, and systems—gets organizations particularly tingly.

Yet the reality for most organizations is they don't have a handle on *little* data. Sure, technology systems may have the ability to capture huge volumes of data, but many organizations either don't know the data is there or don't know how to access it, let alone interpret and use it to make sound business decisions. Data that isn't automatically captured is even less likely to be documented and presented in a way that can be used to assess performance and drive priorities and improvement.

There are three types of data in the context of performance: *demand data* that captures incoming work volume; *status data* on the current work underway; and *outcome data*. Demand data is typically expressed as a quantity per unit of time: 50 customers an hour, 700 orders a week, 12 month-end closes per year. Status data reflects progress on work in queue: six of seven production lines are operational; we're in Phase 2 of the mining project; we've fulfilled 75 of the 87 backlogged orders, and so on. Outcome data looks at performance over time, and ideally against a target, such as 11.5 percent product returns, 25 hospital-acquired infections per month, $2.4 million in sales, and so on. Some refer to these categories alternatively as input, process, and output measures, but regardless of what you call them, every leader should know *at a glance* how well his or her teams are doing relative to all three: the volume of work to be done, at what stage the work is, and how well the work is being performed. Yet they rarely do.

A case in point: During an engagement with a wind energy producer, we met with an engineering team that was struggling to meet project deadlines. Most of our questions centered on status data: "How many projects are you currently working on?" "What stage are those projects in?" "How many are in queue?" "What's your average completion time?" No one could answer our questions. The information was there in the collective minds of the team members involved in delivering value to customers, but the organization had not established the expectation that project work be documented and tracked, nor was there any method for doing so. The consequence was a complete lack of clarity about how this team was doing in terms of fulfilling promises made to customers.

We are not seeing clarity emerging as a result of all the data organizations are able to capture and store in their technology systems. On the contrary, for every conversation I have with clients about the possibilities of Big Data, I have two or more about the lack of data around business fundamentals and the difficulties they have ensuring the basic data they do collect is clean—meaning free of duplicates, inaccuracies, anomalies, recording errors, and inconsistencies that make it unreliable. Even organizations with clean data have difficulty accessing it and analyzing it for critical insights.

Don't misunderstand—leaders *need* to seek and use data about context and performance to fully understand the current reality of how the organization is doing. Accurate, clearly presented data is a powerful tool for giving everyone involved the same information about how the organization is doing and where it wants or needs to go. But organizations need to nail little data before they set their sights on Big Data. For clarity, that means focusing on collecting, analyzing, and presenting the data that communicates what you need to know to properly manage the work and improve performance.

Lest you think that all organizations are drowning in data, the opposite is also true: some organizations have a dearth of meaningful data. We regularly ask for datasets to analyze client performance and set the direction for problem solving, and our clients are rarely able to produce all of the data on our wish list. This includes data that would provide fairly fundamental insights, especially concerning the customer experience.

A hospital couldn't tell us how long patients were in queue waiting for elective surgery because it didn't capture the original date the decision was made that surgery was needed. A financial services firm couldn't tell us its turnaround time for complex customer correspondence because the mail room only tracked the date it opened the correspondence, not the date the correspondence was received. A manufacturer couldn't tell us its median on-time delivery percentage because each time it shipped part of an original order it overwrote the order received date with the date of shipment, making all shipments appear to be on time. And as I write this, we're two months into an engagement with the technology department of a midsize company and working hard to extract fundamental data that the client needs to run its business. The fact that it has been making major business decisions without this data is concerning for all parties.

Getting clear about reality is the only way to manage work and close performance gaps. It is worth investing in creating the means to collect the data you need, or clean the data you have, and use it to drive decisions and actions. I offer the following guidelines on using data to achieve clarity.

Define What You Need to Know

Effective use of data to drive performance starts by asking what you need to know—the answers to which are situational. If you're a hospital, emergency department wait times and hospital-acquired infections may matter. If you're a hotel, capacity utilization and repair requests may matter. If you're a manufacturer, on-time delivery, inventory turns, and scrap may matter. If you're a sales team, customer conversions may matter. A call center? Hold time, abandon rates, and first call resolution may matter.

Each organization needs to identify the data that relates to aspects of the business that matter *now* based on what the organization wants to accomplish. What you *don't* measure is equally important—you don't want to take the time to collect data that's irrelevant for moving the organization toward its goals. More is not necessarily better, given that analyzing the data you collect takes time and resources.

Be intentional about what you *don't* need to know. Choosing not to collect data on a particular process or operational component doesn't mean that the process ceases to exist, of course, but you don't gain clarity by measuring everything that happens in the organization. Leaders need to make choices about which performance metrics make sense to track, and it's equally important to be clear about what *not* to measure.

The best way to assure that you're collecting the data you need—no more and no less—is to begin with questions. What data do you need to meet customer expectations, staff work teams with enough people and the needed skills, budget appropriately, prioritize problem solving, make decisions, and plan for the organization's future? Answering questions such as these requires deliberate thought. Is the data "gettable," meaning it has been collected and can be retrieved? What type of analyses do you need to do to gain insights from it? How will you visually display the results so that the insights are easily understood?

Make no mistake, what I'm suggesting here takes time. Leaders have to know how the operation is doing and make clear choices about what matters to customers, the balance sheet, and employees. That clarity gives back to the organization in the form of better decisions. We saw that from a hospital laboratory director who said that collecting and presenting performance data was like getting eyeglasses for the first time. She had no idea how handcuffed she had been by that lack of knowledge and how unclear she had been about the operation she oversaw. A call center vice president said that his performance data revealed how many assumptions he had made that were dead wrong. A CEO finally understood the details behind why his company's EBITDA[1] had been slipping.

---

[1] EBITDA—a measure of profitability—is an acronym for earnings before interest, tax, depreciation, and amortization.

Learn the Sources of the Data You Need

Once you've defined what you need to know, you need to determine where that information lies. We commonly encounter two clarity obstacles: either it's wickedly difficult to obtain the data an organization needs or there are multiple systems, often disconnected, that contain pieces of the story it needs to learn.

In the first case, the data needed to understand performance simply isn't attainable. Either it's not entered into a system, or the cost to collect it outweighs the return for an initial round of analysis. In either case, systems need to be developed that enable future data capture that's relevant to understanding performance.

In other organizations, we find parallel (and sometimes conflicting) systems, all of which produce their own data relevant to the questions we seek to answer, and some of which are "stealth" systems that few people know about. This situation can create two distinct data problems: the first is redundant data, whereby the same information gets counted twice, giving a false impression of volume, status, or performance; the second occurs when the organization only considers information coming from some of the relevant systems and not from all of them.

A government service agency we worked with dealt with the latter situation during an effort to improve how it delivered value. Early in our work with this client we asked for data on the monthly volume of customer requests, or tickets. The organization sent us a spreadsheet showing a median of 18,000 customer requests (tickets) coming in every month. This number determined staffing. As we worked with this client to understand its value streams, however, we discovered that it had arrived at that demand rate by counting incoming work only from its primary source, the customer service call center. As seen in Figure 5.1, we discovered three additional avenues for incoming requests, and once duplicate requests were removed, the median monthly demand rose to 33,000 tickets— almost double the volume the process was designed to handle. Even

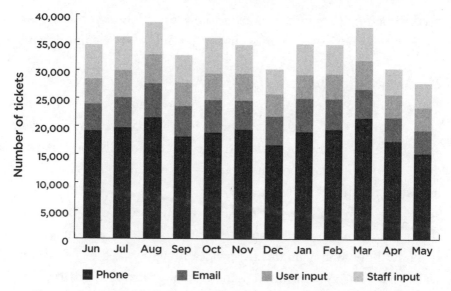

FIGURE 5.1 Monthly volume of customer requests from all sources

worse, our client was missing out on a significant chunk of funding that was based on total work volume.

This situation isn't rare. Fifty percent of our clients estimate the demand they need to serve as much higher or much lower than reality—and that's if they have enough clarity to provide a number in the first place. A financial services firm we worked with had never quantified the number of requests it received from customers seeking to change beneficiaries in complex legal situations. An engineering firm hadn't counted the number of change orders it processed per month. A design firm didn't track the number of incoming projects it outsourced to a third party. A tech firm had no idea how many billing disputes its team was handling.

Clarity requires organizations to know the full picture. In this example, the government agency needs to know how much incoming work it has so that it can design processes to handle that work, properly staff work teams to do the work, know how well the relevant work teams manage demand, and understand what adjustments need to be made. Numbers substantially too high or too low compared to reality create internal chaos that only clarity can mitigate.

Understand What the Data Says

Once you have taken the time to identify the data you need, you'll need to gather that data and confirm that the information you *want* and the information you *have* are the same. Initially look at your data with skepticism. Does it mean what you think it means? Does it answer the questions you have?

Things can get very fuzzy—and this is very common—when the information you need isn't currently captured. You may want to know how long a financial services request takes to fulfill, and learn that your system only begins tracking turnaround time once the request is "in good order." The time spent clarifying information from the customer is not measured, but from the customer's point of view, the service clock began ticking when he or she submitted the initial request. Or you may want to know how many people have been injured on the job in the last year, but your system may only keep a record of people who end up on disability. Knowing the difference between what you want to know and what you have can save a lot of time and avoid the risk of misinterpretation. The best way to assure that you get what you need is to collaborate with someone who has deep knowledge of the dataset from which you need to pull. That person can answers questions such as: What does a blank field mean? What does a certain time stamp represent? Does the data tell you what you think it does?

Information that is manually recorded or subjective requires an extra level of scrutiny. Manual systems are vulnerable to missing data and interpretation errors resulting from inconsistencies in the way team members gather data. Gaming that skews data is also common when organizations set performance goals that are unrealistic without improvement in processes.

This issue came up recently with a hospital we work with. The facility was trying to deal with a growing queue for elective surgery, and we asked the leader for data on the surgeries the hospital had performed in the last three months. Our team wanted to understand the current state volumes and surgery times, but when I opened the file, a simple glance suggested something was wrong. The data showed surgeries regularly lasting 17 and 18 hours. Extremely complex procedures do sometimes last that long, but the majority of the surgeries clocking in at more than 10 hours were appendectomies, breast biopsies, and other types of common surgeries that generally range from less than an hour to as long as 6 hours.

When I asked my client about it, team members could only recall one surgery lasting more than 10 hours in the past few years. More questions and conversation uncovered a range of problems with the data, including high variation for how people tracked start and stop times; the same data entered in multiple places, resulting in a perception that they had twice as much volume as reality; and intentional gaming, for example by staff members who prematurely moved patients from the waiting area into an empty surgery room to stop the "wait time" clock. This practice started the surgery time clock prematurely, which produced significant skewing of the data on surgery length.

As this story captures, organizational data is commonly dirty, misunderstood, and misinterpreted, so leaders should not blindly accept that the data they have is clean, nor that the conclusions drawn from it are factual. When leaders declare, "We need data!" we often reply with, "You need facts."

Learning whether you have facts or not takes deliberate study. You can also "sniff it out" by performing "gut checks." Ask someone who's intimate with the work if the numbers seem reasonable. For example, are the order fulfillment times logical given the product, the order volumes, and so on? Is the customer service call volume at the right scale for an organization of that size? Or in the above case, do surgery length times reflect that person's experience of reality? Leaders shouldn't operate with gut alone, but gut is often a reliable indicator of a data problem that requires attention before any meaningful analysis can occur.

Leaders also need to turn a trained eye on data gathered by third parties. Don't rely solely on the word of large reputable consulting firms or specialty analytics firms. If the data is from a data entry system, find out exactly which data fields were pulled to conduct the analysis. If relevant, learn what calculations were used. When reviewing survey data, get the specific questions that were asked. Make sure to understand what the question was, how the data answers it, and what the data does *not* say before concluding that it offers a useful baseline from which to set goals or make decisions. Drawing inaccurate conclusions from data that is dirty, incomplete, duplicative, or just plain wrong is dangerous business.

Know How the Data Is Calculated

Even when data is clear, clean, complete, and correctly interpreted, organizations may create ambiguity by using nonstandard approaches to calculating various measures.

For instance, consultants, writers, and academics propagate confusion when they differ in their methodology for calculating specific metrics. Overall equipment effectiveness (OEE) is a classic example. This common manufacturing metric is frequently misinterpreted due to differences in how it's calculated—specifically the definitions of the factors that go into the product.

OEE reflects the health of a production line. It's as critical to a manufacturer as heart rate, blood pressure, or body temperature are to a doctor assessing a patient. It provides insight into operating margins, capital utilization, and process efficiency and effectiveness. OEE is the product of three variables—availability, performance, and quality—and is expressed as a percentage.

Sounds simple, right? Nope. We find that many manufacturing leaders can't list the three variables. Even when leaders can name them, they are not always clear how each variable should be calculated, and the same method of calculation is not always used by everyone in the same organization. Availability is typically based on scheduled production time, and yet some teams use a 24-hour clock. Some organizations calculate the quality variable based on end-of-line quality, which can obscure in-line rework that's occurring or scrap that's accumulating, both of which are costly problems. Quality could be 99 percent or 75 percent, depending on who's measuring and how they're measuring. Such confusion can render a critical measure fairly useless as a performance improvement tool. If you don't know what goes into the final number, how can you understand what OEE is telling you? And if you don't understand what OEE is telling you, there's no way to know how well you're doing or what you need to do to improve performance.

OEE is only one example of a common problem we see concerning measurement and performance clarity. Be very clear on what the organization is measuring, what questions the metrics answer, how the numbers are obtained, what the numbers mean, and what conclusions leaders can draw based on what they learn. If multiple departments or levels in your organization do their own calculations, standardize the method across the organization so that everyone is using the same formulas.

Display Data Visually

Data is most useful when it is represented in a visual way that allows everyone to clearly understand the narrative that it reflects. Think back to the scoreboard analogy I used at the beginning of this chapter: the purpose of visual scoreboards is to make sure everyone has the information needed to inform their decisions and actions.

Statistician Edward Tufte is arguably the world's most famous advocate for effective and accurate visual representation of data.

Since the publication of his iconic book, *The Visual Display of Quantitative Information*,[2] tools for visually displaying data have only gotten more sophisticated and user-friendly.

Humans are a vision-dominant species. Our sense of sight is by far our most used sense. The brain's occipital lobe, one of four lobes in the cerebral cortex in mammals, is primarily responsible for processing visual information, and according to current neuroscientific thought it is the only lobe that manages the bulk of its input from only one sense. That amount of brainpower dedicated to this one sense should signal the relative importance of visual acuity in processing information. So why not use that power to achieve clarity by presenting data visually?

A supervisor of a legal team set out to do that when he learned about the power of visual management and wanted to experiment with it. He created a table (Figure 5.2) that tracks the time it takes to complete two segments of a contract amendment: (1) from the initial request for an amendment to creating a final draft that's ready for review, and (2) from a final draft to a fully executed amendment. Study the table, noticing how quickly you understand what the data is telling you.

	Contract Amendment Turnaround Time											
	Target (days)	January				February				March			
		WK1	WK2	WK3	WK4	WK5	WK6	WK7	WK8	WK9	WK10	WK11	WK12
Request to draft	5	10	9	10	9	9	8	8	7	7	7	6	6
Draft to execution	10	12	16	13	20	17	16	16	17	17	14	18	19

FIGURE 5.2 Contract amendment turnaround times: table

[2] Edward Tufte. *The Visual Display of Quantitative Information* (Graphics Press, 1992). See also Tufte's other works: *Envisioning Information* (Graphics Press, 1990) and *Beautiful Evidence* (Graphics Press, 2006).

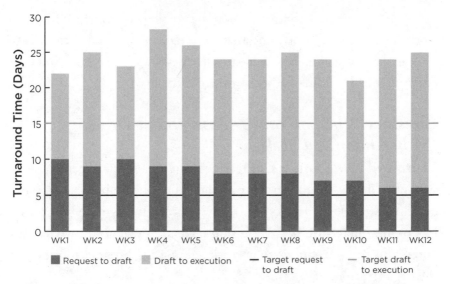

FIGURE 5.3 Contract amendment turnaround time: stacked bar chart

Now take a look at Figure 5.3, which is a stacked bar chart that displays the same data.

How much more quickly were you able to grasp how this work unit is performing? To be fair to the supervisor, tables are a common method for displaying data, and they are far better than not displaying data at all. The table allowed the supervisor to achieve three important goals: (1) Gain clarity about how the contract amendment process was functioning; (2) Accelerate cycles of improvement; (3) Promote greater team member engagement. But the supervisor reached out for our help when a senior leader didn't "get" the story. We helped the supervisor recognize that the table was a good start to visual management, but well-designed charts make it easier to see context, and context is critical for the rapid uptake of information.

In most cases well-designed charts—such as waterfall diagrams, stacked bar charts, line charts, histograms, scatterplots, and so on—are far superior because they allow the eye to see patterns.[3] The range of visual tools available span far beyond what I can cover in one chapter. For additional resources, visit www.ksmartin.com/recommended-reading for a list of my favorites.

Consider Whether Your Measurement Drives the Behavior You Seek

Many years ago, a former CEO turned in-demand management consultant told me: "I know everything I need to know about a company by learning what it tracks and how it incentivizes its employees." His point: make sure that what you measure does not move leaders and teams to take actions that work against the broader interests of the organization.

We see this problem all the time. In one case, a medical device manufacturer changed its incentive program to what it believed was more objective and quantifiable across the organization. A new CEO felt the company lacked discipline and wanted to "hold people more accountable." One of the new criteria this CEO introduced was "meet deadlines." Guess what happened? Everyone met his or her deadlines . . . and the business began to fall apart in the face of repeated recalls and customer complaints. The mandate to meet deadlines caused people to rush product through development and into production, not leaving enough time to surface problems, let alone address them.

In another example of metrics driving the wrong behaviors, one of the "core measures" required of emergency departments by the Centers for Medicare and Medicaid Services is "door-to-doctor time," meaning the median amount of time between when a patient

---

[3] In most cases, line charts (also referred to as run charts) are better for visualizing performance over a continuous timeline and bar charts are better for discrete data. We chose a stacked bar chart versus a line chart for the contract amendment process because we felt it was easier to see the pattern of improvement in the part of the process that the team had control over versus the variation in the part of the process that was customer-dependent and produced no improvement in the overall turnaround time.

arrives and when that patient is seen by a physician. This measurement emerged from the hypothesis that clinical care is improved and patient satisfaction increased when patients see doctors quickly.

We don't see those positive outcomes from faster door-to-doctor times, however. Instead we see ED departments concocting silly ways to meet the requirements, such as by placing a physician in the waiting room when she could otherwise treat patients who need care in an exam room. We also see hospitals improve this up-front piece and ignore the rest of the patient experience, including overall throughput time. Patients are not any happier to see a physician quickly if their total visit still lasts 12 hours. The adage "be careful what you measure" is especially true in healthcare.

More serious problems occur when improper measurement and incentives lead to unethical or even criminal behavior. Wells Fargo offers a notable example of this phenomenon. In 2016, bank employees were exposed for opening unauthorized accounts and credit cards in the names of existing customers. An investigation revealed that bank executives had set unreasonable targets for new accounts and employees began opening unauthorized accounts as a way to meet the quotas.[4] As a former branch manager told me, "People believe that integrity will hold up at all cost. But when an organization places employees in a position where they have to do unethical things to maintain their pay at the level they earned the previous year; and when leadership relies on groupthink so that staff who see peers doing unethical things will conclude that it's OK—in that situation many, many people will succumb. It was a truly awful situation to place employees in."

Data and how the organization uses it shapes behavior, so be clear about the kind of behavior your organization wants to see. Companies that place greater emphasis on gross sales over profit

---

[4] See Michael Corkery, "Wells Fargo Fined $185 Million for Fraudulently Opening Accounts," *New York Times*, September 8, 2016.

often find themselves with sales teams who don't differentiate between low- and high-profit products and will overstate what the company can deliver in order to meet sales targets. Organizations that reward individuals over teams, or functional areas over larger, interconnected areas, tend to have higher levels of "me" thinking and less teamwork and collaboration, even resulting in team members from one part of the company willingly putting work teams in another area in jeopardy just to protect an end-of-year bonus. And so on.

The disconnect between many incentive programs and measuring what matters for overall organizational performance is common and makes performance clarity nearly impossible to achieve. We recently spent months helping a client establish metrics that would allow the organization to clearly see what it needed to do to perform at higher levels, but at the eleventh hour leaders were unwilling to replace its incentive-based metrics with the ones that more accurately reflected the company's health.

If you want to perform at high levels over the long haul, be clear about how you use the data you collect and what behaviors that data may incentivize. And be aware that if you want clarity, your incentive programs may very well need to change.

Clarify the Intent of Required Measurement

Sometimes organizations track metrics they believe their executives, customers, or regulators want, only to find that they misunderstood the request. The cause of these misunderstandings is usually unclear communication. When a director or manager says, "Our CEO wants us to measure X," it is rare for a team member to question the request or ask for more specifics on why and what form that person wants it in. The person responsible for capturing the data and producing reports often lacks access to the person asking for it or is afraid to ask for clarification so that he or she can ensure that the requested metric provides the answer the requester seeks.

A related problem occurs in highly regulated industries that are required to report to government agencies. Team members within these organizations sometimes believe that the oversight body mandates the specific way they gather, analyze, and report information, when more often than not the agency or accreditation body just wants the numbers and doesn't stipulate the method for collecting and reporting them. Even worse, people sometimes assume a measurement is required and go to great lengths to collect and report data only to learn that it was never a requirement to begin with.

Customer intent can also be misunderstood, especially when contracts define performance levels and tie them to incentives. In one example, a construction company was running out of warehouse space and retained us to help determine if it needed to spend capital on additional space.

We nearly always begin a request like this with two questions: How many days of inventory do you have on hand? What is the average lead time from placing an order with a supplier to receiving goods? No one from this organization could answer either question—not senior leadership, not middle managers, and not the warehouse supervisor. When we walked into the warehouse, we were stunned at the amount of paint stored there: enough for one-and-a-half years of demand. When we expressed our surprise, the materials manager shrugged and said, "That's what our customer wants, and they're paying for it."

We donned our operational forensics hats and uncovered five key facts. First, the construction company was paid on a time-and-materials basis, which meant the customer paid dollar-for-dollar for the paint. Second, the company received a bonus from the customer if it met a service-level target to close out work orders within a specified time period. Third, it received a financial *penalty* if it didn't order materials for a job within 15 days of receiving a customer work order. Fourth, ordering material allowed it to place the work order in "pending" status, which stopped the service-level clock.

And fifth, our client had a significant and growing backlog of work orders and was on the verge of not meeting the service-level metrics it had agreed to.

Primary diagnosis? Misinterpreted intention. Our client was given a financial incentive to stock up on unnecessary supplies, whereas the customer's intent was to ensure timely service delivery. Given this context, the solution to the warehouse space constraints had an obvious answer: stop ordering paint. When the client expressed concern about losing the performance bonus, we suggested that the director of materials management talk with the customer to clarify intent. He was understandably nervous about revealing the situation, but with some coaxing he came around to the idea that pursuing clarity was the right move, and his efforts would be seen as a gesture of honesty and would build trust in the relationship, not jeopardize it.

In the end, the customer apologized for setting a measurement system that clouded its intent, and rewarded the construction company leaders for sharing ways to reduce unnecessary expenses. The warehouse crunch was resolved and, interestingly, the order backlog began to drop without direct effort. The level of trust between our client and its customer remains high and has led to more collaboration between them.

Go and See

Even the cleanest, most accurate, and best-analyzed data will not tell you everything you need to know to properly assess performance and understand where improvement is needed. Leaders at all levels, from the senior-most executive to frontline team leaders, need to understand how the work is done to get a full picture of performance. This means frequent visits to those areas where the work is done or where value is delivered directly to customers. In Lean management vernacular this is referred to as "go and see," or going to the *gemba*—the real place.

The technique of observing the work to learn how it is done and understand whether it is performing as designed is often linked to the legendary Ohno circle, an observation technique created by Taiichi Ohno, the industrial engineer who created much of the Toyota Production System.[5] Ohno reportedly brought people to the place where the work was done to teach them how to see waste and grasp the current state of a situation.[6] Ohno would have people stand in the circle and observe for hours or even entire shifts. His instruction was simple: "Watch." When he returned, he asked, "What did you observe?"

Supplementing what you learn from spreadsheets with visits to the gemba brings some obvious advantages. Seeing the reality of the work and talking with those who do the work provides necessary context, at the same time that it shows respect for the people who do the work. That respect creates an environment for them to share their experiences, perspectives, and concerns, without which some data will remain impenetrable. In the case of a clinical laboratory, we learned by going to the gemba that we needed to exclude a particular high-volume test from our analyses because it was performed by a third party. If we had included it, our analyses would have been faulty. People are also far more likely to share the truth with someone they have met in person than someone they have only ever contacted by e-mail or webcam.

The practice of "go and see" is similar in concept to "management by walking (or wandering) around" (MBWA), a practice traced to executives at Hewlett-Packard in the 1970s and popularized in the 1980s by Tom Peters and Robert Waterman in their 1982 blockbuster, *In Search of Excellence*.[7] Going to the gemba carries some differences from how MBWA evolved, however, most notably in intent: the practice of go and see is geared very specifically to

---

[5] Some of Taiichi Ohno's thinking is captured in his book *Toyota Production System: Beyond Large-Scale Production* (CRC Press, 1988).

[6] Jeffrey K. Liker, *The Toyota Way* (McGraw-Hill, 2004), 226.

[7] Thomas Peters and Robert H. Waterman, *In Search of Excellence* (HarperBusiness, 1982).

gaining clarity from a place of curiosity, humility, and a desire to serve. It's very different from MBWA used as a way for leaders to be accessible and visually present, or, sometimes, as a "gotcha" practice with punitive consequences.

"Gemba walks" are a staple for clarity-seeking leaders. I address them here in the context of performance, but gemba walks are vital for nearly every aspect of leadership, and are a key component of *leader standard work*. They are also vital in problem solving of any sort. In nearly every walk we've facilitated, the leader visiting the gemba gains critical insights about the business and how it runs that he or she didn't already know, such as the excessive paint inventory we saw in the warehouse.

To recap, the goal of collecting, analyzing, and presenting data—and supplementing it with visits to the gemba—is to understand reality so you can concentrate improvement efforts on those areas of the business that matter. One way to capture those "areas that matter" is through key performance indicators.

USING DATA TO IMPROVE PERFORMANCE— KEY PERFORMANCE INDICATORS

Improvement begins by assessing how the organization is performing today versus how it wants to or needs to perform. When everyone understands the gap to be closed between current performance and defined targets, they can focus attention on what matters. Team members are in a position to do their best with this type of clear guidance; no one is left to "figure it out" and risk coming to conclusions that may lead them to the wrong play or point them out-of-bounds or toward the opposing team's end line.

Performance metrics in the form of *key performance indicators* (KPIs) presented on a visual, accessible scorecard provide that necessary clarity. This is the organization's version of a sporting event scoreboard. KPIs reflect the overall health of an organization, division, department, or work team. They offer a clear set of goals to be achieved, and they point people at all levels in the same direction with the same inputs. The power of KPIs comes not only from understanding how the organization is performing in individual areas, but in seeing how the multiple aspects of the organization function together. KPIs and the organizational status they reflect give team members critical information about how they contribute to organizational performance, and leaders information to make better decisions about allocating resources and focusing talent and energy where it is most needed.

Ideally, department or work team KPIs are aligned with the main problems the organization decides it wants to solve—the performance gaps it wishes to close—in a defined period of time. Defining and setting cascading KPIs, whereby the KPIs at the highest level guide what the organization tracks further down, should be part of the strategy deployment process outlined in Chapter 3 on Priorities. To review, KPIs may be phrased as, "We want to decrease our product returns from X to Y" or "We want to increase our revenues per month from A to B." KPIs are situational—the ones you monitor are likely different from those monitored by your competition or your suppliers. Likewise, the specific KPIs needed to guide performance at the departmental level will be different from department to department.

For simplicity, we refer to top-level "corporate" scorecards as Level 3 scorecards, and the KPIs they contain as Level 3 KPIs.[8] To keep people focused on what matters, we recommend that Level 3 scorecards include a maximum of nine KPIs, so leaders will have to choose wisely. This limit doesn't mean there aren't dozens, hundreds, or—in a large enough organization—thousands of individual

---

[8] Scorecards can be also referred to as dashboards, and Level 3 KPIs are also referred to as True North KPIs or "wellness metrics."

measurements that should be monitored regularly. The scorecard contains only the most essential information to monitor macro-level performance against a clearly defined target. Figure 5.4 offers an example of a Level 3 scorecard.

To tell a clear story about how the organization is doing, the most effective scorecards present a holistic view of actual vs. desired performance. Consider the measures presented in Figure 5.4, which reflect financial, customer-centric, and employee-centric performance. The physical placement of these eight KPIs on the scorecard isn't coincidental. No matter if a viewer reads charts horizontally or vertically, operational metrics are the first ones the eye lands on. This intentional placement reinforces the message that financials are an *outcome* of operational performance; and you will get the financial results you seek more easily if you focus on the enablers of those outcomes versus the outcomes themselves.

Notice, too, how easy it is to interpret the information. By presenting your KPIs in visual form, it is immediately clear how the organization is faring against defined targets. If the scorecard had been formatted as a table with numbers, it would be more difficult to see trends or patterns, form accurate conclusions about performance, and know whether or not adjustments were needed.

When organizations display the data related to KPIs visually, leaders and team members can easily see the direction in which performance is heading—up, down, or flat. Visual displays also allow you to color code scorecards to allow people to grasp positive or negative trends more quickly. Many choose to use red for negative, green for positive, and yellow for "in danger of turning red." We prefer a more binary approach: you're either doing well (green), or you're not and need to take action (red).

For optimum impact, the scorecards must be displayed in a public place. LED monitors are wonderful for those companies with the budget for them, but organizations can also take a low-cost, low-tech route and post KPIs on large-scale printer paper taped

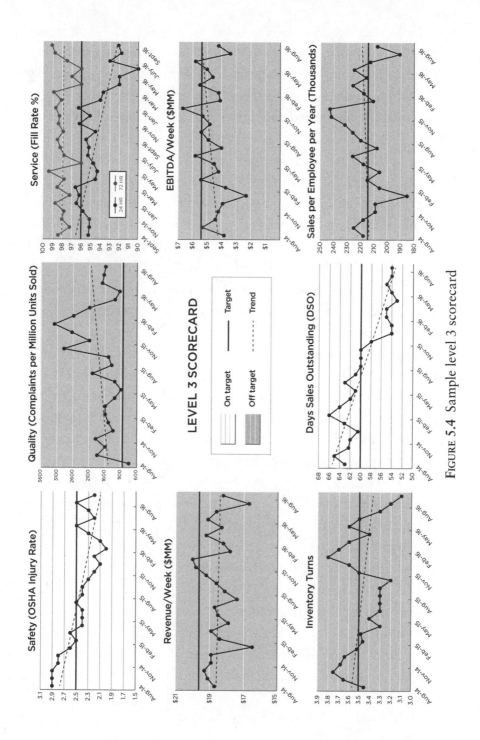

FIGURE 5.4 Sample level 3 scorecard

149

to a wall. Manually drawn charts presented on a whiteboard also work well. The point is for people to see them. When organizations display their Level 3 corporate scorecards publicly, they generally experience performance gains, likely due in some part to the Hawthorne Effect, where people behave differently when they know what's being measured.[9]

The medical device manufacturer that developed the Level 3 board in Figure 5.4, for example, displayed the scoreboard in highly visible locations throughout its headquarters, including the lobby, hallways, office areas, the cafeteria, and in its global factories. This was a bold act of performance clarity given that the company was privately held at that time. The tactic worked—in the three years during which the company operated with this level of performance clarity, it grew from $968 million in revenue to $1.2 billion and became one of the most desirable employers in its region.

The tactic *worked*—past tense. A new CEO took over in 2011 and initiated a results-at-all-costs management style. The CEO did not seek or communicate with clarity and didn't believe in the transparency that the Level 3 boards offered, and so he had all the Level 3 boards removed. It got worse: long-term senior leaders were forced out or resigned and were replaced with people who shared the CEO's mindset. Strategy became murky. When a former senior leader asked the new CEO what the corporate strategy was, the CEO replied: "Our strategy is growth."

In just a few years—and during a period in which the market grew overall—the company's revenue dropped from $1.2 billion to $1 billion and EBITDA fell from $280 million to $220 million. Voluntary employee turnover at headquarters rose from between 1 percent and 2 percent per year to between 8 percent and 9 percent. While cause-and-effect ties are difficult to prove, nearly every senior leader I've talked with since the company's days of peak performance cites

---

[9] https://en.wikipedia.org/wiki/Hawthorne_effect.

the lack of clarity around goals, targets, and current performance as the largest contributor to the company's downward spiral.

Another seemingly trivial action that points to the power of visually displaying data occurred during a transformation effort we facilitated at a technology firm. One of the functional areas in the organization invested in two dry-erase boards on wheels in order to visually display KPIs and track progress. The team we worked with designed how the KPIs would appear on the first board, but the morning they were scheduled to design the second board they couldn't find it. It turned out that a team from another area had taken the board because they liked what they saw and wanted to begin using visual management themselves. Why they felt entitled to "borrow" another team's board and not purchase their own is a different question. The point is this: once organizations experience the clarity that comes with visually displaying performance data—and after working through concerns about showing a work area's "dirty laundry"—they typically want it everywhere.

Cascading Measurement—from Level 3 to Levels 2 and 1

Level 3 scorecards present the highest level performance metrics needed for clarity. Leaders operating at different levels of the organization will also need to collect and display data relevant to the work areas they oversee. Senior leaders focus on Level 3 performance. Level 2 scorecards typically include those Level 2 KPIs relevant to a business unit, division, or department, depending on organizational structure. Level 1 scorecards reflect the relevant Level 1 KPIs for a department or work team.

As an example of how the different levels of KPIs can be used, consider EBITDA and its variants. The CFO will likely track the inputs contributing to gains or losses in EBITDA. One level down, a plant general manager may monitor the percent capacity utilization for each production line under his or her control. At Level 1, a supervisor may monitor overall equipment effectiveness (OEE), and so on.[10]

The relationship between Level 3, 2, and 1 KPIs is an example of the *cascading measurement* I referred to earlier. Establishing performance clarity in this way creates organization-wide alignment from the senior-most leaders to the people doing the work. Such alignment ensures that tactical performance and improvement priorities contribute to overall organizational performance. Enabling such alignment of course requires that *everyone* in your organization understands your Level 3 KPIs. Level 2 and Level 1 KPIs need to be clear to those involved in the work they reflect. All team members need to understand what the KPIs mean, what the targets are, and how the organization references those targets.

Here's another example of how cascading measurement works, this one from the healthcare industry. Senior leaders of a health system that owns multiple hospitals and facilities may need to reduce medication errors across its network. To measure its performance in fulfilling that priority, they would need to understand how many errors occur, and then set a Level 3 KPI to reduce error from the current rate to an identified target (the gap). One level down in the organization (Level 2), each hospital would monitor errors in its facility and use the results to drive improvement efforts. Another level down at the departmental level (Level 1), the pharmacy and nursing departments would track errors in dispensing and administration, respectively.

Cascading measurement provides varying levels of granularity from macro to micro. They enable people to understand the

---

[10] Remember that EBITDA is a measure of overall profit and therefore carries many variables. Percent capacity utilization, one component of EBITDA, reflects whether equipment is producing the output it's capable of (assuming there's demand for that output). OEE presents an even finer look at problems on specific production lines that can negatively affect capacity utilization (and therefore EBITDA), including equipment that's not running when it's scheduled to run, equipment that's not producing as much output as it's capable of due to speed issues, and equipment that's not producing as high quality output as it should due to product quality issues.

organizational goals, where the organization is now in terms of meeting those goals, and what targets they and their peers need to meet in order to improve overall organizational performance.

Three levels of cascading KPIs are sufficient for most organizations. Smaller organizations may only need two levels, while very large organizations may need four to create alignment. Just keep in mind that more is not necessarily better.

Choosing Which KPIs to Track

There is no one set of KPIs—or even categories of KPIs—that can capture the needs of every organization (and anyone who suggests so is someone you should avoid). Below are some criteria you can use to select relevant KPIs for your organization, department, or work team.

Select Balanced KPIs

KPIs tell a story of how the organization or team performs over a period of time. Similar to how we measure blood pressure, glucose levels, and weight to assess overall health, an organization needs holistic and balanced measurement. To tell a complete story, an organization's KPIs should reflect a broad range of relevant performance areas: financial, operational, customer experience, employee experience, supply chain performance, safety, and so on.

There are a number of models that can help stimulate discussions about which metrics are most relevant for establishing a balanced view of performance. Two of the most common models are the classic QCDSM (quality, cost, delivery, safety, morale) model that evolved from the Total Quality Management and Lean management movements, and Kaplan and Norton's Balanced Scorecard approach.[11]

---

[11] Robert Kaplan and David Norton, *The Balanced Scorecard* (Harvard Business Review Press, 1990).

However, don't just copy and paste these categories into your performance measurement system. Every organization is different. When we work with clients on performance measurement and KPI selection, we begin with two overarching categories: *critical to customer* metrics and *critical to business* metrics, which include operational performance, employee-centric, and financial performance metrics.

Clearing Up the Leading/Lagging Indicator Confusion

Metrics have long been classified as either leading or lagging indicators. *Lagging indicators* are similar to looking in a rearview mirror; they reflect performance that has already occurred. *Leading indicators*, in contrast, are predictive in nature and allow the organization to alter performance and address an issue before the next occurrence. Most scorecards, from this perspective, contain only lagging indicators.

Many people new to measurement believe that each metric is either leading or lagging by definition. However, lagging and leading are matters of perspective. A yellow traffic light is lagging in that we know the green light is gone, but it's leading in that the red light hasn't appeared yet. Similarly, quarterly earnings are lagging indicators of financial performance for the quarter that passed, but they are leading indicators for the following quarter. Producing 75 percent quality against a target of 90 percent isn't good, but that metric serves as a leading indicator that should drive improvement. Leaders definitely want metrics that enable the organization or work team to make improvements, and what really matters is active problem solving to close the gaps revealed through measurement.

As you continue to consider the balance of the metrics you choose, be aware of *vanity metrics* that look good, but can mask performance gaps. For example, in digital industries like online publishing or gaming, organizations care about how many customers visit a website or download an app. Those metrics are referred to as vanity metrics because they reflect first-level interest from customers and can make an organization look like it is in demand and worthy of advertisers. When it comes to performance, however, the number of visitors or the number of downloads is only part of the story. As important is the number of minutes a visitor spends on the site or the number of people who actively use the app after download.

With that in mind, the metrics you choose should be those that are both relevant based on your current priorities and will motivate your organization to take proper action.

Be Willing to Change Them

Some of your KPIs may never change; the *targets* should, but the specific KPI you track may stay on the Level 3 scorecard over the life span of the organization. Some KPIs should change, however. We part company with consultants and academics who believe that organizations need to keep all KPIs static year-over-year in order to measure performance over time. On the contrary, if your strategy changes, or your new problems arise, your KPIs need to change to reflect these new conditions.

For example, imagine your organization has spent several years improving an area of your operations that needed attention. You set goals, took steps to work toward them, and over time you reached the desired level. At that point, you may have a new gap you want to focus on. In that situation, you may choose to swap the former priority KPI for a new Level 3 KPI that needs more organizational attention.

That said, we recommend that organizations stick with their KPIs for at least one full fiscal year. The organizational learning and habit formation that results from consistency is more important than perfection in helping build performance measurement discipline. You may consider changes when you begin the next round of strategy deployment.

Another area that should remain flexible is how different departments measure what matters to them. Don't try to standardize in this area. We see this frequently, and it's a dangerous practice. Mandates and templates are tempting, especially for large organizations, but overstandardization is as damaging as understandardization. The metrics needed by one department are not the same as those required by another. Relevance is key; requiring the exact same measurement categories is often counterproductive.

For instance, if you are a manufacturer, you should track safety in your production areas. But the finance department probably doesn't need safety as one of its KPIs. Each department needs to decide what matters in terms of its contribution to corporate performance, and then measure it.

CONCLUSION

So, how *are* you doing? My goal with this chapter is to spur leaders to take the time and effort to develop a clear answer to that question. Organizations need to know where they are today in order to set performance goals for the future. And understanding where the organization is in meeting its goals allows everyone, from leaders to frontline workers, to focus their effort and make proper decisions. In short, clarity about performance is a foundational requirement for improvement, and reliable data that is accurate and visual is the foundation for that performance clarity. Organizations that take the time to gain that clarity never see it as wasted effort. Not once have I had a leader say to me that she wished she had *less* insight into the workings of her business unit.

Case in point: one of the organizations we work with recently adopted the practice of using KPI scorecards and began displaying them in break rooms and common areas around the work space. Prior to that, the members of the organization couldn't see how the organization was doing overall. Now that they can, they have been able to make decisions that have preserved product quality and customer satisfaction during a period of massive growth. A leader of the organization had this to say about the impact: "One of the greatest benefits has been making people think about which metrics matter the most and gaining cross-functional consensus around them. Problem solving, improvement, and decision making are now focused on moving the numbers."

Collecting, scrubbing, analyzing, and publicly displaying performance data in a highly visual way can also make it clear when areas of the organization are working at cross-purposes. For instance, the organization may have set a goal of reducing inventory turns while maintaining an agreed-upon service level, but if your vice president of sales then strong-arms your production planner to increase days of inventory to assure you never have an out-of-stock situation, you lack alignment. This kind of misalignment is usually resolved through the catchball process described in Chapter 3, but if leaders did not reach true consensus, measurement can surface issues you didn't see before.

And to repeat, knowing how you are performing creates the greatest value when it drives your improvement efforts. In the next chapter, I focus on the other side of the performance coin—problem solving.

6

Problem Solving

*Most people spend more time and energy going
around problems than in trying to solve them.*

—HENRY FORD

Leaders spend much of their time dealing with problems—from big problems like an unexplained drop in sales to smaller problems like misspelled words on customer correspondence. The constancy with which leaders deal with these kinds of issues makes many confident that they are pretty good at problem solving. My friend Joel (not his real name) certainly feels that way. Joel is the CEO of a hospital. During a recent dinner he mentioned a pernicious problem that periodically reared its head at his hospital. I suggested that, given the recurring nature of the problem, he and his team weren't tackling it methodically enough.

Well, that was the content of what I said. Because he's a good friend, my actual words were more direct: "You don't know how to solve problems," I said.

He put his fork down. "Yes, I do. I problem solve all day, every day. I wouldn't have my job if I didn't know how to problem solve."

I shook my head. "What you do is not problem solving. It's problem mitigation."

We went back and forth like that for a few minutes until I made him an offer: I would coach him gratis on a problem of his choice to show him the difference between disciplined problem solving and his—and his leadership team's—usual approach. "Deal," he said.

For our experiment he chose to work on the problem to reduce the "door-to-bed" time for patients who went to the emergency department (ED) and were ultimately admitted into the hospital. The hospital's target was to have those admitted patients settled in an inpatient room within 240 minutes of entering the ED. Joel's hospital had a door-to-bed average of 270 minutes.[1]

During my first problem-solving session with Joel, I started with the question, What's the problem? Only once you know the answer to that question can you find answers to the subsequent questions— How do you know it's a problem? How big is it? For whom is it a problem? What are the reasons for the problem?—and experiment with alternative approaches to eliminate the reasons. In fact, defining and understanding the problem should be the most time-intensive aspect of problem solving. Yet many assume they know what the problem is and leap to solutions before they have clarity about what's really going on. CEO or not, Joel was no different. He assumed from the get-go that the cause of the problem lay with the ED, and in our first problem-solving session he jumped over my questions and started suggesting "obvious" process changes that should be made. All this before he even made a visit to the ED! Joel was certain that one of two issues was at play, and possibly both: lab work and CT scans were taking too long, and/or the ED doctors were taking too long to diagnose and admit patients because they

---

[1] This problem wasn't technically Joel's to own—nor would it be any CEO's. Ownership for results belonged to someone on his leadership team. In responding to my challenge, Joel chose a problem he knew was significant and persistent and owned it for learning purposes.

had too many patients to juggle. I smiled and suggested that he go to the ED and observe patient flow for at least two hours.

"Two hours? I don't have two hours to observe one problem. I've got dozens."

"And you'll have dozens more if you don't learn how to stop mitigating and start solving."

I return to Joel's story later in the chapter, but I use him to make a point: Since problems are an organizational constant, knowing how to solve them is the single most effective way to improve organizational performance. That is not a controversial statement, yet few organizations adopt a disciplined approach to problem solving and invest in developing problem-solving capabilities in all their people. I seek to change that.

This chapter offers an overview of clarity-driven problem solving, with a particular focus on the question-based approach I recommend for working through problems large and small. This approach facilitates the process for problem owners at all levels of development.

PROBLEM SOLVING AND CLARITY

Joel's problem-solving behaviors—and his lack of awareness about those behaviors—are common. People at all levels regularly jump to conclusions and take action long before they have clarity on the problem, let alone the reasons for it. In other words, they react before they understand, a common form of hubris.

The same issues that lead to organizational ambiguity as a default state also lead to sloppy and undisciplined problem solving: people think they know when they don't; they feel pressure to be seen as decisive and action-oriented and thus don't take the time to understand the issue deeply; and they don't operate with enough curiosity. Outstanding performance only occurs when an organization makes substantive improvements in the areas that matter. That requires leaders to focus on the right problems and to solve those problems well.

Without the clarity that comes from disciplined problem solving, organizations are not solving problems but mitigating them—and reactively at that. A colleague of mine calls this approach "kissing boo-boos." It makes the involved parties feel like they are doing something, and it makes others think that important actions are under way, but it doesn't result in the most effective and longest-lasting resolutions.

I know this may be a hard reality to swallow. The various roles leaders have had in their careers may have given them extensive experience from which to see patterns. Their guesses about the cause of a problem may be right more often than they would be without that history, but that doesn't mean they are solving the right problems, consistently finding the root cause, or landing on the best countermeasures. Nor will amassing more experience addressing problems without proper coaching make anyone better at problem solving.[2] In fact, it can make you worse.

How could people possibly get worse at something they do all the time? K. Anders Ericsson, professor of psychology at Florida State University, is perhaps best known as the scientist behind the theory that it takes 10,000 hours of deliberate practice to achieve mastery of a skill, an idea popularized in Malcolm Gladwell's book *Outliers*.[3] In his book *Peak*, Ericsson emphasizes that for almost any field, attaining expert status requires not just many hours of practice but many hours of purposeful and deliberate practice during which the practitioner focuses on specific points of weakness, usually *with the guidance and corrective help of a more experienced coach.*

---

[2] Problem-solving coaching is addressed later in the chapter.

[3] Malcolm Gladwell, *Outliers: The Story of Success* (Hachette Book Group, 2008).

Ericsson shares that people who reach a certain level of proficiency and then stop engaging in deliberate practice with a coach often see a decline in their skill level, even if they continue to perform the skill. He documents this phenomenon with amateur tennis players and, more alarmingly, practicing physicians who show an erosion in skill the longer they are out of medical school because no one challenges their approach.[4]

Acquiring problem-solving skills and continually improving them follows the same development trajectory as Ericsson sees in people learning to play the piano or perform an appendectomy. Problem owners become experts at problem solving by first learning how to do it using an established methodology and under the guidance of a coach, and then consistently practicing, often with ongoing coaching. As people get better at problem solving, they may need more intermittent coaching or switch to more experienced coaches.

Leaders in particular benefit from personally investing in becoming better problem owners. Don't delegate problem-solving expertise to work teams or to the organization's improvement professionals and neglect yourself. *You* need to know how to properly solve problems. I provide the means to start in this chapter, but leaders at all levels have to commit to becoming a skilled problem owner and become committed to building problem-solving capabilities throughout the organization.

There is no way to learn superficially or quickly, just as there is no way for me to talk about problem solving in a general way. I provide a framework in this chapter, but problem solving is situational. You will need deliberate and consistent practice to build the breadth of experience that will enable you to solve problems well. Over time, this investment will also put leaders in a position to

---

[4] K. Anders Ericsson, *Peak: Secrets from the New Science of Expertise* (Houghton Mifflin, 2016), 136–137. Read from p. 137 to learn about the problem with learning environments that value knowledge over skills. As I alluded to in Chapter 4, revering knowledge is a rampant problem in the improvement profession as well.

coach team members. In fact, problem-solving skill building is the most important aspect of people development. Viewed through this lens, problem-solving coaching is *the primary role* of the leader.

Disciplined problem solving is most powerful when it becomes an organizational expectation. Organizations benefit from deeper and more relevant resolutions when they adopt a standard method for problem solving and commit to raising everyone's level of proficiency in it. Problem solving should be the number one capability development priority in every organization.

This said, building capabilities is only one aspect of becoming an organization that consistently solves problems well. Developing a culture of clarity that embraces problem solving also plays a crucial role, since solving problems well is far easier when everyone is working to be clear. Organizations operating with a culture of ambiguity, in contrast, are going to have to put in the effort to remove the obstacles to clarity outlined in Chapter 1 in order to create a culture in which problem solving is celebrated. Fear in particular can interfere with the need to discover the truth about the current state and the root causes for it. Taking the time to remove fear from the workplace, approach problems with humility and curiosity, recognize one's biases, and give problem solving the time that's needed all combine with improved capabilities to make an organization outstanding at problem solving.

What Exactly Is a Problem?

The word *problem* often evokes a range of emotions. If you grew up in a household or have ever worked for a company where problems are viewed as necessarily bad, then the word may carry an emotional charge that stirs a range of negative emotions. Some organizations have even banned the word and promote sugarcoated alternatives, such as "issues" and "opportunities for improvement."

Poppycock. A problem is merely a gap between where you are and where you would like to be or need to be. Problems vary in size and complexity, and in degree or urgency. They can affect a narrow or wide range of stakeholders, and can span short or long periods of time. Some problems require game-changing countermeasures to have any impact; others will represent a need for more modest improvements to meet a less aggressive performance target; still others relate to long-term strategy. Some problems relate to existing situations, whereas others deal with the creation of a new capability, process, or product. No matter the type, scope, or urgency of a problem, solving it doesn't need to carry an emotional charge: it's simply a gap to be closed.

Problems are best defined in the same measurable from-to terms I discussed in Chapter 5 on Performance, which define where you are now (from) and where you would like to be or need to be (to). For example, "Reduce product returns from 12 percent to 6 percent." "Increase talent retention from 70 percent to 85 percent." "Reduce new product development time from 36 months to 12 months." And so on.

In these examples, the gap is objective and quantifiable. For more subjective issues, the gap may be defined in ways that provide directional—but not precise—means for measurement. For example, we helped one of our clients develop a "pain index" to measure a team's progress toward solving a customer service problem that had been putting significant pressure on staff. The improvement team reduced the variation inherent with subjective measurement by clearly defining each rating on the index and surveying staff at the same time each day. Objective measurement is always better, but that doesn't mean that subjective measurement has no value.

In defining the from/to measurements, the language of "need" and "want" reflects a difference in the purpose for and degree of urgency in solving a problem (closing a gap). Joel *needed* his organization to shorten the door-to-bed time because an at-capacity ED resulted in incoming patients being diverted to other hospitals (causing loss of revenue and reputation) and reduced patient satisfaction scores from the patients waiting to be moved to an inpatient room. It also led to significant tension between the ED and other departments in the hospital. If, instead, the problem he'd identified had been to increase his hospital's regional market share for a certain procedure, it would have been an important business goal, and would have represented a "want" gap—no less important to the business, but perhaps lower in priority.

In *The Toyota Engagement Equation*, colleague Tracey Richardson differentiates between the two scenarios by referring to the gaps as "caused" or "created." As depicted in Figure 6.1, a *caused* (need) gap occurs when performance deviates from an established standard (also referred to as a performance target). A *created* (want) gap occurs after a current standard is met consistently, and the organization wants to raise the bar and start another problem-solving cycle to close a new performance gap. Leaders view the new defined standard (target) as *proposed* until it's put through problem-solving paces and deemed achievable. The cycle of closing gaps and defining new ones is the essence of continuous improvement.[5]

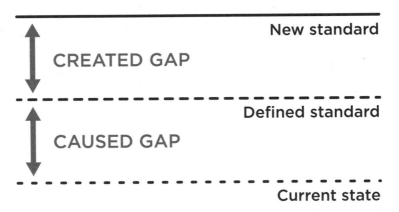

New standard

CREATED GAP

Defined standard

CAUSED GAP

Current state

FIGURE 6.1 Caused and created gaps

[5] Tracey Richardson and Ernie Richardson, *The Toyota Engagement Equation: How to Understand and Implement Continuous Improvement* (McGraw-Hill Education, 2017), pp. 190–192.

While I'm defining terms, there are a few more I'd like to clarify. One that regularly causes confusion is the word *solution*, a word we shy away from. Yes, I know, it is problem *solving*, but the word *solution* implies a level of permanence that is antithetical to the iterative nature of disciplined problem solving. Business operates in a fluid world. Conditions change. One gap closes and another one appears. The impermanence of problem solving is best captured with the term *countermeasure*, which we use instead of *solution*. Problem solving is the search for the best means to counter a defined condition.

Another term I've already used is *problem owner*—the person who leads a problem-solving effort. I use this word in its singular form because all problem-solving efforts should have a sole "owner" who is committed to and accountable for the results of the problem-solving cycle. There are practical reasons for this. First, the problem owner works with various people, functional areas, and/or work teams at different stages of the process. While many people may be involved, only one person "owns" the problem-solving effort and is accountable for results even though the mix of people who need to be involved changes many times throughout the problem-solving cycle. Organizations that approach problem solving with a fixed team may be less willing or able to flex as needed.

Another reason why problems need a dedicated owner is because someone needs to become the *expert in the problem* and be accountable for taking action. Unless there is a sole person who knows with absolute clarity that it is his or her job to uncover the cause of the problem and resolve it, you're at risk of segmented knowledge where no one fully understands the problem. Additionally, your efforts could be vulnerable to the bystander effect.[6] This psychological phenomenon occurs when witnesses to a crime or other events know that others also saw it take place. The more witnesses there are, the

---

[6] B. Latané and J. M. Darley, *The Unresponsive Bystander: Why Doesn't He Help?* (New York: Appleton-Century-Croft, 1970).

more likely each witness is to stand by and not intervene. Everyone thinks that someone else is going to take action. This phenomenon leads to the adage that I see in practice a lot: when everyone is accountable, no one is accountable.

The last reason that problem solving requires a single problem owner relates to the way problem owners develop proficiency—namely, through focused practice with the guidance of a more experienced coach. The coach–problem owner relationship is one-on-one; I discuss this later in the chapter.

CLEAR PROBLEM SOLVING

Some of the earliest problem-solving models included John Dewey's Six-Step Method and Colonel John Boyd's Observe, Orient, Decide, and Act (OODA) loop. Companies such as Ford and Toyota developed models they've dubbed Eight Disciplines (8D) and the Toyota Business Process (TBP), respectively. The Six Sigma approach to improvement and problem solving centers on Define, Measure, Analyze, Improve, Control (DMAIC), and Lean management is based on Walter Shewhart's Plan, Do, Study, Adjust (PDSA) cycle and its cousin, Plan, Do, Check, Act (PDCA).[7] Niche approaches to problem solving include Lean Startup and Design Thinking.

All of the frameworks have clarity shortcomings because they're structured around high-level labels for each of many stages, and those labels do a poor job of reflecting the details. For example, we see many problem owners in the "Plan" stage of PDSA begin by creating a plan to implement, whereas that stage is designed for the problem owner to define and deeply understand the problem as a preliminary step *before* he or she creates a plan to "Do" something

---

[7] I cover the history of PDSA and PDCA and why I don't refer to either as the "Deming cycle" in *The Outstanding Organization*, pp. 128–129.

about it. In another example of linguistic misinterpretation, the "Control" stage in DMAIC is often interpreted to mean that, once implemented, organizations should stick with an improvement for a period of time to stabilize and measure the improvement. While both actions are vital for any improvement cycle, many practitioners fall into analysis and stabilization paralysis rather than moving relatively quickly into a new cycle of improvement. This mistake is common in part because many treat problem solving as if it were linear, whereas the best results come by treating it as iterative and cyclical.

Other clarity issues arise around sequence and missing pieces. TBP has problem owners set a target for improvement as a third step, whereas I find that challenging people to define the target earlier in the process results in deeper problem solving. 8D is the only method to include an explicit step focused on preventing scope creep. And none of the models address a common point of failure: how to roll out an improvement once it's proven to address the problem effectively.

Given the above inadequacies—that none of the problem-solving models to date have been explicit enough nor comprehensive enough to establish the full range of thinking processes and actions needed to solve problems well—I developed a question-based approach that I refer to as CLEAR problem solving. CLEAR can be used alone if your organization hasn't yet adopted one of the existing models, or you can use it alongside PDSA, DMAIC, or another established method to clarify meaning and drive deeper critical thinking, result-ing in better outcomes.

CLEAR isn't meant to be prescriptive, nor strictly linear. The questions are intended to spur deep thought and move the problem owner away from the common fallacy of thinking about problem solving as a one-way, simplistic process on par with baking a cake or cutting a two-by-four.

To demonstrate what I mean by that, consider the request we received from the CEO at a client of ours. He asked us to provide one or two days of classroom training so that his team could learn to solve problems more effectively. We explained that gaining problem-solving proficiency is not a classroom exercise, nor does one learn deeply in only one or two days. It requires people to receive ongoing, real-world, one-on-one coaching—an apprenticeship—to build proficiency. He resisted that idea. "They just need to follow the steps!" he snapped.

No, they don't *just need to follow the steps*. That's not how robust problem solving works. Sure, one might fare better following prescribed steps than none at all, but that doesn't mean the outcomes will be as deep and lasting as they could and should be. Problem solving requires deep thinking and a patient willingness to learn as much as possible about the problem and test as many alternatives as is warranted—none of which can be cultivated by simply following steps.

The foundational mindset that effective problem owners bring is one of humility and curiosity. If I had to capture that mindset as a one-sentence motto it would be: "I don't know, but I want to learn." With curiosity, the problem owner accepts the problem—the gap— and approaches it with the desire to learn and understand, moving from ambiguity about the problem to deep clarity, as illustrated in Figure 6.2. Effective problem owners exhibit dog-after-a-bone tenacity when it comes to answering the overarching questions of What? Why? and How? Their role is to understand the situation as clearly and objectively as possible, after which the most effective countermeasures often reveal themselves. As John Dewey noted, "It is a familiar and significant saying that a problem well put is half-solved."[8]

The final requirement for effective problem solving is patience. Like a crime-scene investigator gathering and following clues, problem owners need to follow the facts where they lead, and paths don't always lead to the place the problem owner thought he or she was headed. Sometimes problem owners have to double back and find a new path, and there is no way to know what they will find as they

---

[8] John Dewey, "The Pattern of Inquiry," in *Logic: Theory of Inquiry* (Saerchinger Press, 2007; originally published in 1938).

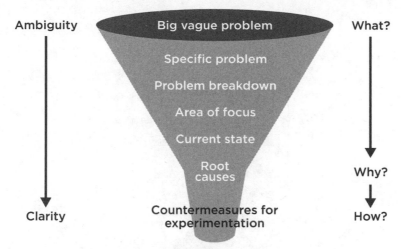

Ambiguity · Big vague problem · What?
Specific problem
Problem breakdown
Area of focus
Current state
Root causes · Why?
Clarity · Countermeasures for experimentation · How?

FIGURE 6.2 Using CLEAR problem solving to move
from ambiguity to clarity

follow a clue to its conclusion. This is the reason why we advise that our clients not try to predict the exact timeline for a problem-solving effort, nor force other problem owners to do so about their efforts. Problem owners never know what they're going to uncover until they start digging.

With curiosity, humility, and patient persistence in mind, let's move on to learn the questions needed for CLEAR problem solving.

Figure 6.3 identifies the CLEAR phases and common questions the problem owner needs to answer in each. Since problem solving is situational, the questions may vary depending on the type of problem and what problem owners learn at each step.[9] The process is also iterative. You may believe that you're clear about the problem, and then learn during current state analysis that the problem is different than originally thought.

---

[9] The questions in this model are best suited for solving problems with existing products, processes, environments, and so on (i.e., going from something to something else). Different questions may be needed when creating new products or processes, entering new markets, and so on (i.e., going from nothing to something).

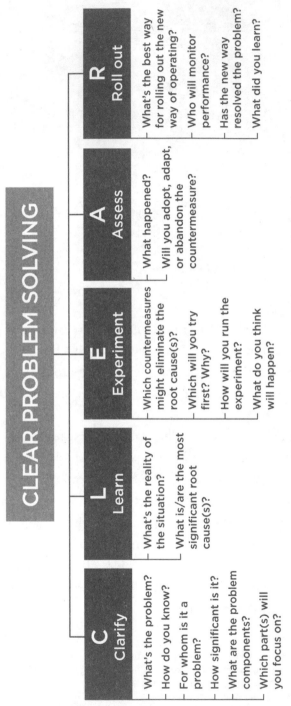

FIGURE 6.3 CLEAR problem solving phases and questions

This occurred recently with a client of ours, whose data indicated an erosion in turnaround times. Only later did we learn that the way the data was collected and analyzed changed in the middle of the time period we were tracking, creating what appeared to be—but was not actually—a change in the trend line. The CLEAR questions enable you to "serve the problem" by letting facts guide the process.

The following sections explain each of the CLEAR phases, with detail on the questions asked in each and the answers problem owners should expect to have before moving on to the next.

C: CLARIFY AND BREAK DOWN THE PROBLEM

The C phase of problem solving centers on clarifying and breaking down the problem. This phase walks you through a set of questions needed to deeply understand what problem you are trying to solve. Many problem owners rush though this stage, thinking they already know what the problem is—after all, didn't someone choose to focus on this problem in the first place? Well, yes, but that doesn't mean you have clarified it, nor that you fully understand its component parts. The C phase can require proportionally more time than any of the other CLEAR phases.

Clarify has three distinct parts: defining the problem, clarifying its significance, and, for many problems, breaking them down. In more colloquial terms, the Clarify phase addresses the questions, What's the problem? How do you know it's a problem? For whom is it a problem? How significant is it? What are its component parts? Which part will you focus on?

What's the Problem?

Answering these questions enables clarity on what the problem actually is, as distinct from what people think it is. The answers also help convince people who may not believe a problem exists that there is a gap in need of closing.

In this early phase of problem solving, the answer to "What's the problem?" often begins as a vague notion. What are you trying to stop or enable? What outcome(s) would you like to create or change? What does the problem prevent a person, team, or the entire organization from accomplishing? What could be accomplished if the problem was solved?

The answer should be presented in the "from-to" terms I introduced earlier, which serve to define the measurable gap you want to narrow or eliminate. Some example answers might be: grow market share from 15 percent to 22 percent; reduce returns from 25 per week to 15 per month; improve quality consistency from 82 percent to 94 percent; reduce lead time from 18 weeks to 10 weeks; and so on.

The examples I have used so far are simple by design. Many problems are like these, meaning it is possible to use simple, objective measurements to define the gap. Not all are as easily quantified up front, however. Some require the problem owner to move on to the Learn stage and capture current state data before he or she can establish the baseline from which to improve. In this case, the problem owner can begin by defining the problem qualitatively. For example, if the organization is losing customers and the problem owner does not yet have objective insights into that loss, the problem can be framed as "Reverse customer churn" early in the process and become quantifiable as data is collected. If the company is facing multivariate quality issues, the problem might be "Improve product quality."

After the problem owner has progressed through the Learn phase in which he or she learns more detail about the problem, it may be possible to circle back and redefine the problem in more concrete terms. This is an example of the iterative nature of problem solving—you may need to cycle back to a previous phase as you gain deeper understanding of the problem and the reasons for it.

People new to disciplined problem solving make a few common mistakes in the definition phase. Number one among them is defining the problem as *the lack of a solution.* For example, a leader may frame a problem as, "We need a new enterprise resource planning system." Based on what? Framing problems as a lack is assumption-based and dangerous.

Any problem whose definition guarantees investment in a new resource—*especially technology*—should raise a red flag, because you can't possibly know what you need until you have done the hard work of understanding the problem. Believing at the outset that resources of any sort will fix your problem—whether people, equipment, physical space, or technology—places an organization at risk of spending more money than it needs to. We see companies spend millions of dollars on new IT systems only to find that their performance problems followed them into their more technologically advanced environment. The same applies with assuming that automation is a solution. One of our common warnings is: "When you automate waste, you get automated waste."

Another common example of defining a problem as a lack of something occurs when inexperienced problem owners define problems as a lack of foundational process design features: "We need standard processes." "We need pull scheduling." "We need fewer batches." While these are all features of robust processes, and therefore worthwhile pursuits, they aren't clear problem definitions. A problem instead needs to be defined in *outcome* terms: What occurs as a result of not having this thing, whether it is a process feature, a piece of technology, a person, etc.? Problem owners are far less likely to make false assumptions or predetermine the path of the problem-solving effort if they form the habit early of carefully defining problems in from-to, outcome-driven terms.

The second definitional mistake problem owners make is defining a problem based on superficial understanding of the cause, not based on tangible outcomes. Typically, organizations understand they have a problem because they experience undesirable outcomes. For example, a client asked us to coach an order entry manager through a problem the company was having with late deliveries. Early efforts to define the problem revealed that some of the order entry team members were entering incorrect e-mail addresses into the contact field of the order form. The error made it difficult to communicate with the customer about the order after it was placed, which caused delayed shipments. With that information, the problem owner defined the problem as "Putting wrong e-mail into order form." The problem was more accurately defined as an outcome: delayed shipment. Incorrect e-mails, in contrast, were a potential cause.

Errors of perspective like this are common. To prevent them, problem owners early in their learning cycle—no matter their role in the organization—need to work with a skilled problem-solving coach. The coach can point out when problem owners jump to conclusions or rely on habitual thinking, and help them course correct and adopt new critical thinking habits.

A corollary to the question "What's the problem?" is "How do you know it's a problem?" Problem owners best answer this question using hard data that captures the negative outcomes resulting from the problem. In the absence of data, problem owners can rely on anecdotal data of sufficient sample size, if it provides consistent insights. Either way, qualifying the problem in this way allows problem owners to advocate for solving it. In organizations with unclear priorities and in those with limited resources, time, and attention spans, advocacy plays an especially important role in this phase of problem solving.

How Significant Is the Problem?

Problem owners will need to position a problem in context with all other competing issues vying for attention in the organization.

Doing that effectively requires problem owners to understand how significant the problem is. Significance gives the problem owner—the problem advocate at this stage—hard data to make a case for committing time and resources to solving *this* problem before another one. The specific questions that help clarify the significance of a problem are: How big is it? How urgent is it? How long has it been a problem? What will or won't happen in the future if the problem continues? Why should anyone spend time or commit resources to solve this problem? In other words, who cares?

Sizing the problem requires relevant data, the right unit of measure for communicating that data, and context. A number alone does not help people understand relative significance. People need to understand that number in context.

Consider this example from a financial services team we worked with. The team could not get leaders to care about a problem they felt prevented their business unit from earning an additional 2 percent in annual revenue, even though increasing revenue was one of the organization's annual goals. No one seemed to think that 2 percent was relevant until we helped the team see that using only a percentage made the numbers seem too small. Including the raw number of $1.3 million alongside the 2 percent figure caused the leadership team to sit up and take notice. Resources were no longer quite so constrained, and the team got what it needed to address the issue. More than that, solving the "2 percent problem" had a ripple effect in that business unit, resulting in a jump in sales of additional products to existing customers. When relevant, use both raw numbers and percentages to provide greater context and, by extension, a clearer picture of reality.

It bears repeating: in most organizations, a problem owner's problem is only one problem of many. Part of the problem owner's role is to convince leadership and peers that the problem is worth solving based on the benefit of solving it—whether it provides a better customer experience, cost savings, or greater revenue—and the quantifiable risk of not solving it.

To do that, construct concrete answers to the questions, So what? and Who cares? as clearly as possible to help others see why this particular problem warrants attention. Doing so creates a sense of urgency that might not otherwise exist. Explicit details about how a problem affects a customer or the organization itself create a shared understanding and deeper commitment to solving it.

Many readers may also recognize that there's a direct tie between garnering support for problem solving and the strategy deployment process outlined in Chapter 3. If an organization's problem-solving efforts are aligned with a well-designed strategy deployment plan, problem owners will not need to do much convincing—the problems they work on already align with known and identified priorities. If the organization does not practice strategy deployment, problem owners may need to lobby for resources and convince peers and colleagues to help. Defining significance allows leaders to make informed decisions about whether a problem warrants a shift in resources. It allows peers to recognize a need for improvement and to support it. For organizations that don't have robust priorities and alignment, communicating significance through data is even more important. It can cut through organizational apathy to amass resources for a relevant problem.

What Are the Problem Components? Which Part(s) Will You Focus On?

Problems vary widely in their complexity. "Mechanistic" problems have a clear cause-and-effect relationship. Joel's hospital and the door-to-bed issue was a mechanistic problem. Complex problems, in contrast, may not have a single cause-effect dynamic and often need to be broken down to allow problem owners to focus on solving one component—or problem aspect—at a time. If you fail to break a complex problem down you risk trying to achieve too much with a single problem-solving cycle, or applying superficial solutions, both of which slow results.

A manufacturing team we worked with, for example, faced a multifactorial problem when it needed to reduce the price of a product that had become commoditized. Pricing, cost, and market share problems are typically complex, with many components. Understandably, the company didn't want to reduce the profit it earned from the product, so it needed to reduce the manufacturing and administrative costs it incurred to be able to reduce the product price and still meet the organization's financial goals. Before we got involved, a team had spent significant time trying and failing to address the problem as one issue.

Through our coaching, the team broke the problem into its component parts—costs related to raw material, labor, utilities, transportation, sales, and so on—and selected a relevant area of focus. With that, the team was able to remove costs in multiple areas. Eventually, by improving equipment utilization, redesigning packaging, and increasing productivity to reduce overtime expenses, the organization was able to reduce the sales price while *increasing* the percent profit it earned. If the team hadn't broken the problem down, studied each of the components, and learned the root causes of each, the countermeasures likely would have remained elusive.

Figure 6.4 shows an example of a problem breakdown tree drawn from a technology client we worked with to grow its market share. We coached the team to create product, revenue, and market channel categories and show the percentages for how much revenue and profit it draws from those categories. The dark blocks represent the specific problem the client decided to focus on for an initial round of problem solving.

With a defined problem and scope, problem owners are ready to move to the next phase in CLEAR problem solving.

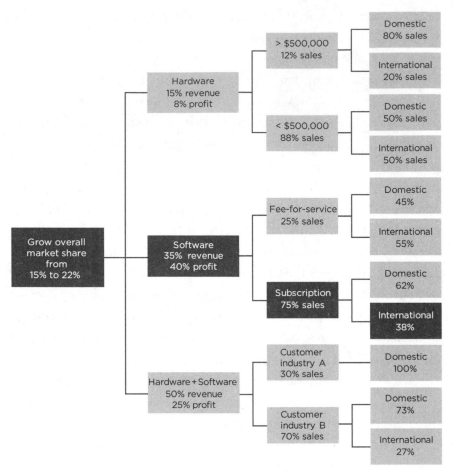

FIGURE 6.4 Sample problem breakdown tree

L: LEARN ABOUT THE PROBLEM AND WHAT'S CAUSING IT

Once the problem owner has defined the problem and broken it down, it is time to move into the Learn phase, the goal of which is to gain a deep understanding of why the problem exists. The Learn phase has two subphases: understanding the problem more deeply— the reality of the situation—and understanding the reasons, or root causes, for the problem.

Stay alert to signs of bias, assumptions, and hubris in your own thinking. The human mind is naturally inclined to give meaning to events. This tendency was appropriately dubbed *sensemaking* by Karl Weick and can lead to faulty or incomplete views of the world.[10] Using the questions I outline below in the spirit of deep learning will help you develop the habit of making sense of things in a fact-based nonbiased way.

What's the Reality of the Situation?

Gaining a deep understanding of reality as it relates to the problem enables you to see more clearly the obstacles that stand between where you are and where you want or need to be. This reality—commonly referred to as the "current state analysis"— begins and ends with facts that help problem owners move out of the uncertain world of opinion and theory into a more objective environment within which everyone is operating with the same information. Learning how to discern fact from fiction is a critical skill. Facts are stubborn things. As U.S. founding father John Adams put it, "Whatever may be our wishes, our inclinations, or the dictates of our passions, they cannot alter the state of facts and evidence."[11]

We see a lot of knee-jerk assumptions in organizations about what is knowable or not knowable about a situation. In Chapter 5, I discussed at length the thorny issues organizations face pertaining to the data they have or don't have. It bears repeating: organizations usually have far more data and information about a situation than they think they do. In this phase of the problem-solving process, the information is often hidden from view, either because no one has yet engaged in the level of excavation needed to find the data and

---

[10] Karl E. Weick, *Sensemaking in Organizations* (SAGE Publications, 1995).

[11] John Adams, in remarks to the jury at the Boston Massacre trial on December 3, 1770; quoted in William Gordon's *The History of the Rise, Progress, and Establishment of the Independence of the United States of America*, Volume 1, 1788.

make it usable, or because the data has been suppressed for some reason. Making problems visible is a central tenet in Lean management and in any organization seeking to operate with greater clarity. Aldous Huxley said, "Facts do not cease to exist because they are ignored."[12] Your only way to learn is to go find them.

At this stage of the problem-solving process, it's helpful to begin with the question, "What do you *not* know?" to define a proper path to the facts. There are three primary methods for discovering the facts: observing, talking with people, and analyzing data and other information.

Observing is a powerful method for learning the truth, and involves going to the physical work locations that play a role in the problem—the gemba—as described in the previous chapter. Methods of observation include watching how the work is done in real time, videotaping a problem process or task, and taking photographs as the work is performed.

Going to the gemba to learn about the problem is nonnegotiable. If the problem lies in a secured area, get the problem owner clearance, or choose a problem owner who already has it. If the problem occurs in a plant in France, send the problem owner to France, or find a skilled problem owner in France. Don't let logistics limit your investigation.

A second way to gain clarity on the current state is to talk with as many people who are familiar with the work and the related problem as is logistically reasonable. These conversations are best held at the gemba, where you can talk directly to people with intimate knowledge about the problem and its potential causes. Also talk with people upstream and downstream from the problem, people affected by the problem, people in areas that may be associated with the root causes of the problem, subject matter experts, external customers, external suppliers—whoever can provide insights that

---

[12] Aldous Huxley, "Note on Dogma," *Proper Studies*, 1927.

will allow you to grasp the current state. Be aware of ambiguity in these conversations. People may sugarcoat, deflect, or intentionally hide information. Help them feel safe (assuming they are, that is!) so they will reveal details about the current state as they experience it. If you receive conflicting information, know that you have not yet learned enough about the issue and you need to verify and validate.

The third way to become clear about the current state situation is to gather and analyze data and other sources of information. It bears repeating: the data or information needed is highly situational, so problem owners want to think deeply about the status, demand, and outcome data needed, and ignore data that only adds noise. We use two techniques for narrowing the pool of data or information needed in the course of problem solving. One is through "forward thinking" questions: "What do I need to know that I don't currently know about this problem?" The other approach involves "reverse thinking": construct a theory about the problem in your mind ("I believe that . . ."), ask, "Why do I believe that?," and then find the information or data needed to confirm or refute the theory. In either case, always begin data collection with very clear questions about what you want to know. Problem owners will save themselves and those providing data a lot of time and wasted effort.

Information needs will likely shift as the problem owner learns more about the current state. As in a crime investigation, let the facts lead the way. If the problem owner discovers surprising information early on, he or she may need to dig deeper to understand it. If information leads to a different path than originally imagined, pivot to the new path and let it lead the way to clarity. Problem solving requires a healthy dose of trust and tenacity—and a good nose for nonsense. If you search for the truth and follow the facts, they won't fail you.

Knowing and getting the data you need is the first step. Learning how to distill and synthesize information—and display it in the clearest way—is an equally important skill all problem owners need to develop. The data visualization techniques I introduced in Chapter 5 are also helpful for gaining clarity in problem solving. Problem owners should use the best one to represent the insight the data reveals and get help from someone with data visualization experience if needed. The results will be worth it. The problem owner and everyone who sees the clear, well-presented data will be better able to see trends and patterns, information flow, and whether a problem is clustered in one location, time of day, or with a specific customer segment.

Figures 6.5, 6.6, 6.7, and 6.8 illustrate four of dozens of ways to visually represent current state findings.

Figure 6.5 is an example of an *information spaghetti diagram*. The abbreviations around the circle's circumference represent leaders who receive information in an approval process. This type of diagram can help visually communicate the number of people involved and handoffs in a process so that stakeholders can easily see the results from simplifying the process. In this case, the client successfully implemented the future state process design, which eliminated more than 30 handoffs, shaved nearly two months from the lead time, and reduced process time by 50 percent, which created around 3,000 hours of annual capacity. Prior to creating the

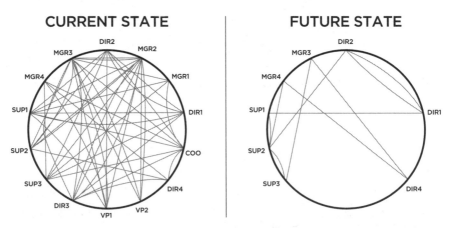

FIGURE 6.5 Information flow and handoffs in an approval process

diagram, the team had struggled to see this overly complicated portion of the process they were improving.

We used the information in Figure 6.6 to help a hospital client solve a two-pronged problem in one of its outpatient clinics: overcrowding in the early morning hours and long wait times to see a physician. We helped leadership see the problem more clearly by layering three data types onto one chart: patient arrival times, physician schedules, and patient exam start times. By displaying the facts in such a clear way, previously resistant physicians agreed to begin seeing patients earlier in the day. The client also designed and implemented a new scheduling system to level patient demand more evenly throughout the day and provided incentives to motivate walk-in patients to schedule appointments.[13]

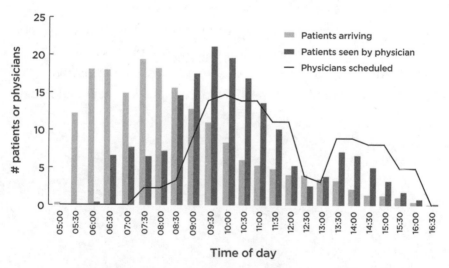

FIGURE 6.6 Patient arrivals versus physician staffing

---

[13] Load leveling is a Lean management technique that's used to reduce or eliminate unevenness (mura) resulting in smoother flow throughout a work system. In manufacturing, it's also referred to as production smoothing. Leveling incoming demand is a critical improvement for achieving flow, and the problem is often ignored because teams believe they can't influence customer behavior. That may be true in the case of seasonal goods and services, but organizations can often influence customer behavior in other circumstances.

Another client set out to transform its highest volume value stream. It wanted to reduce lead time and expense, increase capacity, and create a less stressful work environment for team members. While one improvement team focused on converting the value stream's production scheduling approach from a forecast-driven "push" model to "pull" based on real-time customer demand, a second team focused on leveling incoming orders from the customer. The organization had never studied demand variation, nor had it ever looked at its operation holistically. By visually displaying the facts around its demand spikes (Figure 6.7), leaders were able to see that internal decisions about when to offer product rebates had created the demand variation and placed significant stress on the operation. With this insight and some creative thinking, the client designed, tested, and implemented a new incentive program that leveled incoming customer orders to a large extent.

A client wanted to reduce product movement to improve productivity and reduce transportation expenses, product damage, and worker injuries. The *product movement map* shown in Figure 6.8 helped the team visualize product movement so they could make

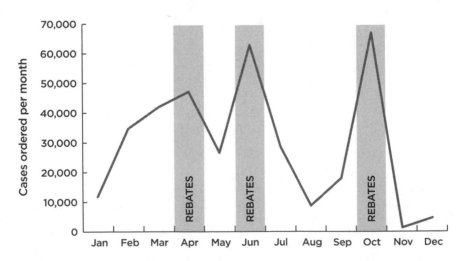

FIGURE 6.7 How rebate programs affect customer ordering patterns

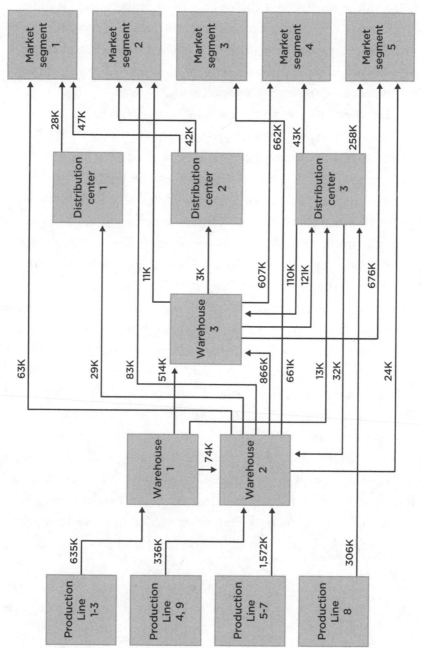

FIGURE 6.8 Product movement map

fact-based improvement decisions. Clarity about the current state also led to an unexpected discovery: the numbers didn't add up. This aha spawned a separate investigation into whether the data was incorrect, or whether product was moved and not tracked. Both situations turned out to be true, which led to an additional round of improvement that solved both problems.

Again, these are just four examples of the myriad ways to visualize the current state insights gained from data analysis. While problems with any degree of complexity typically require some sort of data review, collection, and analysis, others benefit from drawings, photographs, and video. Some problems require value stream mapping to grasp the situation. Others require process-level mapping. Some problems require both—or neither. The key to choosing a path that will get you what you need is to begin with clarity about what you're trying to learn and why.

A common danger in problem solving is turning only to those analytical tools that you're familiar with, even when they might not help. Overreliance on a known tool is a cognitive bias known as familiarity bias. Psychologist Abraham Maslow captured the human impulse to rely on familiar thought patterns when he quipped, "I suppose it is tempting, if the only tool you have is a hammer, to treat everything as a nail."[14] We saw this recently with the manufacturing client I mentioned earlier that had the problem of needing to reduce the cost of goods sold (COGS) for a product that had become commoditized. After defining the expense gap the organization wanted to close, the problem owner needed to grasp the current state. Two weeks later, the problem owner asked us to take a look at his progress.

He had assembled a leadership team and spent a full day creating a current state order-to-delivery value stream map for the

---

[14] Abraham H. Maslow, *The Psychology of Science: A Reconnaisance* (Joanna Cotler Books, 1966), p. 15.

product in question. We were puzzled by his decision to create a value stream map to solve a cost problem—it seemed like over-kill—but we kept an open mind and asked him to share what the mapping process revealed. He said they discovered that low overall equipment effectiveness (OEE) on the relevant manufacturing line was adding product cost. We asked him more questions and had him calculate how much improving OEE would affect product cost. When he realized that the OEE improvement gains he had targeted would only reduce the product cost by a penny per unit, he said, "Well, that doesn't help much!"

Indeed. He had made a common mistake of turning to the only thing he knew—value stream mapping—and focusing on an area he was familiar with, OEE. He succumbed to familiarity bias. He would have made better and faster progress had his first step been to explore which expenses contributed to COGS via problem breakdown.

To help him get back on track, I suggested that he take a step back. "What do you need to know?" I asked. With coaching, he created a list of the information and data he needed. Starting with this question might have helped him avoid a time-intensive activity that is most effective for solving flow problems across complex work systems. Using reverse thinking might also have worked if he had used it early on and started with the hypothesis "I believe that improving OEE will lower COGS in a significant way" and set out to understand what percentage of cost is produced by OEE.

Put the Problem Where It Belongs

The Learn phase sometimes reveals that a problem believed to "belong" in one part of the organization actually resides somewhere else. This often occurs when people are shunting blame. We've seen construction firms point to their suppliers as the reason for delayed project completions, for example, and defense contractors blame regulatory requirements for low productivity numbers. In both cases, the facts proved otherwise.

The opposite can occur as well: one part of the organization can take on a problem that belongs elsewhere out of a sense of loyalty or simply "trying to help." We encountered this situation during an engagement to help a 900-bed teaching hospital improve its performance by adopting Lean management practices. As the region's only trauma center, the hospital had a very busy emergency department (ED). The hospital also had a large outpatient department with many specialty clinics (cardiology, obstetrics, dermatology, orthopedics, etc.).

One of the problems that rose to the top of a priority list was timely and error-free decisions about the level of care a walk-in patient needed. The hospital staff used long-standing criteria to determine whether these patients should be directed to the emergency department or to one of the outpatient clinics. They got it right 97 percent of the time, but 3 percent of patients—60 patients per day—were directed to the wrong area. Three percent may seem a small number, but 60 misdirected patients who require medical care creates internal chaos, clinical risk to the patient, and poor patient experience.

As the problem owner and a few key stakeholders began to problem solve, they discovered that the problem was larger than they had thought. In addition to the 3 percent of patients whose initial assessment was wrong, they also discovered that the busy emergency department, which struggled to deal with its large volume of patients, had created a fourth category of patients: those who were clinically worse off than the criteria for directing patients to the outpatient clinic, but clinically better off than the multitude of patients crowding the ED. For years, the outpatient clinic nursing team had been quietly accepting these "borderline" patients because they felt the ED needed capacity more than the outpatient clinic did. Despite their well-intended efforts, the concession didn't make a significant dent in ED overcrowding. The nurses had merely moved the problem from one area to another *and* compounded it by creating two new problems: increased risk to patients and outpatient staff burnout from taking on patients with acute medical needs.

I use this case as an example of why taking the time to learn about the problem is so important. The hospital had a real issue with the 3 percent of patients who were unintentionally directed to the wrong department, but it had no idea about the volume of patients *intentionally* misdirected. Only with deep learning could it uncover the full scale of the problem and the workaround that had been created.

The problem to be solved resided with the ED, not the outpatient department. As vexing as complex problems such as ED capacity can be, it serves no one for another department to mask the problem and its root causes by moving it elsewhere.

What Are the Most Significant Root Causes of the Problem?

Once you understand the current state reality, you have the clarity you need to learn why that reality exists: the root causes—reasons—for the gap you've identified. Notice that I use the plural version of the term. Simple problems may have a single root cause.

More often, problems have multiple causes that may require different countermeasures.

Root-cause analysis, also referred to as gap analysis, is a fundamental skill set that *everyone* in the organization should possess, from C-level leaders to frontline workers, and everyone in between. While it's helpful to have a few internal people with deep experience in the full range of gap analysis methods, everyone needs to have at least moderate proficiency in three basic tools that can be used to understand the problem more deeply and begin to shed light on the root causes for it.

Five Whys

The five whys is probably the best known among the three gap analysis methods I discuss here. As the name suggests, it involves repeatedly asking why a problem exists to move from the highest-level causes of a problem down to the most essential, or root, level.

To demonstrate, imagine I am trying to solve a simple problem like missing an important meeting. First why: "Why did I miss the meeting?" Answer: Because I got to work late. Second why: "Why did I get to work late?" Answer: Because I overslept. Third why: "Why did I oversleep?" Answer: "Because I forgot to set my alarm." Fourth why: "Why did I forget to set my alarm?" Answer: Because I fell asleep watching television. The essential root cause is forgetting to set the alarm, but distraction was the reason why I forgot in the first place. I'd likely need to experiment with countermeasures that both reduce distraction and increase the likelihood that I remember to set my alarm.

As this very simple example demonstrates, *five* whys is a guideline. The root causes may become clear after three. Or the problem owner may need six whys to find the true root.

With complex problems, relying solely on five whys for root cause determination isn't enough. In this case, a problem analysis tree (also referred to as an issue tree) is a more effective choice. Problem analysis trees can be arranged either vertically or horizontally. Figure 6.9 provides a vertical example of a problem analysis tree.

The blocks below the target problem of deteriorating river water quality represent the range of causes contributing to the pollution. A problem analysis tree helps identify those causes. The tree doesn't tell you which causes you should seek to eliminate, however. That decision requires deeper discovery into which causes have the biggest impact on the problem, followed by prioritization of those causes.

The example of river water quality also highlights a common issue that arises in problem solving—namely that root causes can be viewed as problems themselves. Problems and causes lie on a continuum, which sometimes confuses people. In the deteriorating water example, the blocks above the target problem are the ultimate outcomes of the problem, and the blocks below it are root causes. But that's only because we're viewing the blocks in reference to the target problem (deteriorating water quality). If the target problem was, instead, waste dumping, river water quality would be an outcome and the four blocks below waste dumping would surface as the root causes.

To avoid confusion, problem owners should stay focused on the problem defined in the C phase of CLEAR, and consider the root causes in relation to that problem. When it's time to identify effective countermeasures, it may be necessary to go down a level to eliminate subcauses as you work to iteratively close the gap defined as the problem.

There's another important consideration related to the problem-cause continuum: the problem owner's level of authority in the organization and experience with problem solving. The bigger the problem, the more authority a problem owner needs to have to gather proper facts, engage all relevant parties in problem solving, and so on. Asking a junior team member to solve a market share problem is not only unwise, it's disrespectful to that team member.

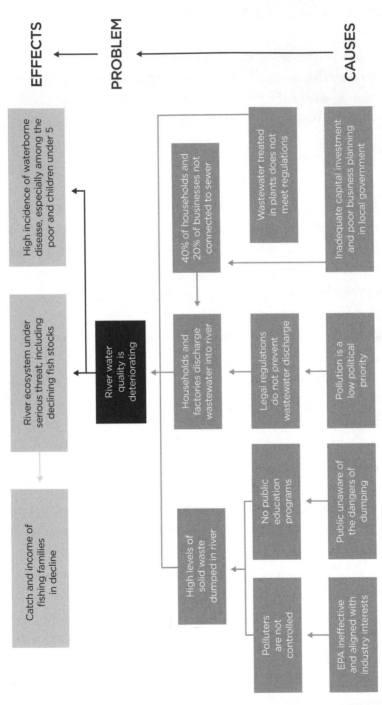

EFFECTS

PROBLEM

CAUSES

High incidence of waterborne disease, especially among the poor and children under 5

River ecosystem under serious threat, including declining fish stocks

Catch and income of fishing families in decline

River water quality is deteriorating

40% of households and 20% of businesses not connected to sewer

Households and factories discharge wastewater into river

Wastewater treated in plants does not meet regulations

Legal regulations do not prevent wastewater discharge

Inadequate capital investment and poor business planning in local government

Pollution is a low political priority

High levels of solid waste dumped in river

No public education programs

Public unaware of the dangers of dumping

Polluters are not controlled

EPA ineffective and aligned with industry interests

FIGURE 6.9 Analysis tree for river pollution

© 1995–2016, European Union. Reprinted with permission. European Commission, EuropeAid Cooperation Office, *Aid Delivery Methods, Volume 1: Project Cycle Management Guidelines*, March 2004, 68, Figure 21, https://ec.europa.eu/europeaid/sites/devco/files/methodology-aid-delivery-methods-project-cycle-management-200403_en_2.pdf.

Make sure that beginning problem owners work on problems with a narrow scope. Those small problems may be causes of a larger problem, but the problem owners will make more progress if they work to improve those problems scaled to their level of authority and experience.

Fishbone Diagram

Another fundamental tool to facilitate the process of uncovering root causes is a cause-and-effect diagram, also known as an Ishikawa diagram or a *fishbone diagram* because the completed diagram resembles a fish skeleton with bones radiating from its spine. This brainstorming tool is used to identify a broad set of possible root causes and, in many cases, subcauses and sub-subcauses. The "head" of the fish is the effect—the problem you'd like to solve—and the bones are categories of causes.

As seen in Figure 6.10, the traditional cause categories used with a fishbone diagram are the six M's:

1. **Man.** Or for our more egalitarian times, *people*.
2. **Material.** The physical and information inputs used to perform the work.
3. **Method.** The process used.
4. **Machine.** The equipment involved.
5. **Measurement.** The ways in which work demand and performance are being measured.
6. **Mother Nature.** Currently framed as the *environment* internal and external to the problem.

Don't feel too wedded to the traditional six M's. Many problems benefit from different categories. For example, if your organization is exploring market share loss, you might want to look at possible root causes related to the product itself, as well as possible reasons related to pricing, sales strategy, brand identity, the competitive landscape,

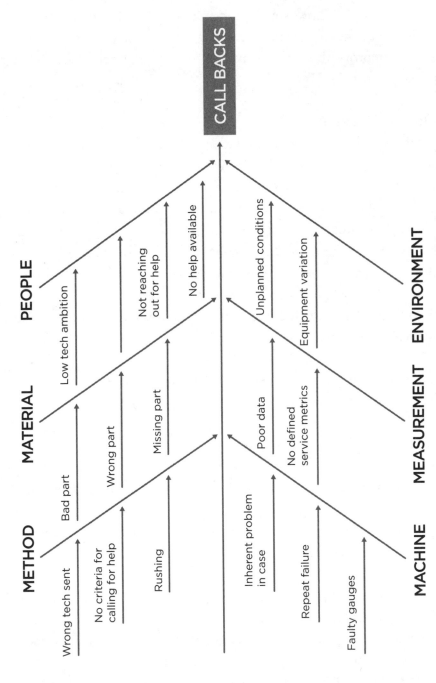

FIGURE 6.10 Fishbone diagram for excessive customer call backs at a repair company

and the customer experience. Product subcauses could include safety, how current or outdated the product is, physical attributes (size, taste, color, texture, etc.), maintenance requirements, and so on.

Brainstorming is an effective way to open people's minds about the full range of possible root causes of a problem. However, the word *possible* is key. Once the brainstorming session is done, the problem owner needs to set out to determine which ones are *the* root causes—and when there are a number of root causes, which ones will be the focus for that round of problem solving.

To guard against opinion- or hubris-based problem solving, data is helpful here. In rare cases when no data is available, you can ask key stakeholders to rate the root causes on their fishbone diagrams based on their experience and what they *believe* is most likely. Multivoting methods, while not typically based on objective data, can be an effective means to narrow the set of options that will be subjected to experimentation. That said, turn to opinion-based vetting only when data is difficult to come by. Well-designed experiments reduce the risk of resolving a problem based on opinions alone.

Pareto Analysis

Pareto analysis is a prioritization tool. It's useful when problem owners need to uncover the myriad factors contributing to a problem and determine which ones warrant further exploration. Based on the 80/20 rule, a Pareto analysis allows problem owners to identify the relative few instances—often 20 percent—that likely cause the majority—often 80 percent—of the negative outcomes the problem owner seeks to eliminate.

Figure 6.11 shows the results of a Pareto analysis for errors that occur during medication administration.

The 15 causes this hospital uncovered are too many to focus on in one round of problem solving. The Pareto analysis allowed the problem owner to make a prioritization decision based on which

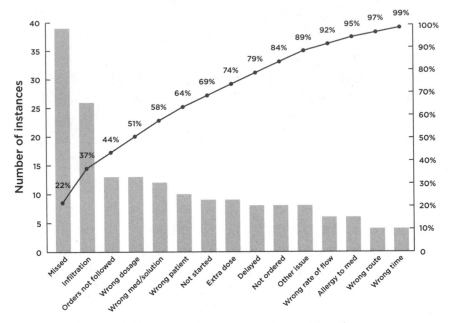

FIGURE **6.11** Pareto chart that ranks problem factors

causes seemed to have the biggest impact on the problem, and which were the most complex. From these results, the problem owner decided to focus on the first two causes, as they resulted in a relatively high number of incidences. After some deeper evaluation, the problem owner also included the third cause for medication errors (orders not followed) because the countermeasure for cause 1 would also eliminate cause 3. This example illustrates how Pareto analysis can be used as a guide—but only a guide—for prioritization. You have to apply judgment as well, and effort-benefit considerations are often a judgment call.

The other judgment call problem owners need to make is in those circumstances where a low incidence root cause causes more harm to the organization than a higher incidence cause.

There is no prescriptive way for a problem owner to know when he or she has done all the deep study needed to learn about the problem. Some problems reveal their root causes easily; others are more stubborn and hidden. Yet there comes a point in every Learn phase when it becomes clear that going any deeper will not benefit the problem—either because it will not teach you anything new, or because the new information you could glean by continuing to dig is irrelevant for solving the problem. Problem owners want to achieve clarity about the problem. They don't want to go so far that they become mired in irrelevant detail and mitigating anecdote to the point that they are afraid to act. Finding the clarity sweet spot between ignorance and information overload is a skill that comes with experience. With practice, problem owners will know when it's time to move on to CLEAR's Experimentation phase.

E: EXPERIMENT WITH COUNTERMEASURES

Many problem owners are relieved to reach the Experiment phase—the action phase—where they begin experimenting with countermeasures to close the performance gap. As mentioned earlier, if you've done a good job during the Clarify and Learn phases, selecting the proper countermeasures for root causes often comes quite easily.

During the Experiment phase the problem owner forms a hypothesis, identifies the countermeasures he or she believes would eliminate the root causes of the problem, and designs and runs a series of experiments to test the countermeasures. When identifying and choosing countermeasures, ask the following questions:

- Which potential countermeasures might eliminate the root cause(s) of the problem? Identify as many as seem relevant.
- Which potential countermeasures should you try first? Why those over others?
- How should you run the experiment?
- What do you think will happen?

There are a few possible risks that problem owners face when deciding which root causes to address and which countermeasures to experiment with. One is suboptimization—this occurs when the problem owner chooses to focus on a small segment of a larger problem. He or she may discover and experiment with countermeasures that completely resolve the element in question, but make little to no difference to the larger problem. This isn't always a terrible thing. Selecting a small area for practice can be a low-risk way for a beginning problem owner to learn how to run experiments. The small issue needs to be consciously selected for this purpose, however, and the problem needs to be viewed more holistically on the next round.

To aid in selecting a countermeasure with which to experiment first, we use a simple two-by-two prioritization grid to rank each possible countermeasure based on its relative ease of implementation and the benefit it will likely have, as shown in Figure 6.12. The problem owner used this grid as a visual tool to select countermeasures most likely to close the gap with the least effort (which includes lowest risk, lowest cost, least logistically challenging, least organizational resistance, and so on). The "ease-to-benefit" rule

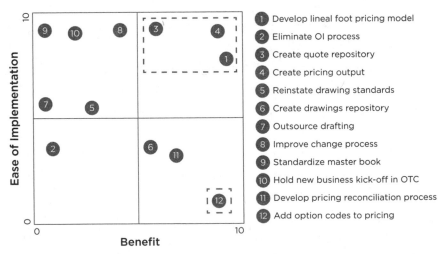

FIGURE 6.12 Prioritizing countermeasures based on ease and benefit

can't be applied rigidly, however. Many problems require countermeasures that are difficult to implement yet provide significant
benefit. In some cases a difficult-to-implement countermeasure
provides a foundation for subsequent rapid improvement. The best
rule of thumb is to carry a bias for successful outcomes, regardless of how much effort the countermeasures to achieve them might
require. Otherwise, you risk implementing easy Band-Aids that
never solve the problem.

Another consideration is whether to conduct one experiment at
a time or run concurrent experiments. When you want to test multiple countermeasures, it's often best to run concurrent experiments
so you can more quickly eliminate some options and validate others.

However, when possible, avoid introducing multiple countermeasures into a single experiment as it clouds the problem owner's
ability to draw clear cause-and-effect conclusions. *Single-factor
experiments* test countermeasures in isolation from one another to
create clarity about the cause-and-effect relationship of any change
you see to the gap. If you alter more than one variable at a time it can
be difficult to learn which one of them was responsible or if it's the
combination of the two that resulted in successfully closing the gap.

With that background in mind, the first step in running an
experiment is to establish a *hypothesis*—or series of hypotheses—
and run an experiment to test each one. Frame your hypotheses as
if/then statements about what you believe will happen: "If we do
this . . . then we expect that to happen."

With a clear hypothesis, you enter the phase of running the
experiment to confirm or disprove your hypothesis. Opt for rapid
cycles of prudent experimentation. Keep the time frame short and
the number of people involved small. For optimum learning, experiments should meet the following design criteria:

1. **Well thought out.** We often coach problem owners to
   adopt a "let's try!" mindset to create a bias toward action.

However, experiments are not akin to throwing spaghetti at a wall to see if it sticks. That's reckless experimentation. Aim for deliberate and disciplined experimentation with clarity about what's being tested and why, and what the expected results are and why. Without that precision, you can't rely on the results, no matter what you find.

2. **Relatively low risk.** Experiments shouldn't carry undue risks. They should not cause the organization to risk losing a key client, cause harm to people, or break any moral or legal codes. You want to establish boundaries within which to run lower-risk experiments. When possible, run the experiment on real work during live work periods to learn how a countermeasure will perform in a real-world environment. When that isn't possible, experiments may need to be run during off-hours or, with high-stakes experiments, in simulated environments. After all, you wouldn't want a pilot to test new landing gear during a commercial flight filled with passengers, right? In either case, you want to establish a test area and use defined methods to mitigate risk. IT experiments are best run on a test system or in a "sandbox."

Experiments also need to be as low risk as possible in terms of the capital needed to run them. When possible, experiment with low-tech versions of the ultimate countermeasure to refine the countermeasure before spending money on it. You can test and refine a new order entry screen design, for example, using cardboard and markers before anyone begins to write code.

3. **Relevant.** You want to prove or disprove your hypothesis, so the parameters of your experiment need to cover those bases that will allow you to draw clear cause-and-effect conclusions.

4. **Conclusive.** The results need to be data-based. Unclear or subjective conclusions indicate that you need to go back to the drawing board and design another experiment.

5. **Repeatable.** One test of clarity is whether the same experiment repeated under demonstrably similar conditions produces the same results. If the countermeasure seems to work, test it again to confirm that its success was not a fluke of circumstance or execution.

It's important to keep an open mind about the experimentation process and the results you get. Successful experiments go beyond merely proving that a certain countermeasure will close the gap. Success means that the problem owner has learned something. Experiments where a hypothesis is disproven are as powerful as those that prove it. Problem owners need a "no fear" environment in which it is okay for a thoughtfully designed experiment to produce disappointing results. If you and your organization don't embrace this thinking, problems will never be solved as well as they could be. The number of experimentation cycles needed depends on the situation. Problem owners want to strike a balance between over-experimenting (a more active form of analysis paralysis) and not experimenting enough. Also seek balance between "good enough" and "perfection." Lean management is a perfection-seeking philosophy, with *seeking* as the operative word. Too many problems go unaddressed because people wait for perfection instead of making progress and then moving into another cycle of improvement. This concept is similar to *satisficing*.[15] Decision makers *satisfice* when they feel that they know enough to make a reasonable decision from available information, even while acknowledging that they don't know everything they would need to make sure that the decision was the best one possible.

---

[15] Herbert Simon, a psychologist and expert in decision making and one of the original theoreticians of artificial intelligence, first refers to satisficing in his book *Administrative Behavior* (Macmillan, 1947). Simon viewed the "rational choice theory" proposed by classical economics as an unrealistic reflection of how people behave in real-world environments defined by uncertainty.

A: Assess the Results and Adopt, Adapt, or Abandon

Assess results throughout the experiment so that you can make real-time adjustments if needed, or abandon a countermeasure that doesn't solve the problem or causes new problems that are worse than the original. At some point, however—often at the end of an experiment—the problem owner needs to take a step back, formally study what happened, and decide whether to adopt the countermeasure as is, adapt it, or abandon it altogether.

The questions that enable this decision include: What happened? What did you learn? What was the effect on the gap? If your hypothesis was proven, what will it take to fully implement the improvement? If the hypothesis wasn't proven, do you adjust the countermeasure and try again or abandon it altogether?

If the countermeasure worked but didn't close the gap fully, could be simplified for greater effect, or has a minor flaw that needs to be addressed, you can adapt it and rerun the experiment. When adapting, you may need to return to the Clarify and Learn phases— or at least review your findings—to make sure you're clear about the root causes. In that review, you may come to the conclusion that you set a "to" metric that was too aggressive. Be careful here: don't adjust the gap simply because you're tired, running out of time, or worried about pressure from the organization. Change it only if your knowledge of the problem suggests it should be changed. If you choose to adjust the countermeasure, form another hypothesis and run another experiment to be sure it works as intended and your new hypothesis is proven.

If the results indicate that you should abandon the countermeasure because the gap didn't close at all, and the evidence suggests that adapting the countermeasure won't fix it, go back to the Clarify phase of CLEAR and make sure you defined the problem properly. Pay particular attention to problem breakdown and make sure you didn't try to tackle too much. You should also review what you found during the Learn phase and make sure you know enough about the current state. Finally, make sure you're clear about the root causes that prevent the process, equipment, or people from performing at the "to" level today. Once you have done that review, use that learning to choose another countermeasure and run another experiment.

If an experiment is highly successful and you choose to adopt the countermeasure that was tested, move ahead to the Roll Out and Reflect phase.

R: ROLL OUT AND REFLECT

This section tackles the question of how to formally change a process or the work environment once you've identified a countermeasure that addresses the problem. Execution matters—it makes the difference between a closed gap and one that stays decisively open because the people who do the work don't understand what the countermeasure is for and don't know how to perform their work with it. It also makes the difference between a closed gap that remains closed and one that reopens. You cannot claim victory in solving a problem that recurs because the improvement wasn't sustained.

So let's get clear about what it takes for a successful rollout: you need a detailed rollout plan that answers *a lot* of questions, such as: What's the best way to implement the new way of operating? Who will monitor performance? Has the "new way" resolved the problem? What did you learn?

More detailed rollout questions include: Who "owns" the new process? How will you document the new way of operating, both for training purposes and in the spirit of standardization? How will you assure that all workers have high degrees of competence and confidence about the new way of operating? Who needs to be trained? Who will train them? What type of training is the most effective way to assure that people can operate in the new way, error free? Who needs to be informed about the change? What's the "go-live" date? What's the "cut-over" plan for migrating to the new way of operating? Who will be available to help people adjust to the new way of operating during the go-live period and beyond?

Beyond the rollout, you also want a plan for measuring ongoing performance leading to continuous improvement. Some of the questions that need to be answered in this plan include: Which KPIs will be monitored to ensure the gap remains closed, and signal when it's time for another round of improvement? Who will measure them? How frequently? How will that person communicate results?

Rolling Out with Ownership, Documentation, Planning, and Training

I've mentioned the importance of clear ownership, and it appears again at this stage of problem solving. For most of the problem-solving cycle, the problem owner acts as the "problem expert," and is accountable for clarifying the problem, learning about it, experimenting with countermeasures, assessing the results, and rolling out the change. When rolling out new improvements, however, ownership begins to shift from the problem owner to leaders in the functional areas that will need to operate differently. More specifically, ownership will often shift to an identified "process owner" who isn't necessarily the problem owner. The handoff from problem owner to process owner should involve a transition period that's well defined, but situational. The problem owner doesn't merely toss the responsibility and walk away; he or she stays engaged throughout the rollout and a bit longer to witness the full cycle of improvement and help as needed.

Successful handoff, training, and overall management of the improvement begins with clear documentation of what the new way of working is and who is affected by it. Recall in Chapter 4 on Process, I discussed the importance of documented standard work for all processes in the organization to create consistent outcomes and provide the foundation for ongoing improvement.

When we facilitate countermeasure rollout, we use a very detailed Excel template with sections for each of the rollout components, including the creation of standard work and a detailed training plan that includes when and where training will take place, who's delivering it, what the learning objectives are, which KPIs will be used to track process performance, and so on.

The most effective rollout plans also include a robust communication plan. Keep in mind that if you are the problem owner or somehow involved in the problem-solving effort, *you* know why a improvement is needed and why it's this particular process change over another. It isn't obvious, however, to people who weren't involved in the problem-solving cycle—many of whom are doing the work. They need to understand *why* first and foremost, followed by *what*, *when*, and *how*. Don't overlook the value that comes from giving people context. Tell them what the problem was, why it matters, what you learned about it, and what the chosen countermeasure will do. *Do not communicate this type of information by e-mail.* To create any level of stickiness for a new way of operating, *conversations* need to take place that communicate "5W1H" information: why, what, when, where, who, and how.

Proper rollout enable two outcomes: less resistance to change, and a gap that stays closed until conditions change and a new cycle of improvement begins. If people don't understand what the new work looks like, how to do it, and why they are expected to do it *this* way versus another, you risk either a failed rollout or a strong supervised launch followed by a rapid return to the prior state.

Review, Regulate Performance, Repeat the Cycle, and Reflect on the Process

Very few improvements continue to operate well if you simply set them and forget them. Countermeasures need care and feeding to perform well. Without attention and ongoing monitoring, processes often revert to their prior state.

The aspects of clarity discussed in previous chapters of this book enable organizations to stabilize and maintain the improvements they realize through problem solving. Real-time clarity about performance informs organizations early on when the work begins to deviate from the standard, or when it's stable and proven to the point that the organization can set a new, higher bar to reach. Also, remember that problem solving is cyclical, not linear. Once you reach a new level of performance and are achieving it consistently, it's time to define a new created gap and problem solve to reach that new, improved state. In the event that you reach a new level that will not stabilize, you acknowledge that the countermeasure you chose is not fully closing the gap and initiate a new cycle of problem solving. That is the intended progression. In practice, many organizations improve once and move on. When they do that, the improvement rarely sticks, and the problem-solving effort is wasted.

Each cycle of problem solving serves as a cycle of learning for both the problem owner and the organization at large. While the problem owner should reflect throughout the problem-solving cycle, we recommend that he or she holds formal reflection sessions following the rollout. Attendees typically include the problem owner, people who played a key role in solving the problem, leadership of the work areas where the improvement was made, and representatives from the organization's internal improvement team, if you have one.

Relevant reflection questions include: What did we learn about the problem, the problem-solving process, and the organization? What surprised us? What went well that we want to repeat in the future? What didn't go well that needs to be adjusted in future problem-solving cycles? How well did we communicate during the process? Were there pockets of resistance that, looking back, could have been avoided?

To aid in deeper organizational learning and to build a problem-solving culture, we also recommend regular, formal case-study sessions where problem owners present summaries of problem-solving cycles to a broad cross-section of the organization, similar to the "grand rounds" case study approach used in medical education.[16] In these sessions, participants can learn about the full cycle from problem discovery and definition through resolution and rollout. To reduce fear in the organization and build humility into organizational culture, the problem owner should also candidly share what didn't go well, lessons learned, and what he or she recommends be done differently during subsequent problem-solving cycles.

BUILDING PROBLEM-SOLVING CAPABILITIES

Developing proficiency in disciplined problem solving isn't just for a few improvement people in the organization or your more scientifically-minded staff. *Everyone* in the organization—from frontline workers to C-level leaders—needs to learn how to solve problems more effectively. To do that, problem owners need to work with a skilled problem-solving coach.

Remember Joel, the hospital CEO whom I offered to coach to demonstrate how discipline problem solving works? When we left him at the beginning of the chapter, he was resisting going to the gemba of the ED to understand firsthand the reality of how the work was done. He eventually relented, and what he found, over several weeks and multiple coaching sessions, is that the root cause of the slow door-to-bed time did not reside in the emergency department, nor the laboratory, nor the diagnostic imaging department. The primary root cause was slow acceptance of the ED patients by the inpatient units—even when beds were available.

---

[16] For more information on grand rounds, see https://en.wikipedia.org/wiki/Grand_rounds.

Without coaching, Joel could have spent a lot of time and money increasing ED staffing or further streamlining lab and imaging's processes, which might have helped shave off a few minutes, but it wouldn't have resulted in a 240-minute "door-to-bed" time. For that, he needed to discover the true reason for delays, and he only got there because I didn't let him leap to solutions before he was clear about the main reason for the problem.

Reflecting on the process I walked him through, Joel admitted, "I jump to solutions too quickly. I think I know, but I don't. You repeatedly pushed me back to problem definition and cause analysis when I thought it was time for action. I learned that taking more time defining the problem saves time in the long run because it means we implement the right solution the first time, and you don't have to spend time convincing people when the root cause is so clear."

Early in this chapter I cited research by K. Anders Ericsson, the researcher behind the 10,000 hours theory. To recap, his findings show that building skills of any sort requires purposeful and deliberate practice. What did not make it into the popular understanding of the 10,000 hours theory is Ericsson's emphasis on the vital role of a teacher or coach in building proficiency: "To assure effective learning, subjects ideally should be given explicit instructions about the best method and be supervised by a teacher to allow individualized diagnosis of errors, informative feedback, and remedial training. The instructor has to organize the sequence of appropriate training tasks and monitor improvement to decide when transitions to more complex and challenging tasks are appropriate."[17]

Problem solving is a complex skill set to develop. A proficient problem owner needs development in the mechanics of problem solving (analytical skills and when to apply a wide range of potential

---

[17] K. Anders Ericsson et. al, "The Role of Deliberate Practice in the Acquisition of Expert Performance," *Psychological Review* 100, no. 3 (1993): 363–406.

countermeasures), time management, advocacy techniques, and how to counter resistance. Even more critical is the development of critical thinking and becoming aware of habitual thinking that interferes with effective problem solving. Building proficiency is faster and deeper in those organizations that adopt an apprenticeship model in which skilled coaches with high proficiency in both problem solving and coaching techniques work with less experienced problem owners. Organizations that rely on self-development or invest in coaching sporadically have less consistent results, similar to the results most people achieve if they try to learn how to play a new sport or musical instrument on their own. They may learn to swing a golf club, but that doesn't mean the ball will land in the hole.

Leaders, improvement professionals, and organizational development teams often underappreciate the role of problem-solving coaching in building proficiency. They see one-on-one coaching as a slow and expensive way to build organizational capabilities. They view classrooms and training programs as a more efficient avenue for learning. While group learning offers efficiency, it is best suited for heightening awareness about a topic, helping people understand concepts and terminology, introducing skills, and creating a call to action: cognitive benefits. It misses the mark when it comes to building proficiency. The real learning comes through practice and application in the real world through one-on-one work with an experienced problem-solving coach.

If that feels too slow and expensive, consider how much time people currently spend in your organization mitigating problems without really solving them. Consider the time and money spent addressing recurring problems or confronting problems again when the first solution didn't work. Consider the risk to the organization's reputation and market share every time a customer complains on social media about a quality issue that thousands of others have had, but remains unresolved. Consider the avoidable errors made every day, resulting in delayed shipments or flawed products or poor customer value delivery that would not happen if you got to the bottom of them. Consider the productivity drain and costs of losing talented staff because they're tired of dealing with the same problems.

Now consider how much more successful your organization could be. From that perspective, investing in organization-wide problem-solving proficiency is one of the least expensive investments you could make. Will it take your organization years to build deep problem-solving proficiency? Yes. Is it worth the investment? That depends on whether you want to be far more successful than you are today, or if you're comfortable with where you are—likely closer to mediocrity than excellence. The choice is yours. If you choose success, you need to invest both time and money. There are no shortcuts, and no substitutes for working with skilled problem-solving coaches.[18]

The Coach–Problem Owner Relationship

Coaching is one-to-one, not one-to-many. When working with clients, we often allow small stakeholder teams to attend coaching sessions, but we find that the learning is slower and more superficial when an audience is present. We now require one-on-one sessions with problem owners as well. The reason is that problem owners aren't as comfortable when others are present during the candid reflection periods we encourage, since those sessions often involve exploration of thought patterns and habits that get in the way of effectiveness.

One example of the importance of the one-to-one coach–problem owner relationship comes from an experience I had with a

---

[18] A warning: the most common use of the term "coaching" is in the leadership space. Effective problem-solving coaches are skilled in disciplined problem solving (and have proven results to show for it), coaching to build *technical skill sets*, and coaching to shift mindsets and behaviors. Many traditional leadership coaches do not possess the technical skills and experience to serve as problem-solving coaches.

problem owner I personally coached. She was afraid to ask for help from other functional areas, and had difficulty advocating for the countermeasure she believed would address the root cause of the problem most effectively, both of which slowed her progress. I knew we needed to explore why she was hesitant to ask for support and advocate for what she believed was right. It turned out that earlier in her career she'd had a heavy-handed boss who wanted her to stay squarely in her lane. He also made clear to her that when she asked others for help she was signaling to leaders that she and her team couldn't handle the work. I doubt we would have been able to work through the difficulty she had asking for help if a team had been present. She grew exponentially after she faced her fear, found that other departments were more than happy to help when she asked them, and became a stronger leader for the experience. They also responded well to her new approach to advocacy, which delighted her supervisor at that time.

The Role of A3 Reports in Problem-Solving Coaching

In terms of structure, there are as many ways to structure problem-solving coaching sessions as there are coaches, problems owners, and problems. A3 reports have been widely used to facilitate problem solving and the coaching process since they were popularized in John Shook's *Managing to Learn* and Durward Sobek and Art Smalley's *Understanding A3 Thinking,* both of which describe how Toyota uses A3 reports to develop deep problem-solving capabilities across its workforce.[19] A3 reports provide insights into a problem owner's thought processes. They double as a communication and consensus-building tool and, used this way, help all stakeholders understand the problem and the the progress that has been made to solve it.

---

[19] John Shook, *Managing to Learn* (Lean Enterprise Institute, 2008); Durward Sobek and Art Smalley, *Understanding A3 Thinking* (Productivity Press, 2008).

Visually, the A3 report should reflect the specific problem being solved. Yet some organizations use A3 "templates" and treat the A3 as a static one-size-fits-all form to be "filled out." A3 reports were designed to be iterative storyboards created by the problem owner to provide insights into his or her thought processes. These insights enable the coach to better help the problem owner develop more disciplined thought and critical thinking, the skills to distill and synthesize information, the ability to advocate, and the know-how for defining and executing next steps in the process. Used properly, A3 reports are clarity-enabling tools.

As powerful as proper A3 reports can be, we often have new problem owners learn how to visualize the problem on flip charts or large whiteboards. After they get comfortable and build skills using this larger-form visual tool, we "graduate" them to the A3 report to help them learn how to tell their problem-solving story more efficiently within the confines of an 11-by-17-inch piece of paper. We see confidence grow and distillation skills develop more quickly when we use this stepwise approach to learning.

Coaching Skills

One of the paradoxes about Toyota's organization structure is how it looks on paper versus how it operates in practice. Toyota North America, for example, has 10 levels from the CEO to frontline operators. This design enables leaders to have no more than six direct reports so that each leader has sufficient time to develop his or her team members. Readers with more than six direct reports likely understand the logic behind this. When organizational structure results in leaders having 12 or 20 direct reports, it's impossible to give each team member enough attention to develop them to their potential.

Problem-solving coaching is very different from the executive or leadership coaching most common in business. It's also very different from the "coaching" that occurs when an underperforming employee is put on an improvement plan. A problem-solving coach is most similar to a sports coach and should only work with a limited number of "students" at a time. To show why, I'll describe what we mean by *coach* in this context.

Problem-solving coaches play several roles and wear several hats. The first hat is that of the expert: problem-solving coaches *must be proficient problem owners themselves.* Coaches cannot be beginners. Would you hire a piano teacher who could only play "Heart and Soul"? Would you hire a driver's education teacher who had just received his driver's license? Get proof of their expertise by seeing it in action in your own organization, or by hearing about it from people you trust who have had firsthand problem-solving experience with the person. The coach should be able to demonstrate the various skills needed throughout the problem-solving process, such as distilling and synthesizing information and data; data analyses, including collection methods, analytical approaches, and options for visualizing data; asking questions in a way that shows respect and uncovers critical information; problem breakdown; choosing one analytical tool or countermeasure over another; habitually visiting the gemba; displaying curiosity; and so on.

Another hat worn by the problem-solving coach is that of a proficient teacher. Effective teaching requires deep knowledge of both the problem-solving techniques themselves and of adult learning. The problem-solving coach often introduces problem owners to analytical, brainstorming, and prioritization tools; data display options; and countermeasures with which the problem owner is not yet familiar. When teaching in this way, the coach *shows* and *demonstrates* the mechanics of problem solving in the same way a soccer coach may show and demonstrate proper shooting technique or a golf coach may demonstrate the best way to hold a club.

A skilled problem-solving coach teaches as much as possible through humble inquiry and Socratic questioning—in other words, by asking open-ended questions such as what, why, and how to learn how the problem owner is thinking and to stimulate more critical analysis, in contrast to closed-ended questions that can be answered with a binary yes or no, or other one-word answers. The coach needs to adjust the approach based on the problem owner's threshold of knowledge and experience, however. Socratic inquiry is best when a problem owner already has the knowledge and experience she needs to solve the problem at hand. It's disrespectful and can confuse the learner to ask questions for the sake of asking questions if the learner does not yet have the knowledge or experience to answer them. The problem-solving coach needs to show and, yes, sometimes tell.[20]

In addition to the role of teacher, the problem-solving coach also serves as a mentor. The coach helps the problem owner learn to think deeply and rely on facts and advises on when to involve key stakeholders, how to communicate findings to affected team members and leaders, and other people-related elements of good problem solving. Wearing a mentor hat, the coach helps the problem owner celebrate successes and reassures the problem owner at frustrating junctures that he or she will get to the end of what can feel like a circuitous road.

In an organization where this type of coaching is new, the fastest and most effective way to build expertise is to have two coaches working together. One coach coaches the problem owner. The more experienced of the two coaches the coach. The coach's coach provides feedback after observing coaching sessions with the problem owner. Together, the coaches reflect on the session and discuss what went well, as well as what could be improved. The second coach highlights patterns he or she noticed that the coach may not be aware of. Both coaches improve coaching proficiency through this process, while also developing the problem owner.

---

[20] This is similar to how I described the difference between reflective and directive development in *The Outstanding Organization*, pp. 116–119.

This model works, but only if leader-coaches are given the time to coach and coaching is considered a significant part of their role. The time needed for coaching depends on the problem owner's degree of proficiency and the stage of problem solving he or she is in; beginners require more coaching time, and the early stages of Clarify (defining the problem) and Learn (understanding reality) typically require more hands-on coaching time than later phases. Early on, we often meet with problem owners multiple times a week. Over time, the problem owner may only need one hour per week, which we recommend as a minimum. As Anders Ericsson found repeatedly in his research on developing expertise across disciplines, even people with high proficiency need periodic coaching to maintain their skill set.

Once the organization has built strong problem-solving capabilities across its leadership team, including the executive team, each leader then serves as the problem-solving coach for his or her team members.

CONCLUSION

Disciplined problem solving brings myriad benefits. From the outside, organizations that value problem solving and invest in building deep capabilities—organizations like Toyota, Danaher, Autoliv, ATC Trailers, ThedaCare, and many others—are known for long-term growth and operational excellence. On the inside, these organizations operate with high degrees of clarity. Everyone, from frontline workers to the senior-most executive, understands that it is his or her job to identify gaps between where the organization is and where it wants or needs to go, and apply a disciplined problem-solving process to reach the new level of performance. Results come in the form of better understanding about the business and better decisions driven by clarity about the current state and the root causes for performance obstacles.

In our practice we have seen hundreds of organizations across all industries experience significant gains from committing to disciplined problem solving as an organizational requirement and investing accordingly in building deep capabilities.

Good problem solving takes time. Leaders are often impatient due to pressure from customers, shareholders, regulators, and others, but speed is not your friend in problem solving. Problem owners need to move toward resolution as quickly as possible, but "as quickly as possible" may be longer than a leader wants it to be and more quickly than a problem owner's capabilities allow. As with all clarity pursuits, organizations can only reach as far as their talent, culture, and commitment allow.

Which brings me to the final clarity factor addressed in this book: you! An organization is only as strong as its people, and as a result, each individual must operate with a high degree of personal clarity. Clarity begins with you.

7

You

Clear thinking requires courage rather than intelligence.

—THOMAS SZASZ

"**A**sk vague questions, you get vague answers."
It's been 30 years since I heard those words and they changed my life. I had just moved to Los Angeles, and a new friend convinced me to join her on a visit to a celebrated astrologer. I was new to SoCal culture and my friend seemed hip and sophisticated, so I said, "Sure, why not?" But as I sat with the astrologer and he answered the questions he had asked me to prepare for our session, I began to feel frustrated. His answers were unspecific. When I said as much he stopped and looked at me with great kindness and said those seven words. His message? It's not me, lady. It's *you*.

His words cut through me. I've always been frank, sometimes haltingly so. I equated direct with clarity. I am the person who listens deeply and with absolute empathy as you talk about the issues you are dealing with, and then I'll push you to face the hard truths. Tough love, some call it. Several senior leaders have told me that I am one of few people who present them with evidence of how their leadership practices contribute to ambiguity and organizational chaos. That astrology session was the first time in my life someone told *me* that I didn't have clarity about myself and my goals. Why was I was there? What did I want to learn? What did I hope to do with the information?

Up to this point this book has focused on how to operate with greater organizational clarity. In this chapter, I shift focus to personal clarity, without which organizational clarity is impossible. Personal clarity manifests in how you think, what you say, what you do, and even how you feel as you interact with customers, peers, leaders above you, staff, and internal and external stakeholders. It's about the individual commitment you make to clarity.

The five P's of Purpose, Priorities, Process, Performance, and Problem Solving that I have highlighted as the hallmarks of organizational clarity also apply at the personal level. What is your personal purpose in life and in your work? What is the purpose of the e-mail you wish to send and the meeting you wish to hold? What do you wish to achieve in the conversation you are about to have? What priorities have you set for yourself? How aligned are your personal purpose and priorities? Have you set clear goals and targets for your personal and professional growth? If so, how are you performing? Perhaps, most important, how well do you do at surfacing and solving problems?

These can be hard questions to ask, and the answers can be even more difficult to hear. You cannot afford to turn away from what you learn, however—not if you believe in the importance of clarity. Your personal current state as it applies to the five P's indicates both the potential and the limits you face as a leader. You cannot remove yourself from the equation. As shown in Figure 7.1, wherever you go, there *you* are—including at work.[1] If you embrace clarity and

---

[1] *Wherever You Go, There You Are* is the title of Jon Kabat-Zinn's seminal book on mindfulness meditation (Hyperion, 1994). His premise is that people go through life emphasizing the need to take action, and thus fail to simply *be* in the moment they are in. The title is both a warning and a celebration of the fact that you always bring yourself to every situation, and the key to full experience and joy is to embrace that.

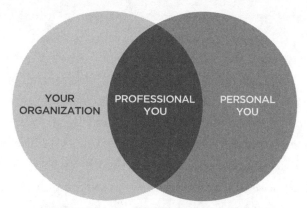

FIGURE 7.1 Your role in the organization

actively seek to achieve it, there are no bounds to how much you can achieve and how well your team can perform. You cannot remove yourself from the clarity equation. Organizational clarity begins with *you*.

To begin operating with more personal clarity, start by being clear about yourself: What is your personal clarity type?

YOUR CLARITY TYPE: PURSUER, AVOIDER, OR BLIND

New York Times journalist Adam Bryant spent years interviewing more than 75 CEOs for his column, "Corner Office." He summed up the common patterns revealed in those conversations in his 2011 book *The Corner Office*. One of the patterns he saw was that CEOs have what Nell Minow, cofounder of the Corporate Library, called "passionate curiosity."[2] They want to understand the world around them and the people in it, and ask questions relentlessly—sometimes

[2] Adam Bryant, *The Corner Office: Indispensable and Unexpected Lessons from CEOs on How to Succeed* (St. Martin's Griffen, 2012).

revealing an opportunity or an organizational blind spot in the process.

This passionate curiosity may be so noteworthy because it is not a universal trait in all people who find themselves in leadership positions. Even those who have it may find it difficult to maintain over long periods and in work environments that resist it. A leader may be curious, but if his or her peers are not, and if the board he or she serves discourages that curiosity, then eventually curiosity will begin to feel more like a personal liability than an asset. Eventually that leader will stop showing curiosity in the same way that children lose their curiosity when teachers and parents criticize them for it.

Whether your natural instinct is to be curious, or whether your instinct is to avoid seeking information, people—like organizations—fall into one of the three categories of clarity I introduced in Chapter 1: *clarity pursuers*, *clarity avoiders*, and the *clarity blind*.

To recap from Chapter 1 and apply these concepts at the personal level, clarity pursuers are people who consistently operate with and seek clarity. While some clarity pursuers are naturally inclined this way, the most important aspect of clarity pursuit lies in *actively choosing* clarity. Like the CEOs Bryant interviewed over the years, clarity pursuers are curious; they ask questions and they want to know the answers.

Clarity avoidance is also a choice and comes in three forms. Type 1 clarity avoiders use *deceit* to achieve a defined purpose. Grifters, or con men and women, are classic clarity avoiders. Within organizations, Type 1 clarity avoiders put personal advancement ahead of ethics and decency. A Type 1 clarity avoider will easily lie to "throw a colleague under the bus" and gain favor with a higher-up. In the film *Wall Street*, the duplicitous character Gordon Gekko is a Type 1 clarity avoider of the worst kind.

Type 2 clarity avoiders operate, in contrast, with *strategic ambiguity*. This occurs when people avoid clarity on an issue that—if

clear—could force one side to take a position that damages a relationship, initiates a conflict, or limits future options. Politicians
and diplomats may operate with strategic ambiguity in order to
maintain support from certain constituent groups, or to maintain a
middle position amongst multiple governmental allies with conflicting interests. However, it often seems that politicians know no other
way of operating—employing strategic ambiguity in the absence of
any degree of clarity is a problem.

In business, negotiators may employ strategic ambiguity to get
more favorable pricing. Strategic ambiguity may also lead leaders to
sequester new product development teams and/or refer to projects
in code to prevent leaks. You may employ strategic ambiguity while
negotiating an acquisition if you want to control messaging around
details of the deal. While strategic ambiguity is legitimately called
for at times, it should never be used as an excuse when clarity is
possible.

Type 3 clarity avoiders engage in *willful ignorance*, typically as a
defense mechanism to avoid likely conflict or the need to take some
sort of action. In our experience this head-in-the-sand choice is the
most common type of clarity avoidance. We see it when leaders
avoid gathering current state data to learn the truth about performance, and we see it when leaders resist visually displaying data for
fear that they'll be judged or will be forced to address a problem.
We see it when leaders don't ask candid questions of customers, suppliers, staff, peers, and board members because they don't want to
hear the answer. Willful ignorance is an active choice to live in a
fog-like state and violates clarity on all fronts. Personally, I'd rather
receive the worst possible news than not know the truth about a
situation. At least you know what you're dealing with. And how else
can you engage in effective problem solving if you don't know the
truth? If you want to operate with high levels of clarity, you need to
be relentless in surfacing problems.

FIGURE 7.2 The blind men and the elephant

People who are clarity blind fall into two categories: those who don't recognize the importance of clarity and those who do but can't perceive when they don't have it. It's like the parable about the blind men and the elephant. Illustrated in Figure 7.2, each of the blind men touches a part of the elephant and draws inaccurate conclusions based on the limited information he has. Clarity blindness is like that—business leaders think they have the whole picture when they don't.

Leaders of siloed departments or functions are particularly vulnerable to clarity blindness. They may have complete knowledge of the work done in their part of the organization yet be completely unaware about how their area's work affects those downstream. This is one reason why value stream management is such a powerful practice for enabling the delivery of higher levels of customer value at lower cost: it reduces clarity blindness and creates a clear call to action.

Hal Gregersen, executive director of the MIT Leadership Center, posits another reason why leaders may know less than they should about the organization. Gregersen argues that leaders often find themselves in an information bubble constructed by staff who are afraid to share bad news. The consequence is that leaders may only get information that is good or neutral, or hear about problems only after they have already been addressed. To counteract this effect, leaders have to actively seek information. You will receive it if you ask, but only if you also create a low-fear environment in which people are rewarded for being candid—no matter what the content of that candor is.[3]

Whether someone pursues or avoids clarity—or is blind altogether—is often situational. You may pursue clarity in business dealings, for instance, but be blind when it comes to some of your personal relationships. You may avoid clarity when it comes to your area's performance, but actively pursue it to highlight another area's performance. On average, I find that people tend to spend far less time pursuing clarity than they do avoiding it or staying blind to it. It often takes a clarifying event that provides awareness about a problem and presents them with an opportunity to choose clarity—or not—before people see their own patterns. The left pie chart in Figure 7.3 illustrates directional proportions for the default modes I find many people operate in and a visual goal for shifting the proportions.

Where do you currently lie? Becoming aware of the degree to which you operate today with clarity helps you gauge the size of the gap you need to close, and measure your progress as you begin to lead with greater clarity.

Set aggressive goals for operating with greater clarity, but be kind to yourself as well. It's not only unrealistic to think you can achieve perfect clarity-pursuing behavior in all situations and at all times, but there are also valid circumstances when avoiding clarity

---

[3] Hal Gregersen, "Bursting the CEO Bubble," *Harvard Business Review*, March-April, 2017, https://hbr.org/2017/03/bursting-the-ceo-bubble.

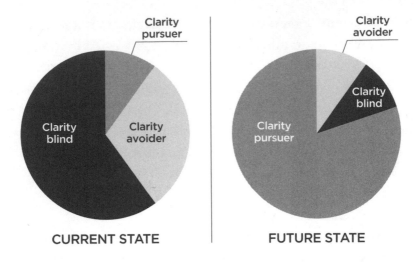

FIGURE 7.3 Current and suggested future state proportions
of clarity-related behaviors

is the right strategic choice. There will also be situations where you simply don't notice the lack of clarity. Instead of perfect clarity your aim should be to reduce the frequency of situations in which you are not seeking to think, speak, and operate from a place of clarity.

THINK

I've never met a leader who didn't believe in the importance of having clear ideas about the issues that matter to him or her and to the organization. Despite such widespread consensus on the importance of clear thinking, however, leaders are lauded far more often for decisive action.

Yet clear thought is a precursor to making good decisions, acting decisively, solving problems, and seizing opportunities in a way that consistently fulfills the organization's goals. Leaders understandably feel pressured to *do*, but it's critical to first give oneself the time to *think*. Many leaders fail to invest the time needed to assess a situation fully, gather on-point information, and develop a thoughtful position.

I see it frequently: smart, well-meaning people who have invested significant organizational time and money in business performance improvement, people who insist that their teams develop strong problem-solving skills—but avoid using a disciplined approach *themselves* when confronted with a complex issue. Instead, they make a call based on a combination of instinct and what they think they know.

If this sounds like you, understand that some of those decisions may work out, but many won't. The reason is that you've got too much noise in your head: thousands of thoughts, biases, and conflicting priorities. These include business-relevant concerns about an upcoming customer meeting, product launch, or problem in one of the functional areas you oversee. They also include business-*ir*relevant issues like the road construction that affects your commute, concerns about a loved one, a home repair that isn't resolved, or . . . you name it.

Your brain gives preference to information you need to stay safe, but in our modern, predator-free environment, that leaves a lot left to wade through. In the same way that organizations have trouble choosing among hundreds of conflicting organizational priorities, you may have difficulty identifying personal priorities. Without clarity of thought, you are vulnerable to giving preference to the most recent concern, or the most annoying, or the one that will cause the least amount of conflict or effort to address. Without clarity of thought, it's difficult to navigate through the noise and engage in the type of purposeful action for which great leaders are known.

Clear thought not only helps you prioritize, it also brings advantages in the form of creativity. Research has shown that people who take the time to sift through the noise to gain clarity of thought are qualitatively more innovative. Distraction and overload, in contrast, reduce your ability to engage in divergent thinking.

Neuroscientists Moshe Bar and Shira Baror documented one aspect of this phenomenon in a recent study in which they asked one group to remember a six-digit number while taking a word association test. Another group was asked to remember a two-digit number while taking the same test. The participants with the two-digit number gave more creative and divergent responses than the six-digit group, because six digits tax the brain more, reducing the cognitive power participants had to perform the creative task.[4]

John Kounios and Mark Beeman, both cognitive psychologists, also looked at the underlying factors enabling creative thought in a series of studies documented in their book *The Eureka Factor*.[5] They found that the "aha moment" many associate with the appearance of a creative idea is preceded by two enabling stages. In the first, the person engages in deep immersion in the subject about which he or she is hoping to have a breakthrough. In the second, the person takes a break from the content and does something that allows the brain to relax—like go for a hike or have a work-free weekend. It is the deep knowledge of a subject coupled with a release from it that allows the brain to pull together disparate ideas. People who lack clarity of thought don't take the time to learn deeply about their subject, and don't take the time away so that the brain can free associate and generate creative thoughts.

The conclusion is that clarity of thought results in better ideas, which generate better decisions and actions, which bring better results. Remember that your decisions catalyze action on the part of your colleagues and staff—perhaps thousands of people, depending on the size of your organization and your role within it. If those decisions have a clear rationale that's consistent with the

---

[4] Moshe Bar, "Think Less, Think Better," *New York Times*, June 17, 2016.

[5] John Kounios and Mark Beeman, *The Eureka Factor* (Random House, 2015).

organization's purpose or a problem it is working on, your internal teams and outside stakeholders are more likely to understand them, buy into them, and trust that you are acting in the organization's best interest. If instead you tend to act impulsively, or overreact to certain people or situations, you may find that a decision you make this week will be in direct conflict with a decision you made two months ago. When you do that—intentionally or not—you create confusion, discord between project groups, and, eventually, distrust in your leadership capabilities.

Clear thought cuts through all that, enabling clear action and better results. Even if you are not one of those people who naturally possess patient and disciplined thinking habits, you can develop them. Few people naturally think in methodical, rigorous ways in nearly every context; most of us need to *practice* clarity, especially in situations when we don't naturally embrace clarity of thought, such as when we're dealing with an emotionally charged issue, we're rushing, or someone is demanding a response from us before we're ready.

What Are Your Biases and Assumptions?

As I mentioned in Chapter 1, social scientists have now identified more than 175 cognitive biases that shape how we make decisions, form beliefs, and interact socially. While biases can help the brain filter the 2 million bits of information that bombard it each second, caught unaware, they can trip up even the most deliberate thinker, leading to false conclusions and poor decisions.

As the behavioral psychologist Daniel Kahneman writes in *Thinking Fast and Slow*, we are more vulnerable to biased decision making when we are tired, busy, rushed, overloaded with irrelevant pieces of information, and/or making the types of recurring decisions that lull us into believing we understand the situation and can make a decision without much attention or thought.[6] Unfortunately,

---

[6] Daniel Kahneman, *Thinking Fast and Slow* (Farrer, Straus, and Giroux, 2013).

we experience one or all of these states fairly consistently. Gerald Zaltman of Harvard posits that 95 percent of the consumer decisions we make are unconscious, motivated by our automatic and biased thought processes.[7] Imagine how that translates to the decisions we make in the workplace.

Some biases carry an emotional component that makes them particularly difficult to overcome with countervailing facts. Issues that are tied to our personal identity, such as religion, ethnicity, or political leanings, fall into this category. Biases like these have a psychological and social wall around them, protecting them from our rational minds. Social science research shows that this type of strongly held belief can be very difficult to change. Even powerful and convincing evidence showing that a belief is fallacious or that another belief is equally worthy will not change a person's mind.

The legal scholar Dan Kahan and his colleague Donald Braman suggest that this type of bias formation is grounded in the fact that people often form beliefs and ideas based on the beliefs of others whom they perceive as having the same values they do. They refer to this phenomenon as "cultural cognition" and document its power to guide opinions about a range of issues from mandatory vaccination to climate change.[8]

Sociologist Arlie Hochschild, in turn, refers to a "feels as if . . ." story that people construct for themselves to make sense of their world and their place in it.[9] In her book *Strangers in Their Own Land*, she applied the "feels as if . . ." anthropological lens to understand how the Tea Party movement—which is generally against all government spending except defense and law enforcement—could

---

[7] Gerald Zaltman, *How Customers Think: Essential Insights into the Mind of the Market* (Harvard Business School Press, 2003).

[8] Dan Kahan and Donald Braman, "Cultural Cognition and Public Policy," *Yale Law & Policy Review* 24 (2006), 147.

[9] Arlie Hochschild, *Strangers in Their Own Land: Anger and Mourning on the American Right* (The New Press, 2016).

have its strongest support in the U.S. states that suffer most from poor economic conditions and environmental degradation. Put another way, she asks, Why would those who most need support so adamantly reject it? Her work reveals that community cohesion, a strong work ethic, and a general lack of confidence in the government's ability to spend money wisely have created a bias for these people against government social support. For them, it "feels as if . . ." government programs allow people who haven't worked as hard or lived as morally as they have to "cut the line." Therefore they eschew the system that makes such line-cutting possible.

Assumptions are closely related to biases. They occur when we accept information as true or an event as certain to happen, without proof. Assumptions can cause us to make decisions based on cause-and-effect relationships that don't exist and draw broad conclusions based on too little data. Worse, they lead us to operate with prejudice.

Even without that emotional element that occurs when biases are grounded in our personal or community identity or in our assumptions, overcoming biases is hard because they operate unconsciously. We might not know in the moment that a decision is influenced by bias because biased decisions "feel right" or "instinctive." It can be done, however. In the next section I offer some enablers of clear thought that can help you uncover your hidden biases and assumptions—in other words, allow you to identify your "thinking performance gaps"—and overcome them.

Enablers of Clear Thought

Clarity pursuers make a *conscious choice* to be curious and seek relevant information. They assume they don't know, are eager to learn, and approach unfamiliar territory with humility. But what do you do if you are clarity blind, given that clarity blindness occurs when the blind person doesn't realize that he or she lacks the full picture?

My advice is to assume a situation is *not* clear until you find evidence that it is. Stanford psychologist Carol Dweck offers some useful guidance here. Dweck is the scholar I mentioned in Chapter 1 whose work focuses on learning mindsets. To recap, her studies have revealed that some people have a fixed mindset, which means that they believe they have innate traits from birth that cannot develop or change. Others have a growth mindset, which expresses itself as a willingness to persevere and attain skills through practice. Approaching clarity with a growth mindset—as I believe clarity pursuers do—will set you on a strong trajectory for success. A second enabler is to give yourself the space and time to slow down: be mindful, ask questions, and care for yourself.

Mindfulness

Mindfulness means paying attention purposefully, in the present moment, and nonjudgmentally.[10] It's a state of being that allows its practitioners to lead with greater clarity by developing a more calm and focused mind. Mindfulness and the practice of mindfulness meditation is a trending topic in leadership and management literature for good reason: there's a growing body of scientific evidence showing that mindfulness meditation changes the brain in a powerful, performance-enhancing way.[11] It develops areas of your brain responsible for self-regulation, allowing you to more effectively place your attention where you want it, regulate your mood, and manage your response to information. It also helps create more healthful stress responses and more effective ways for the brain to process a large volume of inputs.[12]

Not convinced? Ask top performers in any discipline about the practices they incorporate into their daily routines. You will find

---

[10] Jon Kabat-Zinn, *Wherever You Go, There You Are*, 10th ed. (Hatchett Books, 2005), 3.

[11] Darren J. Good, Christopher J. Lyddy, Theresa M. Glomb, Joyce E. Bono, Kirk Warren Brown, Michelle K. Duffy, Ruth A. Baer, Judson A. Brewer, and Sara W. Lazar, "Contemplating Mindfulness at Work: An Integrative Review," *Journal of Management* 42, no. 1 (January 2016): 114–142.

[12] Christina Congleton, Britta K. Hölzel, and Sara W. Lazar, "Mindfulness Can Literally Change Your Brain," *Harvard Business Review*, January 8, 2015.

that the vast majority mention some form of meditative practice, and often credit it for their success. Elite athletes, for instance, use meditation to prepare for the stress of competition. The famous basketball coach Phil Jackson, who led the Chicago Bulls and then the Los Angeles Lakers to legendary success, is an avid proponent of meditation and introduced the practice to Michael Jordan and Kobe Bryant. The latter has become an outspoken advocate for meditation as his "anchor."[13] Musicians likewise use mindfulness meditation methods to clear their minds and prepare for a performance.[14] And business leaders use it to alleviate the stress from a high-pressure day, reduce personal tendencies toward reactivity, and put themselves in a position to view business issues and make decisions with greater clarity.

Manish Chopra, a principal at McKinsey & Co. in New York City, wrote about his journey from skepticism about meditation to adopting a daily meditation practice. In his words, "most of today's workers—and senior executives perhaps most of all—lack what they need, whether it's meditation or a different approach, to balance and offset the demands of their anywhere, everywhere roles in today's corporations."[15] Meditation provided Chopra a counterbalance to an always-on way of being. Just as our batteries need to be recharged, our minds need to be cleared. Mark Bertolini, CEO of Aetna;[16] Marc Benioff, CEO of Salesforce;[17] and Accenture's Robert Stembridge,[18]

---

[13] See Daniel McGinn, "This Mindfulness Teacher Gets Results (Just Ask Kobe)," *Boston Globe*, May 27, 2015; and "Kobe Bryant on Oprah. Meditation Dictates My Day," https://www.youtube.com/watch?v=ucNODrsGdx0.

[14] Rolf Hind, "Head First: Mindfulness and Music," *The Guardian*, June 16, 2011.

[15] Manish Chopra, "Want to Be a Better Leader? Observe More and React Less," *McKinsey Quarterly*, February 2016.

[16] David Gelles, "At Aetna, a CEO's Management by Mantra," *New York Times*, February 27, 2015.

[17] Don Clark, "Salesforce.com CEO Marc Benioff Delivers Meditation on Mindfulness," *Wall Street Journal*, October 20, 2015.

[18] "Mindfulness: One Second Ahead," *The CEO Magazine*, August 2016.

managing director of technology, are all active meditators and promote mindfulness as a means to improve focus and enable clarity.

I, too, have been practicing yoga and various forms of mindfulness meditation for more than 20 years and have found it to be a powerful tool for improving my well-being. My performance as a leader, consultant, family member, friend, and citizen has been forever changed by practices that quiet my ever-busy mind. I've included some basic instruction for beginning a mindfulness meditation practice in the Appendix for readers who are curious to try it.[19]

Mindfulness is the most effective way I know to slow thinking processes enough that they become observable. Mindfulness introduces a pause between receipt of information and your reaction to it. It enables you to engage in *metacognition*—thinking about one's thinking—which reveals thought patterns that include biases and assumptions.[20] People in the early stages of developing a mindfulness practice will quickly find that they are able to remind themselves to pause and objectively reflect on a situation when they are reacting emotionally or in a way that seems inconsistent with the facts. I call this a *clarity pause*. It can be used retrospectively to explore one's thinking about a past event. Over time as you develop a deeper mindfulness practice you will find that the clarity pause becomes an automatic, in-the-moment response that allows you to reflect on what you believe and how you act, which will enable you to recognize when you are operating with bias and change course. This ability to create a real-time clarity pause makes you more effective as a leader, colleague, friend, or family member.

For instance, when someone comes to you about a problem, mindfulness and the clarity pause it enables allow you to observe your own reactions: Do you automatically assume you understand the nature of the problem from the first facts given, or is it your

---

[19] For more information, visit www.ksmartin.com/mindfulness.

[20] https://en.wikipedia.org/wiki/Metacognition.

instinct to gather more information before coming to a decision? What about when a customer comes to you expressing a preference or making a request? Do you assume you understand what he or she is really asking you to do, or do you seek clarity first? Do you take the time to discover the root cause for a problem, or do you assume you know and leap to a solution?

If you find that it is often your instinct to assume that you know, mindfulness allows you to recognize when you are doing it. When you notice these habitual ways of operating, you are in a position to ask a clarifying question instead of giving an ill-informed answer or forming a premature conclusion. A small amount of extra attention can provide significant clarity.

Questions

Asking questions is a critical tool for achieving clarity.[21] But learning to lead with questions versus proclamations is initially uncomfortable for many. The causes are myriad and all boil down to two roots. First, asking questions comes with an implicit acknowledgment that you don't know the answer. Many people don't like admitting when they don't know something. This is particularly challenging for leaders, many of whom rose into their roles because they consistently *knew* what to do and then did it. Take comfort from the fact that as a leader, it's OK to not know. In many cases, it's preferable. A leader's job is to develop other leaders, keep the train on the tracks, and inspire all to become the best versions of themselves in service to your customers. Believing that the leader needs to know everything is a challenging mindset to overcome, but it's required if you want to be a leader who leads with clarity and inspires others to do the same.

---

[21] For excellent books on the life-changing value of asking questions, see Michael Bungay Stanier, *The Coaching Habit: Say Less, Ask More & Change the Way You Lead Forever* (Box of Crayons Press, 2016); Warren Berger, *A More Beautiful Question: The Power of Inquiry to Spark Breakthrough Ideas* (Bloomsbury USA, 2016); Edgar Schein, *Humble Inquiry: The Gentle Art of Asking Instead of Telling* (Berrett-Koehler Publishers, 2013).

The second reason people are often afraid to ask questions is that they may have to do something with the answers. This can run the spectrum from relatively innocent situations in which a leader is facing a deadline and doesn't feel that he or she has the bandwidth to deal with something else, to the more extreme end when a leader recognizes that asking the question is likely to uncover an immoral or illegal act, or an expensive or high-risk problem that he or she would rather not know about. Either way, recognize that when you choose to not ask a question that should be asked, you are engaging in clarity avoidance.

Mindfulness plays a role in asking questions as well because it helps you see when you don't have an answer, and it helps remove the fear of admitting it. But you don't want to begin asking questions without deep thought. Good questions are a sign of wisdom and deep thinking. When tackling an issue, take some time to frame what you want to know and why you want to know it. What will you do with the information?

If you're preparing to make a decision, it helps to be specific from the outset about what questions you need to ask to enable clear thinking—in the same way I recommend you think backward in problem solving. As Stephen Covey laid out in his iconic *The Seven Habits of Highly Effective People*, begin with the end in mind.[22] What does clarity of thought look like when applied to, say, the sharp increase in customer returns for a particular product? What stage of clarity are you in right now? Where do you want to go? What does success look like?

Asking too many questions can have a similar effect to asking too few. Clarity pursuers can be vulnerable to falling, like Alice in Wonderland, down the rabbit hole of information, creating ambiguity instead of clarity.

---

[22] Stephen Covey, *The Seven Habits of Highly Effective People: Powerful Lessons in Personal Change* (New York: Simon & Schuster, 1989).

When have you asked enough questions? At some point in the process you will cross over the inflection point after which more knowledge will not result in clearer thought or better decisions. That line is not always obvious. You don't want to jump to conclusions based on limited information. Nor do you want to wade into the world of analysis paralysis from using information gathering as an excuse to avoid making a decision or taking action. Nor do you want to find yourself drowning in data because your questions weren't discerning enough. Finding the sweet spot is the key and is situational.

You will never know everything, but for most questions in most situations you will know enough. Repetition is one signal that you have reached that point. When different sources produce the same information—or different questions produce the same answer—that's a sign that you have gone as deep as you can and should go.

Self-Care

You may be thinking that all this clear thinking requires a lot of time—and it does. You need to schedule time to think, the same way you schedule time for meetings, or for dinner with family or a friend. There is no getting around it. But understand that taking the time to enable clear thought in advance leads to better decision making and less rework than if you jump to make a decision or fulfill a task without taking the time for clarity. Or as I like to say, you need to go slow to go fast. Clarity of thought is impossible if you fill all your time with doing.

Say

The actions we take and decisions we make result from information that has been communicated to us in written or visual form, transmitted verbally, or obtained through one of our other senses. Everything you communicate results in a recipient learning, feeling, deciding, acting—or all of these. That's a big responsibility. You can motivate or discourage, help or harm, provide clarity or produce fog. Words and tone both matter.

We all play two distinct roles in communication: information provider and information recipient. When you are the provider, the words you choose can make or break a meeting with a customer or team member, an acquisition negotiation, or an afternoon at the movies with a loved one. The words and tone you choose can determine whether your listener hears what you are trying to convey or misinterprets your message. Your words and tone can incite anger or garner support for something you wish to accomplish. Your words and tone can accurately reflect what you think, or they can send a message that is ambiguous or confusing.

Here are a few steps to ensure you are getting your message across when in the provider role.

What Is Your Intent?

The first element of clear communication is to be clear about your intent: What are you trying to communicate? To whom? For what purpose? In other words, what do you want the recipient to learn, decide, or do based on your message?

Having intent means you are making conscious choices. Intent is the mental positioning you do before you open your mouth or hit reply on your e-mail. Ideally, you're a clarity pursuer and you intend to communicate as effectively and honestly as you can. There are circumstances that warrant leaders operating with strategic ambiguity, but these are few among the total interactions a leader has in any given day. The vast majority of the remaining communications often end up as ambiguous, however, for one of two reasons. The first is that individuals or teams sometimes hoard information under the guise of "need to know," but for the real purpose of protecting turf or acting as a solo hero. The second occurs as a default state when people haven't thought through their intent before they

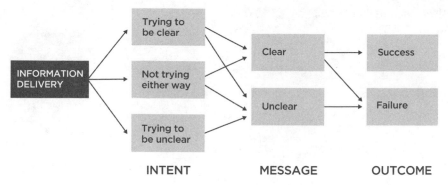

FIGURE 7.4 Seven possible communication pathways

communicate. As a result, the information provider speaks without thinking about what he or she wants to convey, to whom, to what end, and what the best delivery method might be to achieve the level of clarity he or she desires.

Clear communication, in short, does not happen by accident. Without deliberate forethought and purposeful engagement, you're more likely to confuse and obfuscate than to communicate what you intend. As shown in Figure 7.4 there are seven possible pathways for verbal communication. Only two of those result in a recipient successfully receiving a clearly conveyed message.

By knowing your intent and taking steps to shape your message for a specific audience to produce a desired end, you can increase the frequency with which you travel the ideal path represented by the dark blocks in Figure 7.5.

Know Thy Audience

The second factor to keep in mind when communicating or requesting information is your audience. Who are you talking to? Why? What do you want them to know and/or do with the information? What foundational knowledge do they already have? What "state" are they in when you deliver the message? Clarity is in the eye of the beholder, and beholders vary widely based on their level

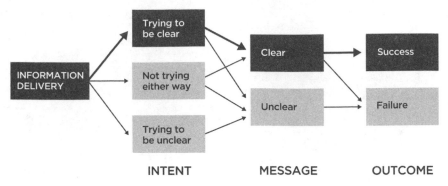

FIGURE 7.5 Ideal communication pathway

of education, culture, beliefs, experience, mindset, emotional state, degree of detail orientation, and readiness to receive a message.

The answers to these questions will sometimes be clear, as when you have a one-to-one meeting with a colleague or when you meet a certain team. The answer is trickier if you have a mixed audience, as you might when presenting to a group of customers or key stakeholders, all with different needs, goals, and aspirations. When your audience is mixed, you have to make even more conscious choices.

Recall in Chapter 2 on Purpose when I talked about creating a persona to represent your organization's typical customer? It's helpful to go through a similar process to define your audience, who are the customers of your message. What is their role? Why should they listen to you? What do they already know about the subject? Are there details they *think* they know that are wrong (including common misconceptions)? What do you want them to know or do as a result of having the information? Are there reasons they will resist doing that? Is there a way that clearer communication can overcome that resistance?

Having your typical audience member in mind when organizing your thoughts can help you filter through all the information you have and highlight only the most important facts you need to make your point *for that person*. More is not better. Recall earlier in this chapter when I referred to *New York Times* reporter Adam Bryant and the interviews he conducted with successful CEOs? Another skill they exhibited was the ability to distill information to its essence, offering only the most important conclusions without getting mired in unnecessary detail. Don't make your audience work to understand your point—give it to them clearly and concisely.

And timing is everything. Consider whether your audience is in a position to receive your message. If you need to share information with a member of your team, and you find him or her head-down solving a problem, is it a good idea to interrupt, or is it better to wait? Savvy communicators are particularly strategic, especially about when to have difficult conversations.

Knowing your audience is not just about who they are and what they need to know. It's also about timing and attention. Suppress the urge to say, "But I told them . . ." or "If they'd just listen . . ." if members of your team have not applied a change as you communicated it. It's possible they weren't listening, but it is far more likely that you didn't tell them in a way or at a moment when they were able to hear you.

Last, unless you have a very good reason not to be—a reason that shows respect for the information recipient—please be honest. Show people the respect they deserve by leveling with them. People often avoid sharing uncomfortable truths because they think sharing them will be stressful and lead to unpleasant interactions or conflict. While that may be true, research shows that people who set out to communicate honestly experience a stronger sense of personal well-being even than those who set out to communicate with kindness. In addition, the recipient of honest communication is far less likely to react negatively than the communicator thinks.[23] So know your audience and be clear—and honest—with them.

---

[23] Emma Edelman Levine and Taya R. Cohen, "You Can Handle the Truth: Mispredicting the Intrapersonal Consequences of Honesty and Kindness," *SSRN*, February 1, 2017.

Word Choice

In nearly every client meeting I facilitate, someone in the room takes his or her turn to speak and launches into an explanation using terminology with which others are not familiar.[24] I often see body language that indicates that someone doesn't understand a term; I wait for a few moments to see if anyone asks for clarification. Very often, no one says anything and I ask for clarification on behalf of the person who doesn't seem to know the term. I can only assume that this type of unclear communication occurs when I'm not present. Multiply that by all the communication that happens in your organization—e-mails, meetings, process documentation, and so on—and you get a sense for how important the words you choose can be for clarity.

The use of acronyms, esoteric terms, business jargon, and elitist language increases the distance between you and your listener and creates ambiguity. More than that, ambiguous language can erode trust.[25] Few people are going to interrupt you to ask for clarification on a term they were not familiar with, and the more obscure or unknown the terms you use, the less clear your message.[26]

It's easy for speakers to brush off such concerns by saying, "Well, if people don't know something, they should ask." This is the wrong way to think. The speaker has a responsibility to her listeners. As a leader, *you* have a responsibility not to waste people's time by creating a situation where they have to seek clarity about communication that could and should have been clear in the first place. In the following sections I highlight the most common types of word choice problems that you—and everyone in the organization—should avoid.

---

[24] In his book *Writing Without Bullshit* (HarperBusiness, 2016), author and writing expert Josh Bernoff has a useful section on industry-speak and how it makes writing less clear and persuasive than it could be. He also discusses jargon in his book.

[25] See Jena McGregor, "Sick of Workplace Jargon? Cite This New Study to Get Your Boss to Stop the Lame Lingo," *Washington Post*, July 12, 2011.

[26] See also Roger Trapp, "Why You Should Avoid Jargon and Talk Like a Leader," *Forbes.com*, February 24, 2016.

Acronyms

Acronyms can enable more efficient communication, but that efficiency is lost if people don't understand what you are saying. In the same way that terminology can be unfamiliar to people, so too can acronyms. When that happens among members of our client teams, more than 50 percent of the time we don't learn that the acronym wasn't clear to everyone until later in the session when it arises again. Even worse, the clarification discussion often reveals that team members who thought they knew what an acronym meant were wrong.

As much as I "preach" about this issue, I recently fell into the trap as well. During a conversation with one of my team members about a client of ours, I asked her the dollar value of the client's average "MSA." She responded with a detailed explanation of how the organization recently changed the structure of the regions, moved a number of leaders, and changed the service process for customers. I listened carefully to find relevance to my question and was lost. When she paused I asked, "But what about the MSA?" She said, "You want their salary range?" I was still lost. What did salaries have to do with my question about the project I had been working on to shorten the customer's contracting process? I asked, "Are you talking about the master sales agreement?" to which she said, "Ohhhh . . . I thought you meant medication solution architect!" referring to the new title for their sales representatives.

So what's the fix? I'm not suggesting that people stop using acronyms. EKG is much more efficient than "electrocardiogram," after all, with little potential for confusion. Acronyms are OK, but only under the following conditions:

1. Only use an acronym when you are 100 percent certain that everyone listening to or reading your words knows what the acronym means, and has no chance of misunderstanding.

2. Adopt a consistent habit of defining acronyms immediately after using them for the first time with a particular audience, whether in conversation or writing. Example: "What's the average value of an MSA, meaning master sales agreement?"

3. During in-person communication, adopt a consistent habit of asking the audience if everyone is familiar with the acronym and watch to see if people look puzzled or hesitant.

Business Jargon

Many years ago I worked with the leadership team of a technology company to help them address why they were losing market share of one of their most profitable products. This was our second problem-solving engagement with this company, and I had learned about the widespread use of acronyms and unique terminology in our first engagement. During a rather heated moment in the conversation, the vice president of marketing snapped at one of the product leaders, "The optics won't support that."

I noticed the controller furrow his brow, and assumed his body language was a gesture of disagreement, not confusion. I didn't want to interrupt the discussion because they were in the most critical period of "storming" and they needed to get through it.[27]

A third leader entered the fray, and a rapid-fire three-way back-and-forth went on among them in which the word *optics* was used five times. I noticed the same furrow on the controller's face and also on the face of a software engineer they had called in to help explain a technical issue. Just when I was about to intervene, he asked, "What are optics?" The controller nodded. With a note of impatience, the VP of marketing explained, "It's how something appears, whether it's true or not. You know, the perception."

---

[27] By storming, I'm referring to Bruce Tuckman's classic stages of a team's evolution: forming, storming, norming, performing. Bruce W. Tuckman, "Developmental Sequence in Small Groups," *Psychological Bulletin* 63, no. 6 (1965): 384–399.

OK. Got it. But why do we have to use newfangled words that people may not be familiar with? Why not just use perception, or say, "It won't look good to customers if we do that"? Or "The regulators will think we are hiding something"? Why "optics" and not "appearances"? Buzzwords may be common language to one group and completely foreign to another. Being present and thinking about your audience enables greater clarity.

Actively choosing *not* to use clear terminology is particularly problematic. For example, there is no more specific or urgent word in nuclear energy than *meltdown*. It is efficient, means something very specific, and generates the proper urgency when applied. Refusal to use it, as happened during the Fukushima disaster, as I mentioned in Chapter 1, likely allowed far more damage to occur than if people had simply spoken the truth. The word *problem* is another example I highlighted in Chapter 6 on Problem Solving. I've run into a number of organizations that have more or less banned the word because "it sounds negative." Banning words that have clearer meanings than alternatives is a silly, wasteful, and, in the case of Fukushima, potentially catastrophic exercise.

Fuzzy Words

I introduced the term *fuzzy words* in the chapter on clarity in my earlier book *The Outstanding Organization*. Fuzzy words are those that seem descriptive but are anything but.

Fuzzy words are subjective, their meaning changeable depending on the perspective of the person who is listening. Adjectives are the usual culprits. For example, people who live in rural areas often have a different view of what qualifies as a "short" drive than their urban-living counterparts. Likewise, a six-foot-tall competitive weight lifter may describe a suitcase that weighs 30 kilograms as "light," whereas that same suitcase will be impossibly heavy for a five-foot-tall woman. The list is long of descriptors such as *fast, a lot, heavy, short, not too much,* and so on, that carry different meanings for different people. Using specific, quantifying language (85 pounds, five minutes, 15 percent, and so on) brings much-needed clarity.

Fuzzy words also include those that have different meanings depending on the context in which they are used. "Cost," for example, can refer to expense or to price. "Income" can be gross, net, pretax—any number of categories. Revenue isn't the same as gross sales, and yet many people use it that way.

Fuzzy words also include references that aren't clear such as the pronouns *them, they, we,* etc. I've asked the question, "Who's they?" more times than I can count.

Acronyms, jargon, and fuzzy words are everywhere, and one antidote is awareness of your audience—not everyone has the same foundational experiences anchoring how they interpret a fuzzy word. Clarity pursuers avoid using fuzzy words and are relentless in asking people to define the fuzzy terms they use.

Answering Questions

In the section on thought I addressed the benefits of asking questions to gain personal clarity. Here I'd like you to flip your perspective and consider how you might answer questions posed to you by customers, partners, peers, your division head, and your teams. Answering questions is one of the best opportunities you have to promote clarity.

If you're asked a binary question (yes-or-no) honor the questioner by responding in the simplest way first: "Yes." "No." "I don't know, but I'll find out." "It depends." If a simple answer warrants details or contextual clarification, provide it *after* you have answered the question. You may be surprised at how uncomfortable it is for you to answer with a simple yes or no, and it bears reflection on why this is.

I understand that some situations are more complex than yes-or-no options capture. In these cases, many people falsely believe that brief answers carry the risk of oversimplification. They do only if you don't add context and details to explain the brief answer. If you think about the questions you face on a daily basis, you will find that most invite a simple response. If you don't give it, it is usually because you choose not to, are in the habit of providing unnecessary detail, or are afraid to commit to a yes or no response.

These are difficult habits to break. When you choose the complicated answer instead of the simple one, you do your listener a disservice and spread ambiguity. You force the person to work too hard to interpret meaning from your answer, and you erode trust if the asker goes away unsure of what you said. If I'm the recipient of a rambling answer to a binary question, I will often ask, "Was that a yes or no?" both to gain clarity and to sensitize the communicator to the fact that he or she is being vague.

Of course, sometimes the asker doesn't frame a question clearly, or the question is unexpected. In those cases, clarity requires you to confirm that you understand what she wants to know before responding. Consider the power of asking questions about questions. A respectful, "I'm curious why you're asking that" can help clarify what the asker really wants to know, and may shed a light on concerns that you did not consider. I find this question to be an extremely helpful tool to diagnose a situation and get into the mind of the person with whom I'm communicating.

Finally, it's a wonderful gesture of respect and a technique that can help you communicate more clearly if you anticipate someone's questions and craft your message accordingly. Preemptively answering an information recipient's questions shows that you've done your homework, you know your audience, and you don't want to waste their time being unclear or having them ask questions you could have addressed up front. One way to do this is to put yourself in the recipient's shoes and anticipate what questions you'd have. If you are sharing information about a new policy or process, for example, consider the context and content your audience needs and add the necessary details while removing irrelevant noise. You don't have to become a mind reader. You just need to take a clarity pause and be more deliberate about what and how you communicate.

Tone Matters

The last point to consider as an information provider is the tone you use to convey information. Some people are very good at keeping their tone calm and consistent. President Barack Obama was known as "No Drama Obama," a nickname his aides gave him during his first presidential campaign to describe his seemingly unflappable public response to both significant accomplishments and major disappointments.

Few of us can manage such a consistent public persona. Most people get flustered or angry or frustrated at times, and that frustration comes through in our tone, especially when we view the listener as having less power than we do. Consider the marketing executive's irritation about "optics." The heated discussion he was having with his colleagues had flustered him, and that carried over to his response to the software engineer when he asked for clarification about a jargon word that prevented him from understanding the conversation.

A clarity pause can prevent this. After all, how would it feel for you to get snipped at for an innocent question? How open would you be to engaging with the VP in an open and honest conversation the next time? The marketing executive was unknowingly training people not to ask him clarifying questions, an act that breeds clarity avoidance and is a fundamental act of disrespect.

Your tone affects the recipient's ability to receive your message. If you are patient, calm, and clear, you are more likely to get your message across than if you are terse and snippy. Your tone sets an example. If you don't keep your cool, why should anyone else?

The bottom line is that you should use tone purposefully as a tool of communication. When dealing with someone who you know prefers straightforward no-frills delivery, for example, a frank tone is probably the best approach, while someone who is more sensitive and prone to take issues personally may need you to invest in softening the message while still being candid.

Do

Action is where all your work to achieve personal clarity pays off. Everything I've discussed in this chapter is in the service of your actions. Clear thought allows you to formulate your ideas and positions. Clear speech allows you to communicate them and convince others to support you and your team. But people primarily assess leadership through the actions you take. Action is where you most clearly show what you stand for and what you expect from others. It is *doing* that matters—so act clearly. Model the behavior you want to see, and work to ensure that your actions are consistent with your thoughts and words.

Congruence

You set the standard for action in your organization. If you believe problem solving is a core skill that everyone needs to have, and you have committed to developing your team's problem-solving capabilities, then you need to model disciplined problem solving yourself. If you say you believe in developing people and that it is the job of managers to invest in helping team members realize their full potential, then you need to invest in personally developing the people you oversee.

On the surface, this seems like commonsense, be-the-change-you-wish-to-see thinking. Real-life situations can make congruence very hard, however. We see this all the time while working with clients, most recently while facilitating focused problem solving with a company that specializes in talent management. There were some odd dynamics during a meeting, and when I asked the vice president who had retained our firm what was going on he explained that one of the directors who reports to him was the source of the prickly tension I had perceived.

She was a boomerang employee who had left the company a few years before but was rehired by my client to run a different department. He acknowledged that when she had left for a better-paid role years before there had been an organization-wide sigh of relief. She was widely disliked by her peers and by the team she led. She used abusive language and threatened her staff with performance sanctions for relatively minor issues like failing to invite someone to a meeting. Given that this company is in the business of helping others hire and cultivate talent, I was surprised that he would hire someone who was so indifferent to people and said so. The vice president shrugged and said, "She delivers."

There's the rub—when one aspect of organizational or personal clarity bumps up against another. My client rehired this person because she was results-oriented at all costs, failing to see the incongruence with the organization's purpose and its respect for people—and failing to recognize that the process for achieving results is, in most cases, more important than the results themselves.

Hitting all the right notes can be a stretch goal when it comes to aligning all of your actions with the organizational priorities you have communicated. My client made a compromise. Problems arise when comprises are made thoughtlessly, without concern for clarity. And compromising is a slippery slope. Compromising once makes the next time easier and the next time easier still.

Strive for congruence with your thoughts, your words, and your actions. Don't start each meeting talking about how important the team is, and then disrespect them by checking e-mail while they're talking or asking for feedback. Don't drill everyone on the importance of careful budgeting and then sponsor a boondoggle.

Again, I know this all seems straightforward, but the practice of modeling with congruence can be very challenging for some. A particular source of conflict for many leaders results from the need to relinquish tactical-level control during improvement activities.

An example of this occurred while we were working with a hospital system. With our guidance, the facility's leaders—including the chief nursing officer (CNO)—set clear boundaries for a frontline and supervisor-level improvement team that defined what the team did and didn't have the authority to do. In this case, the boundaries set by leaders were budgetary and technology-based: the team couldn't spend more than $500 and couldn't suggest a technology solution—in other words, they needed to work with the resources they had. With those boundaries in place, the leaders, including the CNO, gave permission to the team to design improvements in any way that moved them toward the performance target they set and didn't increase risk in safety, quality, or regulatory compliance.

The gap they set out to narrow was reducing medication errors. The team focused on the stage during which the greatest number of errors occurred: medication administration. Root cause analysis revealed that the primary reason for administration errors was due to the nurses being interrupted during meds rounds. The team further determined that phone calls from doctor's offices, labs, the laboratory and imaging departments, the admitting department, and so on, were the primary source of interruptions.

With that insight—and in a flash of low-cost creativity—the improvement team bought plastic name badges with clips on them and created a "name badge" for each of the nurses using green card stock. The plan was for the medication administering nurse to give her name tag *before she started her rounds* to the health unit coordinator (HUC) who answered the phone. When a call came in, the HUC would see if she had that person's name badge in front of her. If yes, she'd take a message and clip it to the badge. If not, the HUC would page the nurse to take the call. After the nurse completed administering medication, he or she would pick up the name badge and return the phone calls.

The team tested the idea, and it worked beautifully. It also fit within the boundaries of low cost, low tech, and effective. The team was thrilled with their progress. But when they presented their solution to leadership during an end-of-day report-out, the CNO seemed unhappy. After the team finished presenting, I asked for questions or comments and the CNO raised her hand.

"Why green?" she said. "I don't like green."

I wish I were kidding. In front of 18 peers and the improvement team, the CNO gave not a word of praise or congratulations to the team, but instead made an issue about the color of card stock they used—after leaders had agreed to our report-out rules: no criticism if the team operated within the boundaries. Only questions were allowed, such as "How did the team approach thus and such?" "What are the risks and how will we prevent them?" And so on.

You could feel the air go out of every member of the improvement team. The CNO's peers looked at her incredulously. I decided to address her violation of the rule as gently as I could in front of the entire group assembled. If I didn't, no one would believe in the process. After the meeting, I followed her to her office. While she was upset with me, she eventually understood what she had done and apologized to the team the next morning. I'm not sure she ever regained the trust of the team and respect from her peers. She's no longer with the hospital, in large part because she didn't possess the proper leadership perspective for an organization on a transformation journey.

Ambiguity caused by incongruence between your words and your actions costs the organization time and money. Leaders, especially executives, often forget how much weight their words and actions carry: when you suggest something, people are very likely to take action on it. If you then act contrary to your suggestion, you sow confusion and disagreement, and erode trust. Did she give me permission to address the problem, or didn't she? Can I stick with the countermeasure I prefer, or can't I? That ambiguity costs time on many levels. First, by having people spend time developing a fix that leaders won't accept. Then by having leaders undo changes made after the improvement was already in place.

If you find yourself behaving in an incongruent way, reflect on what you can learn from it. Are there certain circumstances that seem to breed incongruence? If so, how do you prevent that behavioral pattern? If you're cultivating a team culture in which people are encouraged to surface problems, invite your team or peers to call you out when you are not modeling the behaviors you say you want to see in others. Be sure to listen to and respect that feedback when it comes.

FEEL

"It's not personal." I hear leaders say that all the time. Let's be clear: Work *is* personal. How could it not be, given how much people invest in it? Having the personal clarity you need to think, speak, and act with congruence and clarity requires you to acknowledge that your organization is made up of people, and wherever there are people there are going to be feelings. You need to be clear about *your* feelings, and you need to encourage people to be clear about theirs.

We are emotional beings, and it's a direct affront to human nature to expect people to behave otherwise. Accepting and leveraging this fact—that feelings reflect a person's perception of reality—is the most practical, rational thing you can do in the spirit of clarity. I've included some tips for using feelings to accomplish work.

Tip 1: Ask

When I facilitate meetings for organizations and we get to a transition point in a discussion that has some emotional elements to it, I often ask, "How do you feel?" I am not asking what they *think* about the solution. That is a logical, cerebral response, and that is not what I want at that moment. Instead I want to know how they feel—Nervous? Angry? Agitated? Relieved? Joyous? Because people aren't used to being asked the question, it can take a few minutes for them to evaluate whether it's safe to answer it truthfully. Once one person starts sharing, others often begin to as well. The question may surface tension, but it gives people permission to address the elephant in the room that otherwise slows progress. It allows people to ask questions they have been avoiding, or to express concerns they've been keeping to themselves.

Feelings are instructive. Invite people to put them on the table. Better, encourage them to do it—and share your own. Feelings say something about the person who is feeling them *and* about the object of those feelings. If you hear a lot of excitement, that tells you the process was mostly handled with clarity. If you hear a lot of anger or confusion, it might tell you that you have more clarity work to do. What follows is the process I generally follow to use feelings as a means to bring clarity and accelerate results.

Tip 2: Acknowledge, Accept, and Alter

The feelings others have—the feelings *we* have—are indispensable to surfacing issues that otherwise might not have been part of the equation when leaders sat down to make decisions, or might lie buried under a pile of work. Feelings tell us when we are headed in the wrong direction. That nervous sensation you get in your stomach, that edgy irritability you feel in certain situations—those are among the physical and emotional signals we have that tell us when a situation makes us uncomfortable. Feelings work behind the scenes even when our rational, analytical minds are overwhelmed by fatigue or information overload.

When there isn't enough clarity, you still need to acknowledge others' feelings when they are frustrated by circumstances, bewildered by a decision, or fearful about a change. Ask them how they feel and listen to the answer. And don't stop with "how" questions.

Ask them *why* they feel that way. If part of what they have to say includes criticism of you, your team, or another team member, listen carefully to what they are saying and be thoughtful about how you react to it. If the person is upset, some of what he or she is saying may come across as irrational or immature—but that doesn't invalidate the core message.

Acknowledgment goes hand in hand with accepting what a person is feeling at that moment, whatever those feelings are. Please do not approach a conversation about feelings from the perspective that the other person is *wrong*. Feelings are never "wrong." Telling a person that he shouldn't feel a certain way is like telling grass not to be green. We do not *choose* to feel the way we do—feelings just *are*.

Consider an example from an organization we have worked with: Every year during the holiday season the organization gave each of its 5,000 team members a voucher he or she could use to buy a "gift." The gift options included items such as a set of barbecue utensils or a rain jacket with the company's logo on it. If purchased at retail, the items would each cost around $40 or $50. In previous years, the gift options had also included donations to two local non-profit organizations that the team member could choose in lieu of receiving one of the items.

To be clear, the physical gift choices were not in high demand—each year at least 20 percent of team members didn't cash in their vouchers and another 20 percent selected the donation option. So leaders were surprised by the strong backlash they received when a new president announced in an all-company e-mail that instead of giving holiday gift options, he had made a lump sum donation in the company's name to a charity he chose. No more rain jackets.

A behavioral psychologist might say the team members' reactions represented a classic case of loss aversion: people place a higher value on items they are at risk of losing or have lost than they would if there was no loss risk. But when the team we were working with talked about it, their feelings were much more nuanced, and highlighted a broad set of issues that came down to one thing: the organization did not respect its people. There was no organizational emphasis on clarity. The company underwent frequent managerial shifts that came with no communication about their purpose or what they aimed to achieve. Leaders offered little to no development or coaching to middle managers and did not define career paths for people in service departments. The list went on. In this type of environment, those small holiday gifts were one of the last gestures of appreciation from leaders to team members, and the new president took that away.

If leaders had asked team members how they felt about what seemed to them a trivial leadership decision, they would have uncovered a larger set of leadership issues that—if ignored—could have signaled this organization's decline. It was already missing growth targets in a rapidly expanding sector, a clear signal of strategic misalignment.

Did any leaders ask? Did they acknowledge what they heard? Did they probe for the deeper message the team members were sending? Most importantly, did they take steps to alter any of their decisions or actions in response to what they learned? They didn't. The senior management dismissed the complaints as standard resistance to any change and not worth addressing for fear of making a "mountain out of a molehill." For their part, the team members who'd confided in us didn't think there was anything to be gained from communicating their concerns directly to the senior leadership team. They believed—and they may have been right—that leadership would not have heard them about the larger issues underlying their complaints. We encouraged them to try, but they wanted to let it go and we didn't push it, as ultimately they were the ones who needed to advocate for change.

The situation for that company may have been very different, however, had a leader sat down and asked his or her team members to share what was bothering them. That leader might have found him or herself altering a decision or a planned approach based on the conversation. Alterations can come in many forms, large and small, personal and organizational. On the personal level, you may modify your perspective on a situation by learning more about how your team members feel. You may adjust the actions you take in response to an issue.

I am not talking about knee-jerk alterations, like might happen if the organization with the holiday gifts decided to reverse the president's decision and reinstate the old policy. Actions like that are one of the risks leaders face in the world of feelings—feelings may cause you to alter a decision reactively rather than using problem solving to identify the real issue behind those feelings. My client's issue wasn't about the holiday gifts per se; my client's issue was a culturally ingrained tendency to treat people as if they were commodities.

The need to acknowledge, accept, and perhaps alter applies not just to you in your interactions, but also among team members in your sphere of influence. Model the approach you want to see, and then expect it from others. If there is a problem between two colleagues, set the expectation for them to work it out in a context of mutual respect and acknowledgment, using a mediator if necessary.

Tip 3: Attend to Your Own Needs

You are human, which means you will also experience setbacks, disappointments, and personal issues that affect your work. You'll make mistakes and some of your decisions won't work out. Whoever you report to will sometimes have to talk to you about problems or performance issues in your area. You can't be a smart leader if you don't attend to your own feelings about those events and deal with them.

That applies to negative emotions like anger and frustration as much as it does to positive emotions like joy and elation. Rich Sheridan, the CEO and cofounder of Menlo Innovations and author of *Joy, Inc.*, writes about his personal experience with all those emotions. In 1997, when he was offered a major promotion to become vice president of research and development at a rapidly growing tech firm, he turned it down. For him, work had become laced with stress and frustration, troubled projects that were ultimately canceled after years of investment, angry colleagues, internal competition, and other negative feelings that were affecting his life. He wanted less of all that, not more, which seemed inevitable if he accepted the new role.

Did work inevitably have to be more of the negative, or could he take his experience, build his own company, and create the uplifting work environment he wanted for himself and everyone there? *Joy, Inc.* is the story of the choices Rich made.[28] Those may not be your choices, but his experience is worth considering for the insights it provides into how personal attitudes shape experience. Feelings matter—and yes, work is personal.

CONCLUSION

Your potential is bounded only by your willingness and tenacity to develop the skills you need to lead. When it comes to clarity, that includes operating with clear thought, word, and deed that allows people to have confidence in you, understand what you want, and feel comfortable and safe working to achieve it.

Fortunately, the actions that facilitate personal clarity can also bring a great deal of pleasure and fulfillment. As mentioned earlier, mindfulness meditation can provide much-needed *me* time, sooth anxiety and stress, and enable the clarity of thought needed to make effective work decisions. People experience similar fulfillment when they take the time to reflect and take clarity pauses, and make time for the self-care activities of good sleep, healthy eating, and outdoor

---

[28] Richard Sheridan, *Joy, Inc.* (Portfolio, 2015).

exercise, all of which enable clear thinking and action. Asking how people feel and acknowledging those feelings can improve relationships of all kinds, leading to enhanced fulfillment.

How clear do you want to be? The actions you take to generate personal clarity serve *you* first and foremost. They make you a better friend, parent, sibling, child, partner, community member. And they make you a better leader. Desire, skill, and tenacity are your only limits—and all three are within your control.

8

Committing
to Clarity

Individual commitment to a group effort—
that is what makes a team work, a company
work, a society work, a civilization work.

—Vince Lombardi

Mike Nichols was a film, television, and stage visionary who won an Oscar, a Grammy, four Emmys, nine Tonys, and three BAFTAs. Nichols was known as much for his talent as his unshakable passion, commitment to the work, and love of clarity. Four months before he died in 2014, he spent a few days with fellow theater director and friend Jack O'Brien talking about his career. On clarity and how it feels, he said: "One minute you don't know, the next minute you suddenly get it. And that as you know is the great thrill, whether it happens in your life, in your work, in your study, in watching something, when you get it and everything shifts and everything changes and says some simple—at least a clear if not simple thing—that's a thrill, that's exciting. That's why we're here. Because there's nothing else like it. There's nothing like 'getting it.' " [1]

There *is* nothing like "getting it." It is the moment when a problem owner finally understands what's *really* behind customer discontent. It's the moment you find your way through the "mess" of innovation and discover a solution to a design need that had been eluding you. It's the moment in a process improvement session when team members realize that the person upstream from them is not creating the need for rework out of laziness or malice, but because the process is flawed. It is in the surprise cause you uncover for a vexing quality problem. It is the first time you see how work flows—or doesn't flow—from a customer request to delivering on that request. The moment of clarity is like no other. No matter how difficult the truth may be, seeing it is liberating because now you have something tangible to work on.

I understand why people avoid clarity or are blind to it. I also know from my own experience and our work with clients that clarity is better. It is better even when clarity uncovers difficult realities. A client of ours who has started to use KPIs to focus improvement efforts on areas of greatest need is experiencing that discomfort right now. The attitude of one of the managers—I'll call him David—is instructive. One of the KPIs David selected for his area's Level 2 scorecard shows poor current state performance for a critical operational area in which he and his team should excel. Many leaders might have been tempted to keep that number in their pocket, but David understood the spirit of measurement. He trusted that shining a light on the truth would allow his team to find innovative ways to close the performance gap faster than they would if he kept it quiet. He also believed that people in other departments already knew that

---

[1] The Jack O'Brien interviews took place over two days in the Golden Theater in New York, where Nichols had his Broadway debut in the improvisational comedy act "An Evening with Mike Nichols and Elaine May." The interviews were filmed and edited for the HBO documentary *Becoming Mike Nichols*.

his team's performance needed improvement. Being quantifiably transparent about the problem, he figured, could help heal relationships with internal customers affected by their poor performance. David reports that this indeed has begun to occur, with an unexpected side benefit: the frustrated internal customers have offered to help him in any way they can. They want to see his team succeed.

This is how clarity starts—with action. When David took the brave step of putting unflattering data on a KPI scorecard, it sent the message that the organization is serious about cultivating a clarity culture. It takes a bit of courage to take those first actions, but the payback is multifold, because seeking and operating with greater clarity creates a domino effect. When you communicate clearly, you create a pay-it-forward environment in which recipients of clear information pass clearer information on to the next person. In that way clarity is a gift you give, one that generates more of itself as it spreads.

Everyone wins in an environment gifted with clarity. When Mike Nichols "got it," he then passed that understanding to the actors he directed, to the director of photography who shot the scene, to the lighting director who set the visual tone for the production. His clarity provided everyone else with the clarity they needed to do their job to create outstanding theater, films, television, and music.

Because ultimately that is what clarity is about—creating an environment in which individuals and the organizations they work for can do their best and achieve outstanding performance as a result. Everyone wants to be a part of that. Clarity gives a person what he or she needs to shift away from operating as a lone "I" inside a maelstrom of human commercial activity, toward feeling part of a "we," connected and engaged with others in the service of a collective goal.

This book highlights clarity-enabling practices to define your organization's purpose and priorities; promote clarity around processes and performance; enable deeper, more effective improvement through disciplined problem solving, and help you develop the clarity-pursing habits you need to model before you can require it of your teams.

Your organization doesn't need to adopt all of these practices at once. In fact it shouldn't. You cannot force clarity, and you cannot rush it. This is especially true inside organizations with a deeply ingrained culture of clarity avoidance or blindness. You can offer it—give it as a gift, cultivate and feed it, and see it flourish—but be patient. You can commit to clarity in small ways, and deepen that commitment through consistent action before you move on to more complex and nuanced applications of clarity. It is better to progress in a measured and consistent way than to try to do too much too quickly.

The importance of consistency is evident in the famous marshmallow experiment conducted by social scientist Walter Mischel in the 1960s.[2] In Mischel's original experiment, children were brought into a room and given the option of eating one marshmallow at that moment or two marshmallows 20 minutes later. Most of the kids ate the one marshmallow right away. Much has been concluded about willpower from observing those kids who were able to hold out and wait for the larger reward later. Some of those conclusions were called into question years later when a group at the University of Rochester replicated the marshmallow test with an important change: the researchers made sure some of the participating kids viewed the adult promising the marshmallows as unreliable. They did so by having the adult researcher that greeted the child promise that he or she could play with crayons or a toy in the testing room, and then having no crayons or toy once the child was brought in.[3] Kids that were "primed" that way never held out for the bigger reward—they didn't believe it existed.

---

[2] Walter Mischel, *The Marshmallow Test: Mastering Self Control* (Little Brown, 2014).

[3] Celeste Kidd, Holly Palmeri, and Richard N. Aslin, "Rational Snacking: Young Children's Decision-Making on the Marshmallow Task Is Moderated by Beliefs About Environmental Reliability," *Cognition* 126, no. 1 (January 2013): 109–114.

Though the marshmallow test takers were children, their responses were not childish at all. Adults are also primed to believe or not believe in the rewards they can expect based on the reliability of the leaders around them. That is why commitment to clarity and consistency in its application is so important. All it takes is one slip—a promise of clarity not kept—and months of work can be undone.

So take clarity one action at a time, one step at a time, one team at a time. That is often how we see organizations naturally embrace clarity. In our practice, clients might contact us for help with one area—a specific problem-solving effort, for example, or value stream transformation—and get "hooked" on clarity when they see what it can do for them. These efforts show how much easier it is to make decisions, how much stronger cross-functional collaboration can be, how performance improvement can happen faster, and so on. Word travels from strong results, and soon enough everyone is asking for more.

To facilitate the process by which clarity spreads beyond these initial—and admittedly contained—efforts, each leader must pursue clarity in his or her personal interactions, and encourage clarity in his or her sphere of influence. This happens when you reinforce clarity-enabling practices as you define purpose, set priorities, standardize processes and leadership practices, measure performance, and solve problems. Practice and promote clarity every day so that that it becomes an ingrained habit:[4]

- **Pursue** clarity by seeking facts in the form of data and objective information, and using those facts to inform your views and decisions.
- **Observe** the situation by regularly going to the "real place" (gemba) to see how work is done and how customers respond.

---

[4] For more on how repeatedly performing certain actions forms the neural pathways needed to convert actions into habits, see Charles Duhigg, *The Power of Habit* (Random House, 2014).

- **Use** visual management to surface problems and initiate open, blame-free efforts to solve them.
- **Ask** questions to learn the facts, and ask questions about questions to understand what a person truly wants to know.
- **Listen** to what people tell you, even when it reveals an uncomfortable truth.
- **Assess** whether you, your team, and your organization have clarity about a situation before taking action or making decisions.
- **Use** mindfulness and clarity pauses to confront biases and assumptions and communicate with greater clarity.

You will see results as the problems you face as a leader and as an organization diminish and performance on all levels improves at an accelerated pace. Clarity is a gift—go on and give it.

Acknowledgments

Though I've written four previous books, I'm struck again by how collaborative the writing and publishing process is. No book comes to be solely through the work of the author, and I'm deeply grateful to all who've played a role in *Clarity First*.

First, I carry deep gratitude to Laura Starita and Tim Ogden of Sona Partners, the masters of ideas and words. You served as my thinking partners by telling me my last paragraph in a chapter should be the first; helping me strike the balance between tough love, empathy, and actionable advice; continuing to help me find and trust my voice as a writer; and introducing me to new cutting-edge research relevant to the topic of clarity.

Thank you to Anthony Mejean, Shannon Burns, Gordon Schuit, Laura Starita, and Mykell Lirio for creating beautiful images from my chicken-scratch drawings and clunky Excel files.

To the clients we've worked with: hiring a consultant always requires a bit of courage. Those who take the plunge do it because they want to improve, but it is still sometimes difficult to make the changes needed to adopt more effective ways to operate. Thank you for trusting us to guide you in that journey, and thank you for teaching us as much as we teach you.

Thank you to the friends and colleagues who provided insights, feedback, encouragement, editorial suggestions, and the perspective to help me make sense of this demanding topic. You are: Katrina Appell, France Bergeron, Pascal Dennis, Tom Ehrenfeld, Emeline Fort, Darrell Foxworth, Liz Guthridge, Jim Huntzinger, Ed Gwozda, Tina Jackson, Mike Lindsay, Dan Markovitz, Kevin Meyer, Mark Graban, Mark Minukas, Isaac Mitchell, Sammy Obara, Barry O'Reilly, Mike Osterling, Elizabeth Prather, Tracey Richardson, Claudia Russell, Mary Savoy, John Shook, Chote Sophonpanich, Michael Stratford, Rachel Stutts, Chris Talcott, Nampetch Tatiyawong, Cristal Totterman, Brad Toussaint, Tim Turner, Rosa Underwood, Darril Wilburn, Jerry Wright, Daniel Wolcott, those former Wells Fargo leaders and employees who wish to remain anonymous, and The Karen Martin Group subscribers and social media connections who responded to my surveys and polls. Sharing your experience and perspective has made the book all the better.

Thank you to authors Dan Ariely, Josh Bernoff, Anders Ericsson, Ray Kurzweil, Jeff Liker, Richard Sheridan, and Carolyn Taylor for sharing their work and perspectives—and confirming that deep exploration regarding the value of clarity is long overdue.

I'm grateful to those who sparked my early interest in clarity—especially Marianne Williamson, who gave a talk one New Year's Eve in the 1980s during which she shared how Gandhi waited for clarity to lead the famous salt march that drove out the British from India's shores. The story grabbed me by the throat and never let go. Thank you, Marianne Williamson, for telling that story; thank you, Ram Dass, for sharing it in your book; and thank you, Gandhi, for serving as a beacon of clarity.

Another early clarity influence for me is Roger Greaves, chairman and former CEO of Health Net, my first corporate employer. Roger was and continues to be a shining example of how leading with clarity contributes to an organization's success. At Health Net, there was never a doubt about why we were in business, who our customers were, what they valued, what *our* values were, what our priorities and business goals were, how we were doing, and what we should be working on *that day, that week, that month, that year.* Thank you, Roger Greaves.

Thank you to the crackerjack team at McGraw-Hill and its partners: Casey Ebro, Donya Dickerson, Courtney Fischer, Chelsea Van der Gaag, Jeff Weeks, Maureen Harper, Pattie Amoroso, Steve Straus, and Alison Shurtz. Your contribution comes through on every page, starting with the beautiful cover, font and paper choices, and visually pleasing layout. You dealt with orphans, misplaced modifiers, and the perennial debate about whether it's proper to end a sentence with a preposition, and promoted the book so people learn about it.

Thank you to John Willig, the literary agent who's always calm, cool, collected, and connected. Thank you for your enthusiasm for this topic. From your lips to God's ears, Mr. Willig.

Thank you to my team of marketing geniuses—Jill Williams and Hillary Barnes—and to Nick, Christopher, Steve, and their extended team at AlterEndeavors. I also owe special thank yous to the people who provide inspiration and insights and helped us design the clarity assessment: Nicole Forsgren, Sally Hogshead, John Perry, Laura Starita, Will Thalmeier, and Jill Williams.

Last, I have deep gratitude to several people who played a key role in the life- and career-changing journey I refer to as "domino effect." I have long embraced the notion that we need clarity about our overarching goals, but I learned to let life take me where I need to be. That has been far more powerful than trying to plan every step. I can think of no clearer example of how that has benefited me than my sudden decision to move to San Diego 17 years ago.

There I met a powerful group of early-adopting Lean practitioners, consultants, and leaders. They were the real deal. I had been using TQM (Total Quality Management) to help organizations improve their performance. While TQM was close to Lean management in spirit, Lean offered greater practicality with its clarity-building principles, management practices, and tools. So thank you to those San Diego–based Lean pioneers who fly under the radar and yet have contributed to significant organizational transformation and set me on a deeply fulfilling trajectory I had not planned: Mike Osterling, Raju Deshpande, Jim McKechnie, Jerry Wright, and Joe Colarusso. You never know where life will take you. Sometimes you just need to hop on a surfboard, ride the waves, and forget your preconceived notions.

And finally, I offer a note of gratitude to Mike Osterling for our long-standing partnership as coauthors, codevelopers, cofacilitators, and friends. The generosity you've shown by sharing your time and knowledge means more than words can adequately express.

Appendix

Developing Clarity Through Mindfulness Meditation

Mindfulness means paying attention purposefully, in the present moment, and nonjudgmentally.[1] Its gift lies in allowing its practitioners to operate with focus, clarity, and full awareness of what they are experiencing, whether good or bad, desired or not. Adopting a mindfulness meditation practice allows you to develop a clear mind and the wisdom needed to be a trusted and successful leader. This Appendix includes instructions for two types of sitting meditation practices and one type of walking meditation.[2]

Even short sessions—as little as 10 minutes a day—will generate results. Anyone should be able to fit that short amount of time for practice into a busy day. Leaders know that finding windows for reflection and developing oneself is a key success factor.

---

[1] Jon Kabat-Zinn, *Wherever You Go, There You Are*, 10th ed. (Hatchett Books, 2005), 3.

[2] These instructions are designed for both beginners and more experienced meditators who are interested in refining their practice or trying an alternative approach. The instructions are provided courtesy of Elizabeth Prather, an experienced meditator, mindfulness consultant, and trainer. For more information, visit www.ksmartin.com/mindfulness.

SITTING MEDITATION

Traditionally, practitioners meditate in a seated position, as this is a comfortable way for our bodies to relax and for us to focus inward. Nonetheless it's important that you avoid becoming so relaxed that you fall asleep or daydream instead of meditating. The following guidelines will help you prepare for meditation and position your body in a way that strikes a happy medium between too stiff and too relaxed.

Getting Started

First, find a quiet place where you can practice uninterrupted and where you can sit comfortably, either in a chair or cross-legged on a cushion on the floor. Here are some tips for establishing a practice that will enable you to reap the greatest benefits.

1. **Set a timer.** Before you sit down, set a timer for the desired length of your mindfulness meditation practice. Begin with 10 minutes. With experience, you can gradually extend each session to 20 minutes or longer.

2. **Sit with a straight back.** *This is very important.* Sitting straight and feeling balanced helps your mind be clear and alert. You want your back straight, but relaxed. If you're seated in a chair, place your feet flat on the ground, your pelvis and lower back relaxed (not curved in either direction), and your shoulders loose and settled downward away from your ears. Avoid leaning forward, backward, or to one side. Position yourself so that your back doesn't touch the back of the chair, moving forward on the seat if necessary.

3. **Position the hands.** Place your hands in a comfortable position—either in your lap or on your thighs, wherever the hands rest naturally. Some people prefer the palms turned downward, while others prefer the palms turned upward as a gesture to invite in calmness. Those who prefer the palms

facing upward may prefer to touch the thumb to the index finger to create a "closed loop" of energy. Others may prefer to let the fingers relax fully. Experiment and use whatever feels best.

4. **Release tension.** Relax your body. Pay special attention to those places where you typically hold tension, whether it's your neck, shoulders, back, or hips. Notice the parts of your body that are connected to other objects, such as your buttocks on the chair or your feet on the floor, and invite them to relax.

5. **Position the eyes.** You may practice with your eyes either closed or slightly open. If you keep them slightly open, establish a soft, unfocused gaze and look past the tip of your nose toward the floor in front of you.

6. **Relax the face.** Invite all of the muscles of your face to relax, especially those between the eyebrows and around the eyes, lips, and jaw. Gently place your tongue on the roof of your mouth, just behind the front teeth to reduce salivation and the need to swallow, which distracts the mind.

7. **Begin intentional breathing.** Breathe through your nose for both the inhalation and exhalation. Take three slow and deep breaths, breathing in and out through the nostrils, releasing tension from throughout your body as you exhale. Let your awareness permeate your entire body, and note any sensations that arise as you breathe in and out. Allow yourself to relax fully, as this is an important component of the practice and allows sharp focus and clarity to arise.

With your body in position and timer set, select one of the two sitting meditation approaches described below. Meditation 1 focuses primarily on the breath and is designed to develop greater focus. Meditation 2 is designed to build greater awareness of your mental capacities and potential. Both meditation practices help you develop and learn to operate with greater clarity.

Sitting Mindfulness Meditation 1: Developing Focus

In this meditation practice, the breath becomes a tool for anchoring your attention and developing focus. An anchor is needed to tame our "monkey mind"—the restless, agitated, and easily distracted state of mind in which you bounce from idea to idea, priority to priority, and from the past to the future—as you begin to focus your attention on your breath. As you gain more experience, you'll learn to recognize when your monkey mind is taking over and then return your attention gently to your breath. Because the breath is always with you, you have unlimited access to it as an anchor whenever you want. Intentional breathing also stimulates the parasympathetic nervous system, which decreases stress reactions and relaxes the body.

To begin, settle your body in a seated position as described in the "Getting Started" section. Turn your full attention to your breath and follow the breath by choosing *one* of the following "breath objects"—you may want to experiment with both types to learn which is more effective for you to focus your mind.

- **Breath focus.** Focus your attention on the natural movement of your breath as it flows in and out of your body. Don't try to control the breath in any way; just be aware of its movement. Avoid trying to visualize the breath or contemplate its qualities; focus your attention on the experience of breathing as a neutral observer, similar to watching clouds passing in the sky. Avoid evaluating or judging your breath.

- **Belly focus.** Focus your full attention on the experience of the breath in your belly region. Be aware of how your stomach expands when you breathe in and contracts when you breathe out. Let this observation be neutral and effortless. Observe it in the same way you would watch waves roll onto a beach. You don't want to change the pace of your breathing or manipulate the breath in any way.

Just breathe naturally as you maintain your focus on the expansion and contraction of your abdomen.

Do not be concerned about distractions. No matter which breath object you've chosen, you'll notice sensations, thoughts, and feelings arising from one of your senses. Avoid trying to stop these thoughts or rid yourself of the sensations. Instead, be aware of these distractions as they arise. Think of them as gifts, signaling when you've lost focus. Gently acknowledge what took your attention away, let it go, and return to the experience of breathing. Your mind will most likely wander again after a few breaths. Notice the distraction and then return your attention to the breath again. This acknowledgment and return is the heart of practice.

Sitting Mindfulness Meditation 2: Developing Increased Awareness

In addition to becoming more focused, mindfulness meditation can help you develop a level of awareness that allows you to observe more closely your internal reactions to information or events. This ability helps you develop a "one-second pause" between what you think, learn, or experience and your reactions and responses to those inputs. This is the clarity pause I mention in Chapter 7. During these pauses you may begin to see patterns in how certain thoughts or contexts make you feel or behave. As you become more familiar with the workings of your mind, you improve your mental capacity and the ability to respond in more effective and meaningful ways at work and at home.

This mindfulness meditation has three steps:

1. **Follow the breath.** After you've settled your body as described in the "Getting Started" section, spend a few minutes directing your full attention to your breath, as described in Meditation 1, until your mind feels settled and stable.

2. **Notice experiences.** Once you are settled, let go of the attention on your breath and become aware of whatever arises in your mind. In this meditation, anything that arises—thoughts, sensations, sounds, odors, and so on—serves as your anchor of awareness. You should observe whatever arises neutrally, without getting engaged with it in any way. Just be present with whatever arises in your mind. When a thought, sound, or sensation appears, notice when it changes, follow it as it disappears, and be open to whatever arises next. When you get distracted, simply return to your breath to stabilize your attention, and then open up your awareness again. When the meditation is over, try to carry this sense of increased awareness with you through your day.

3. **Label the experience.** If you notice that you have trouble maintaining neutrality on a thought or sensation, and instead begin to engage with it, it can be helpful to give this thought a short mental label. For example, if a thought about tomorrow's important meeting arises, you can label it "meeting" without beginning to think about the meeting agenda or who will attend. You can also use simple labels, such as "thought," "sensation," or "feeling" to keep your mind from engaging further.

Helpful Tips for Sitting Meditation

Though the meditation instructions may be simple, they aren't necessarily easy, and this is definitely true when developing mindfulness. It can be difficult to summon the discipline to get started and to keep practicing long enough to see results. The results are worth it, though, so having a longer-term mindset helps.

Beginning meditators often say they feel sleepy during practice. If this happens to you, sit up straighter and bring a laser-like focus to your breath.[3] When your mind feels clearer, return to the meditation. It's important that you make an effort to become more mindful of your body, thoughts, actions, and emotions. Do this with a relaxed, gentle, and kind attitude—toward both yourself and the practice.

A minimum of 10 minutes a day, five to seven days a week, typically produces good results. In time, you can increase the amount of time to 20 or 30 minutes for even greater benefits. Try to commit to *daily* practice—even if you don't feel like it—rather than practicing once or twice a week for longer durations. Frequency and consistency are more important than the total number of minutes you meditate in a given week.

It bears repeating that it's best to set aside a place where you can meditate relatively undisturbed. Setting aside a specific time and place for your practice will help you establish a more sustainable habit. The good news is that, though your formal mindfulness practice may last only a few minutes, your mindful clarity and focus continue throughout the day.

WALKING MEDITATION

Walking meditation offers a way to bring mindfulness into everyday activities. Before you begin, find a location with enough space to walk a short distance—about 20 steps—before you need to turn around and retrace your path. To begin the practice:

1. **Focus your attention.** Bring your focus to your body and, in particular, to your feet and legs.

---

[3] And maybe commit to getting more sleep! Many leaders I know—and maybe you are one of them—find that the only time they take for themselves all day is the 10-minute meditation. No wonder they're falling asleep as soon as they sit still for a minute—they're exhausted!

2. **Begin walking.** As you walk, notice the sensations of your foot inside your shoe, or on the ground if you're barefoot or in socks. With each step, notice all of the sensations you feel when lifting your foot and moving your leg. Notice the shift in sensation as you transfer your weight from one foot to the other. Take another step and, again, notice the sensations connected with the movement. When you've completed the walk in one direction, turn around mindfully, being aware of your body's movements as you do so. Retrace the path to the starting point, continuing to notice all the sensations of walking.

3. **Find the right pace.** Walk back and forth at a pace that feels comfortable and allows you to notice details. Some days your pace will be slower; other days a bit faster.

4. **End the practice.** After 10 to 20 minutes, stop and notice what's happening in your body; be aware of your legs and feet, and notice your breath. Observe what you see and hear around you with a nonjudgmental mind as you gently end the meditation.

Helpful Hints: Walking Mindfulness Meditation Practice

Walking meditation is especially helpful for people who are more active. This is not an exercise in how many "laps" you can do, however. Instead, focus on the quality of your attention in each step, and in each moment of the practice. It's also something you can do at the office during a break. A combination of sitting and walking meditation can be especially beneficial. Again, as with sitting meditation, you'll gain the greatest benefits with a daily practice rather than weekly sessions, even if those less frequent sessions are done for longer durations.

In addition to this more formal walking meditation practice, take the opportunity to walk in a mindful way whenever you can, whether you are on a daily walk around your neighborhood or in the woods for a weekend hike. Leave all electronic devices behind and enjoy noticing what you feel and experience without distraction. Notice how your body feels (without judgment). Notice how your breath feels and sounds (without judgment). Notice your environment, including the sound of the birds, smell of the trees, and so on. Be present, relaxed, and nonjudgmental about whatever arises.

REAPING THE BENEFITS

Developing mindfulness is extremely beneficial for leaders (and people in general). It has a long history, and ample scientific evidence proves its benefits. With mindfulness meditation, you learn how to manage your attention. Through practice, you are able to find the mental space to respond instead of react. This helps you and those around you be more relaxed and calm no matter the situation. With a more mindful way of operating, you can more easily direct your life and your work with purpose and clarity.

Try to avoid thinking of meditation as another chore on your to-do list, but rather as a private escape and a daily gift you give yourself to reduce stress and become a more effective leader, business partner, decision maker, problem solver, parent, child, significant other, and friend. Find the practice that resonates with you. Experiment and be patient with yourself. With mindfulness and the resulting clarity, you'll become better able to understand yourself, connect more deeply with others, and become more effective in and satisfied with work. Deep joy and happiness can result from this practice. Why not begin now?

Index

Note: Page numbers followed by *f* refer to figures.

About the Author

Karen Martin helps organizations use clarity, focus, discipline, and engagement to achieve higher levels of performance on financial, operational, and cultural fronts.

She is president of The Karen Martin Group, Inc., a global consulting firm. Karen and her team have helped organizations such as Adventist Health, AT&T, Chevron, GlaxoSmithKline, Epson, International Monetary Fund, Lenovo, Mayo Clinic, Prudential Insurance, and the United States Department of Homeland Security learn more effective ways to design work systems, grow market share, solve business problems, and accelerate improvement.

An in-demand international speaker, she is the Shingo Prize–winning author of *The Outstanding Organization* and coauthor of three additional business performance improvement books.

For more information, please visit www.ksmartin.com.